Microsoft

I0112659

Microsoft 365 Copilot Adoption: A practical guide for business leaders and consultants

Mark Smith and Megan Smith

Trademarks

Microsoft and the trademarks listed at http://www.microsoft.com on the "Trademarks" webpage are trademarks of the Microsoft group of companies. All other marks are property of their respective owners.

Warning and Disclaimer

Every effort has been made to make this book as complete and as accurate as possible, but no warranty or fitness is implied. The information provided is on an "as is" basis. The author, the publisher, and Microsoft Corporation shall have neither liability nor responsibility to any person or entity with respect to any loss or damages arising from the information contained in this book or from the use of the programs accompanying it.

EDITOR-IN-CHIEF
Julie Phifer

EXECUTIVE EDITOR
Loretta Yates

ACQUISITIONS EDITOR
Shourav Bose

DEVELOPMENT EDITOR
Rick Kughen

MANAGING EDITOR
Sandra Schroeder

SENIOR PROJECT EDITOR
Tracey Croom

COPY EDITOR
Rick Kughen

INDEXER
Rachel Kuhn

PROOFREADER
Barbara Mack

TECHNICAL EDITOR
Zoe Wilson

COVER DESIGNER
Blair McLean

COMPOSITOR
codeMantra

GRAPHICS
codeMantra

Dedication

For the innovators, the change makers, and the constructive skeptics.

Contents at a Glance

Contents

PART 3   **ESSENTIAL SKILLS TO WIN WITH AI**

Foreword

At Microsoft, our Copilot journey began as more than a product launch, it was a shift in how we work, learn, and lead. One of the most powerful lessons I've learned is that peer influence moves faster than policy. The Copilot Champs Community, thousands of employees across the company and around the globe, became the heartbeat of adoption. These Champs didn't just teach others how to use Copilot, they shared stories, surfaced feedback, and created a ripple effect that transformed how people engaged with AI.

That kind of momentum doesn't come from the top down—it comes from people feeling empowered to lead from where they are.

This book explores AI adoption, but at its core, it's about people. A human-first, AI-enabled approach means helping individuals feel confident and supported. It's about recognizing the parts of our work that are uniquely human—creativity, empathy, judgment—and letting AI help with the rest. When AI fits naturally into your workflow, it stops feeling like a tool and starts feeling like a superpower.

I'm especially grateful to know the authors of this book, Megan and Mark Smith. Their people-first approach to AI adoption deeply resonates with me. They understand that scaling Copilot isn't about technology, it's about trust, empathy, and shared learning. Their research and insights have helped other businesses embrace Copilot not just as a tool, but as a catalyst for meaningful change. I'm proud to call them friends.

At Microsoft, we call ourselves "Customer Zero." That means we're not just testing Copilot—we're living it. We're navigating the same transformation our customers are, learning what works and what doesn't. The Champs Community has played a vital role in that process, helping shape how Copilot evolves internally and externally.

Whether you're beginning or scaling AI adoption, I hope this book reveals what's truly possible—not just with technology, but with people. Because AI isn't just a tool, it's a transformation. When you center change around human strengths, you don't just improve workflows—you unlock greatness.

—Cadie Kneip, Readiness Business Program Manager, Microsoft

Acknowledgments

We need to acknowledge all the people who have been involved in bringing this book to you. These people include colleagues and friends who have profoundly impacted our thinking, created opportunities to test our theories, and generously shared their own knowledge and experience.

First, we thank our children—Connor, Poppy, and Nīkau—and our parents and siblings, who gifted us the belief that hard things are worth doing well. To our friends who have become family and our local village—we appreciate your support more than you know.

To the team at Pearson and Microsoft Press: thank you for backing us and guiding us through the writing and editing process. Special thanks to Loretta Yates, Shourav Bose, and Rick Kughen for your patience and expertise throughout. We are so grateful to Zoe Wilson, our incomparable technical editor, whose input has strengthened the recommendations and frameworks in this book through her experience leading Copilot rollouts for some of the world's largest organizations. To Alan Chai, Tina van Heerden, Brett Gilbertson, and the hundreds of others who have shared their stories on conference stages and podcast platforms. Thank you for allowing others to learn from your experiences. Huge thanks to Cadie Kneip for sharing her experience building Microsoft's own Copilot champions community in the foreword, and to Karuana Gatimu, Jessie Hwang and the whole team responsible for the helpful content published at *adoption. microsoft.com/copilot*. Thank you to Blair McLean, who brought his vision and artistry to this project through the cover design.

Mark would especially like to acknowledge those who have been influential in his career journey. To Jason Ferguson, whose faith in me unlocked opportunities and flung open doors that have forever transformed my life. Working with you and the indomitable Shane Parsons, the technically brilliant Andrew Li, and skilled deal crafter Darren Clark has been a highlight of my career. Special thanks to Steve Mordue for being a relentless challenger and status-quo buster; your uncanny eye for emperors without clothes inspires sharper thinking and bolder action. To my good friends, William Dorrington, Chris Huntingford, and Andrew Welch: your brilliance as natural change-makers inspires me to reach new heights.

Megan is grateful for the people at Microsoft around the world who have embraced and supported her in recent years, especially Suzanne Quinn, who has long been a believer and steadfast encourager for Mark and now inspires us both with her enduring passion for empowering others through technology. Thank you to our friends in the

90 Day Mentoring Challenge community who we have the privilege of learning with. Learning in community is one of the most powerful ways to keep people at the center of technology use and innovation.

Finally, to the Microsoft 365 Copilot MVPs around the globe—and especially those who have contributed their experiences to this book—thank you for sharing your stories and for standing ready as local guides whenever readers seek expert advice. Find your local MVP at *mvp.microsoft.com/en-US/search?target=Profile&program=MVP*.

About the Authors

Mark Smith is the founder of the 90 Day Mentoring Challenge (90DayMC.com), a global program that accelerates careers through structured mentoring, skills development, and community support. Under its banner, he created The AI Advantage—a pathway designed to help any professional develop the skills to become AI-augmented in the Intelligence Age. Known online as nz365guy, Mark is a futurist and co-founder of Cloverbase, where he develops frameworks and advises global organizations—including Microsoft—on AI adoption strategy and skilling. He is a Microsoft AI Platform Most Valuable Professional (MVP), Microsoft Certified Trainer, and host of the Microsoft Innovation Podcast, where he distills practical lessons from technology pioneers. With more than two decades at the forefront of the technology industry, his mission is to help leaders and consultants drive human-centered innovation empowered by AI.

Megan Smith is a digital strategist, change manager, and AI educator. She is the CEO of Cloverbase, an AI adoption and skilling company that guides organizations through tailored learning journeys and mentoring programs to amplify human intelligence and connection. With a career spanning more than a decade at the intersection of technology and transformation, Megan has led Copilot enablement programs for Microsoft's global account teams, equipping organizations to embrace AI-driven change. Together with Mark, she created the 90 Day Mentoring Challenge, a career accelerator designed to empower business leaders and consultants with the practical skills to unlock their full potential and drive meaningful innovation.

Introduction

Artificial Intelligence is not new, but we are living in a hype cycle that has made it the buzzword of conversations around both board tables and dining tables. The hype around AI in general and Microsoft 365 Copilot specifically often starts with the promise to get more done, in less time. For many, it's an exciting prospect to claw back time that's currently spent drafting documents, replying to emails, summarizing meetings, or crunching data. While the advent of AI stirs excitement and opportunities for some people, for others, it generates fear and risk.

How can we learn from the organizations that are leaning into AI and shaping their strategies to take advantage of the benefits it offers? In *Microsoft 365 Copilot Adoption*, we uncover the patterns amongst the early adopters of Microsoft Copilot and organize them into an adaptable framework. This framework offers business leaders and consultants a roadmap for the organizations they are leading into the AI-enabled future. Because the AI revolution isn't really about productivity; it's about possibility.

Many people we've spoken with are already incredibly productive. They're not looking to squeeze more tasks into their days; they're looking for more time to spend on higher-value, meaningful work. They want to stop spending evenings catching up on admin. They want to contribute their creativity, judgment, and insight to the problems that matter most. They want to go home at a reasonable hour, knowing they've made a difference and not just ploughed through a to-do list.

That's where this book starts—not with tasks and tools, but with the why behind Copilot adoption.

The evolving nature of work

The access and scale of generative artificial intelligence are changing how we work. The way people approach work will continue to evolve at an accelerated pace as the development of this technology advances. Organizations that fail to adopt AI technologies will not be able to compete with those that do. This technology-driven wave of change is likened to changes we've seen in the past—the industrial revolution, the arrival of the Internet, the always-online mobile generation. Indeed, it builds on these changes, but one key difference is the timeline of change cycles contracting from decades to years, from years to months. Where companies were once able to take a conservative approach to adopting cloud computing with a "watch-and-learn" strategy, waiting even 12 months to start incorporating AI into organizational processes would place that organization at a severe disadvantage to its competitors.

However, letting "fear of being left behind" drive AI strategy is as likely to fail as doing nothing. It's become a common directive from executives to add AI into every project, but it's important to first understand how AI fits into your organization's vision and purpose so that you can secure the leadership commitment necessary to adopt AI effectively.

From productivity to purpose

Microsoft Copilot is a suite of AI-driven features built into Microsoft 365 and other Microsoft platforms. It uses natural language intelligence to help people create digital artifacts, automate tasks, and collaborate more effectively—without needing deep technical expertise. Microsoft Copilot makes it possible to seamlessly blend AI into everyday workflows, simplifying complex processes and encouraging people to rethink how they work.

When we think about using AI or Copilot for a specific workload or scenario, we need to move beyond a one-dimensional focus on productivity. Time saved is good, but what happens with that time is where real value lives. To move beyond a productivity conversation, it's helpful to frame the intended impact that adopting Copilot will have across a continuum that starts with productivity and ultimately progresses to purpose:

- **Productivity—doing more** Copilot helps individuals accomplish more in less time. It drafts, summarizes, suggests, and automates parts of your day so you can keep moving.

- **Efficiency—doing it smarter** Copilot helps streamline workflows across teams. It reduces friction, shortens cycles, and simplifies complexity in how work gets done.

- **Effectiveness—doing the right things** This is where Copilot becomes strategic. It improves the quality of decision-making, aligns work with outcomes, and focuses energy where it counts.

- **Purpose—doing what matters** This final stage is where Copilot unlocks time and mental space for people to focus on meaningful, human work—whether that's innovation, service, creativity, or connection.

It's important that we make purpose, not productivity, the goal. Say, for example, your organization holds an all-hands question-and-answer meeting every two weeks, offering employees a chance to get answers directly from the leadership team. However, in the pursuit of productivity, this meeting is replaced with an AI-powered chat experience.

The upside of this solution is an hour back for every employee, as well as instant answers to questions outside of the scheduled all-hands meeting. Is it more efficient? Absolutely. Is it more effective? Mostly. But whether the new AI chat experience achieves the purpose of the original meeting depends on the goal.

Sure, the new system streamlined communication, but at the expense of the human connection, cultural reinforcement, or even serendipitous moments that are possible when people get together. Efficiency gains are only progress if we're also paying attention to effectiveness and purpose.

Who this book is for

This book is for business leaders and consultants who are involved in leading, sponsoring, or implementing Microsoft Copilot. It's a practical guide for people responsible for improving the effectiveness of their teams, creating a culture of innovation, and ensuring their organization is ready for the future.

Whether you are a CEO who needs to present an AI strategy to the board for approval or a consultant who needs to demonstrate the value of investing in Copilot, this book guides leaders and consultants through successful AI adoption patterns, frameworks for change management, and AI skill development. It highlights the importance of measuring and celebrating wins and failures, addressing common concerns—such as data privacy or shifting job roles—while staying flexible in the face of rapid AI advancement.

Maybe you're thinking about automation. Maybe you're aiming for innovation. Either way, here's our challenge to you:

1. Don't stop at productivity.

2. Don't settle for efficiency.

3. Push for effectiveness. And lead with purpose.

In the chapters ahead, we'll give you frameworks, stories, and tactics to do just that. But it starts by understanding that Copilot is not a magic wand. It's a copilot to sit beside your people, not in place of them. Its real power is in what it enables your teams to become.

Assumptions

You don't need deep technical knowledge to apply the concepts in this book, but you should have a solid understanding of how your organization collects, stores, and uses data, as well as a high-level understanding of how your organization uses Microsoft technologies.

Foundational knowledge of artificial intelligence and generative artificial intelligence would be beneficial. More importantly, you should be able to answer these questions:

- How has your organization approached AI to date?

- What experimentation has been done?

- What does the organization's high-level technology ecosystem map look like?

- Which mission-critical technologies does the organization rely on to deliver its products and services?

- What relationship does the organization have with Microsoft?

You might be familiar with how your organization uses Microsoft technologies, including Microsoft 365 (for example, Teams, Outlook, SharePoint), Microsoft Copilot, and Copilot Studio. You may also have some knowledge of whether your organization uses Microsoft Business Applications (for example, Dynamics 365, Power Platform), Microsoft Fabric, Microsoft Azure AI Foundry, and Microsoft Purview.

How this book is organized

Microsoft 365 Copilot Adoption is organized into four parts. These four parts include chapters on each of the 12 Cs of Copilot adoption, structured as follows:

Part 1: Preparing for Copilot

- Chapter 1, "Context"   How generative AI is changing the way we work and why your organization needs to have a plan for Copilot adoption

- Chapter 2, "Clarity"   Why it's important to establish how your organization's goals align with a clear leadership-driven AI vision

- Chapter 3, "Commitment"   The role of a representative AI council in creating an organization-wide culture of innovation

Part 2: Driving change and adoption

- Chapter 4, "Change management"   Strategies for managing cultural and technical shifts

- Chapter 5, "Capability"   Building Copilot confidence and AI literacy skills amongst your team

- Chapter 6, "Compliance"   How to plan for data governance, security, and compliance considerations

- Chapter 7, "Champions"   The vital role an internal network of Copilot champions plays in scaling Copilot adoption

Part 3: Essential skills to win with AI

- Chapter 8, "Conversation"—How conversation shapes effective use of Copilot and learning from peers
- Chapter 9, "Critical Thinking"—Encouraging a culture of critical thinking and problem-solving
- Chapter 10, "Communication"—Keeping stakeholders engaged and informed by sharing success stories

Part 4: Sustaining and measuring success

- Chapter 11, "Continuous improvement"—Measuring adoption and impact to build on incremental gains
- Chapter 12, "Culture"—Bringing everyone on the Copilot adoption journey and integrating Copilot into every part of the organization

We recommend first reading the parts in order and returning to the chapters as you complete each stage. You might also find it valuable to ask others involved in Copilot adoption in your organization to read the chapters relevant to the role they will play. Establishing a shared understanding and language can be a powerful tool to realize the benefits of Copilot.

How the "Try this prompt" section works

At the end of each chapter, we've included a section with an example prompt that you can use with Copilot. These prompts can be customized to your unique circumstances, serving as a reminder that an essential part of successfully adopting Copilot is to become a skilled user. Everyone will use Copilot differently because your own unique strengths and experiences amplify the value it offers.

Quick access to online references

Appendixes A through E, as well as the prompts from the "Try this Prompt" sections are available as digital downloads. The playbooks are provided in PDF for easy portability. The "Try this prompt" sections are available as .txt files, allowing you to easily cut and paste the prompts into your favorite AI engine.

Download the companion files at *MicrosoftPressStore.com/MS365copilot/downloads*

Errata, updates, & book support

We've made every effort to ensure the accuracy of this book and its companion content. You can access updates to this book—in the form of a list of submitted errata and their related corrections—at

MicrosoftPressStore.com/MS365copilot/errata.

If you discover an error that is not already listed, please submit it to us on the same page.

For additional book support and information, please visit *MicrosoftPressStore.com/Support*.

Please note that product support for Microsoft software and hardware is not offered through the previous addresses. For help with Microsoft software or hardware, go to *support.microsoft.com*.

PART 1

Preparing for Copilot

Before rolling out Copilot, it's important to first understand why your organization is adopting AI and what role you expect it will play as part of achieving your organizational strategy. In Preparing for Copilot, we look at the foundational steps in the Copilot adoption framework:

- In Chapter 1, "Context," we outline how generative AI is changing the way we work and confront how this shift is creating anxiety amongst many people who fear that their role may become obsolete.

- In Chapter 2, "Clarity," we discuss the important role executive sponsorship plays in driving a clear AI vision across the organization and how to pitch the value of Copilot to executive decision-makers.

- In Chapter 3, "Commitment," we examine the role of an AI Council and highlight how an enduring commitment to transparency and innovation with AI creates trust.

Getting these foundations right significantly increases the value Copilot will create for your organization. Being able to articulate and demonstrate how AI aligns with your organizational strategy will help embed Copilot into how your people operate your key processes.

> **Tip**   "Before Copilot, I spent nearly 40 percent of my day navigating scattered information, digging through long email threads, searching SharePoint folders, and jumping between Teams conversations to piece together context. It was exhausting and often slowed down decision-making. Now, with Copilot, that mental load is lifted. It retrieves relevant details in seconds, summarizes conversations, and even suggests next steps like having a reliable colleague who never forgets anything. It hasn't just saved me time; it's given me clarity. I now spend more time making strategic decisions and less time playing digital detective. For someone juggling multiple clients, platforms, and deliverables, that shift is game-changing."
> **–Stephanie Ideho-Iraoya** is a Microsoft MVP for M365 Copilot, a Power Platform Advocate, and a Community Leader based in Nigeria.

CHAPTER 1

Context

I knew I had just seen the most important advance in technology since the graphical user interface. This inspired me to think about all the things that AI can achieve in the next five to 10 years.

—Bill Gates

In this chapter, you will:

- Understand the importance of context in AI adoption and how it can anchor your organization's goals

- Explore the economic impact of the AI revolution and how Copilot can reshape modern work

- Discover how Copilot can empower your people to unlock new levels of efficiency, creativity, and innovation

- Learn why a formal adoption plan will help you avoid the potential pitfalls of rolling out AI tools like Copilot

Realizing the value of M365 Copilot investment

Imagine a CEO riding the wave of Microsoft's AI buzz, rolling out Copilot across their organization—sales, IT, operations, and every single department. They picture instant wins: smarter emails, sharper reports, and hours saved in the workday. With Copilot's unique access to data in Microsoft 365, they think turning it on will unearth gold in the daily grind of emails, files, and Teams chatter. Six months later, though, the dream sours. Half the team is dodging it, muttering about "another tool," and the $30-per-user-per-month tab burns thousands of dollars with little to show for it. What went wrong? Without effective leadership and strategies to help people change the way they work, the gold stays buried.

This isn't a hypothetical; it's a warning. Software languishes without adoption; studies clock failure rates near 70 percent when new tech lands without a plan. Deadlines slip, costs spike, users bail, and licenses lapse. Despite the promise of AI, Copilot isn't immune to this outcome. New users can be spooked by unease and unfamiliarity with how generative AI works, underscoring the need for a deliberate and considered rollout. That CEO's dream? It fades as the organization wakes up to unrealized potential because no one led an effective adoption plan.

That is why understanding the context is vital; anchor your organization's objectives with an understanding of what is driving and impeding AI adoption. According to the 2024 Annual Work Trend Index from Microsoft and LinkedIn, 75 percent of global knowledge workers are already using AI at work. However, 60 percent of leaders worry that their organization lacks a plan and vision to implement AI effectively.[1] Read the full report at *https://news.microsoft.com/annual-wti-2024/.*

With Copilot, it's possible to overhaul your business processes and trim 10 hours a month of repetitive tasks per employee while improving work quality and creativity, but only with a formal plan and a clear strategy. Launching Copilot without a plan is risking more than the cost of the licenses; it's throwing away an opportunity for future innovation. Take the time to understand the context and tailor your strategy so that you can gain the AI-powered advantage Copilot offers.

Understanding the AI revolution and the role of Copilot

You can't afford to wait on the sidelines of this AI revolution—it's already resetting the playing field. The 2025 Technology and Innovation Report by the United Nations estimates the economic impact will hit $4.8 trillion by 2033,[2] predicting disruption at a scale that will eclipse entire industries. Many knowledge workers already lean on AI tools daily, whether to find more efficient ways to manage their inboxes, deliver excellent customer service, or perhaps reduce marketing campaign timelines.

This isn't a niche play reserved for those working in tech; the AI revolution is causing seismic shifts in every industry. Creating trillions in value and a workplace where repetitive, mundane tasks vanish, freeing space for creativity and strategic thinking. Microsoft Copilot isn't just in the race; it's leading the pack and reshaping the future of modern work. No other vendor—save perhaps Google Workspace—can match its deep access to individual and organizational data through Microsoft 365.

Microsoft's AI platform extends on the existing adoption of Windows, Azure, and Microsoft 365 among many of the Fortune 500 companies, as well as millions of organizations of all sizes around the world. Copilot is embedded in Microsoft 365 apps like Word, Excel, Teams, and Outlook—the tools your team lives in at work. It is more than a basic AI assistant. It leverages the Microsoft Graph, a data powerhouse processing 10 billion API calls daily, mining your digital exhaust: every email sent, file saved, and Teams message ignored. It can help cut through the overwhelming amount of information and inbox chaos to create clarity by drafting emails based on your patterns, building spreadsheets from scraps, and anticipating your next step. Microsoft credits most of Copilot's wins, like hours shaved off grunt work, to this Graph-driven model. If you guide it right, it can become a valued partner.

As shown in Figure 1-1, Rogers' Adoption Bell Curve offers a practical lens through which to understand how Copilot adoption is spreading across organizations. It splits adopters into five camps: innovators (2.5 percent), early adopters (13.5 percent), early majority (34 percent), late majority (34 percent), and laggards (16 percent).[3] The adoption curve offers a model for scaling AI use across

---

[1] Microsoft Corporation and LinkedIn, *2024 Work Trend Index Annual Report: AI at Work Is Here. Now Comes the Hard Part* (Redmond, WA: Microsoft, May 8, 2024), https://www.microsoft.com/en-us/worklab/work-trend-index/ai-at-work-is-here-now-comes-the-hard-part.

[2] UNCTAD, Technology and Innovation Report 2025: Inclusive Artificial Intelligence for Development (Geneva: United Nations, 2025), https://unctad.org/publication/technology-and-innovation-report-2025.

[3] Everett M. Rogers, *Diffusion of Innovations*, 5th ed. (New York: Free Press, 2003).

your organization. Start by fostering the innovators: the AI-curious individuals who may already be experimenting with AI outside of work. Based on the scenarios uncovered by this first group of people using Copilot, you'll recognize the mindset and skills early adopters need as you look to scale your success. Identify and connect with these innovators and leaders early to spark momentum for the broader use of Copilot. Knowing who jumps first and why can give you an advantage when scaling adoption.

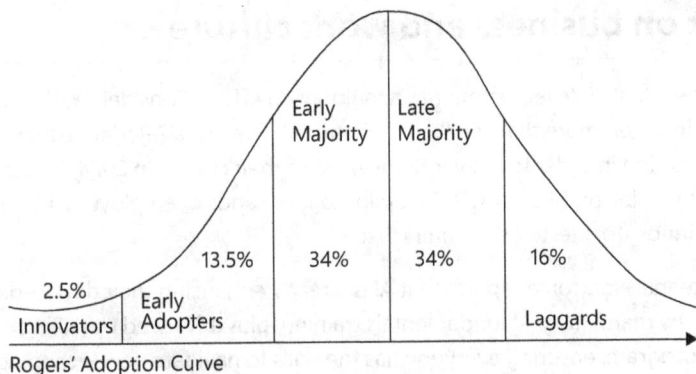

Rogers' Adoption Curve

FIGURE 1-1 Rogers' Adoption Bell Curve

Studies have shown that where the organization does not provide AI-enabled tools, many employees are now "bringing their own," a form of shadow AI. Shadow AI refers to the unauthorized use of AI by employees without the knowledge or approval of the IT department. This practice presents a considerable risk for trade secrets, intellectual property, and even valuable customer data to be inadvertently leaked and used to train public AI models.

Copilot offers another advantage for organizations that use Microsoft 365, beyond the ability to mine that deep organizational knowledge captured in emails in Outlook, chat messages in Teams, and files in SharePoint. It provides a unique level of protection for your critical organizational data. Copilot inherits enterprise data protection from Microsoft 365, which means your user and business data are protected and will not leak outside the organization.

Additionally, because the organization owns and controls its data, it is not used to train foundational models. This security, combined with the scale of access to Windows and Microsoft 365 and Microsoft's recent announcement to make Copilot Chat available for free to all, makes it an ideal starting point to get AI into the hands of your employees safely.

> **Note** Microsoft 365 Copilot has two experiences now. Microsoft 365 Copilot Chat is free and secure, grounded in the data from the internet. Microsoft 365 Copilot is the per-seat licensed experience, grounded in your organizational data, including everything in the Microsoft Graph. Learn more about both at *https://adoption.microsoft.com/copilot*.

Working with AI requires a new mindset and an evolved skill set compared to how knowledge workers have typically operated in the last decade. It takes time and practice to develop these skills. Even before committing to the cost of a per-user-per-month license for Microsoft 365 Copilot, people using

Copilot Chat can start to build their AI skills. And this practical learning is essential. You can't go to the gym, watch others work out, and expect to get fit. In the same way, without opportunities for practical, hands-on experience with AI-powered tools, it's impossible for people to gain the AI skills they need to get it to work for them.

The impact of Copilot on business and work culture

Investing in your people and their AI skill development has a multiplying effect. Consider EY, the global services titan that has recently invested more than a billion dollars in AI. Their goal? Redefine how people work inside their organization in order to deliver more value to their clients. In 2024, EY accelerated its everyday AI rollout by introducing Microsoft 365 Copilot to thousands of employees, but only after leaders and "thrive time" innovators tested the waters first.

Today, 71 percent of EY's Oceania workforce reports that AI is already enhancing their day-to-day tasks.[4] That impact is amplified by mandatory AI fundamentals training, plus advanced upskilling through the global EY Badges program, ensuring everyone has the skills to navigate new technology. EY also launched an internal AI platform that helps people work in multiple languages, tearing down barriers and sparking richer collaboration across different regions. By investing in both AI tools and their people, EY is seeing governance and strategy around AI become a unique differentiator for the firm and for the clients who look to them for future-focused innovation.

This exemplifies the power of Copilot to help people get stuff done and create space to thrive. Microsoft Copilot can help reduce the overtime that chains staff to desks. Formal adoption makes it possible to quickly clear hours of admin so folks can log off and hit the gym or catch their kid's game instead of working late and burning out. Copilot offers an antidote to the repetitive busy work that bogs down our work lives. Endless email threads? Synthesized in seconds. Report summaries keeping you late? A well-crafted prompt sorts it. Finance teams ditch invoice drudgery; IT support desks accelerate ticket resolutions. Adopting Copilot lifts the burden of mundane tasks—scribing notes, answering FAQs, and building slides—that bleed into nights and weekends. Executives can show up to meetings better prepared in less time, and frontline sales reps can build compelling pitches without working late into the night.

Giving people time back to invest in the things that matter to them might be one of the most lucrative benefits a modern employer can offer. Creating a culture where people are incentivized to use AI to be more effective by gifting some of that time back to them to re-invest in themselves is in direct contrast to organizations that use the recovered time to squeeze even more juice out of the proverbial lemon. People who fear their jobs being "taken" by AI are not inclined to engage with and adopt it. Fear kills creativity.

It's about balance, not cuts, and constant learning to reskill and redeploy talented people who already know your business. It's about creating breathing space to avoid burnout. It's about creating

---

4 "AI the EY Way: Inside the Organisation's Holistic, People-Centred AI Transformation," *Microsoft New Zealand News Centre*, March 14, 2025, https://news.microsoft.com/en-nz/2025/03/14/ai-the-ey-way-inside-the-organisations-holistic-people-centred-ai-transformation/.

space to innovate and encouraging people to augment their knowledge and experience to create value in a new way.

Adoption fuels this human shift. Formal adoption is the key to successful execution. It signals that you are committed to walking into the AI-powered future with your people. Without that commitment, Copilot's benefits will be choked by resistance and fear. The AI revolution is shadowed by a psychological hurdle that no past business productivity technology has faced.

The unique psychological challenge of AI adoption

Adopting software has never been simple, but AI, like Microsoft Copilot, brings a twist no one has seen with Teams or Excel: a perceived threat to the user's future job security. When employees learned Teams in earnest in 2020, they might have grumbled about change, but no one lost sleep, fearing it would steal their jobs. Now, though, people are learning to use Copilot at the same time as facing daily headlines that scream about AI replacing millions of jobs. Many workers are afraid it will erase their roles, with a 2025 survey revealing 32 percent thought it would lead to fewer job opportunities for them in the future.[5] What incentive does a person have to train the tool that could rob them of their livelihood?

When it comes to AI, this part of "context" is uniquely human, and unless it is tackled as part of your formal adoption plan, it could become the most significant cause of resistance. In that case, it isn't about mastering prompting—it's about building and sustaining trust.

The media doesn't help. Headlines shout: "AI to Replace 300 Million Jobs," or "Copilot's here, kiss your desk goodbye." This isn't the quiet debut of cloud storage or email; the AI story is loud, constant, and unsettling. It's sparked the fear of becoming obsolete in people across organizations, from executives around the board table to frontline workers. It frames Copilot as a threat, not an aid. Past tools faced "I don't get it"; Copilot faces "Will it get me?" That's why many ditch trials—not just because of a skill gap but, most importantly, because of a trust gap. Formal adoption must reassure, not just train.

The challenge for those of us who are tasked with driving the adoption and use of AI is to replace that mindset of fear with one of curiosity. Curiosity is a powerful antidote to fear. When designing an adoption plan, consider that people may need reassurance before they can trust that Copilot is worth getting curious about. Your organizational change history largely determines the speed at which your employees can make that mindset shift. What technology rollout legacy are you building on?

Lessons from past technology adoptions

It's a commonly acknowledged truth that the best predictor of future behavior is past behavior. Before announcing Microsoft Copilot as a shiny new tool, it's worth investing some time in understanding the successes and failures of past rollouts. Tech adoptions have been stumbling over the same traps

---

[5] Luona Lin and Kim Parker, "U.S. Workers Are More Worried Than Hopeful About Future AI Use in the Workplace," *Pew Research Center, Social & Demographic Trends*, February 25, 2025, https://www.pewresearch.org/social-trends/ 2025/02/25/u-s-workers-are-more-worried-than-hopeful-about-future-ai-use-in-the-workplace/.

forever. Hershey's pre-Y2K Enterprise Resource Planning (ERP) project, which attempted to implement three new tech platforms simultaneously, is often cited as a cautionary tale for large-scale system implementations. The cost of that failure included their inability to fulfill around $100 million worth of orders, which impacted their share price. Imagine being the person who had to front their next tech rollout following that.

Hershey's is not alone. Technology implementation has a 70 percent failure rate when launched without a plan.[6] Many of the pitfalls that cause this are still relevant when rolling out Copilot. Avoid the trap that derailed Hershey's ERP implementation: unrealistic timelines, the pressure of which led to inadequate testing, rushed rollout, and insufficient training. Cautionary tales like this one illustrate how simply purchasing and installing new systems without addressing organizational and process fundamentals can reinforce a productivity paradox: the value of technology remains unrealized (or worse, becomes a liability) if it is not supported by thorough planning, alignment, and execution.

By contrast, when Accenture put Copilot in the hands of their developers, they didn't just organize one training session. They provided ongoing coaching. This dedicated approach to training delivered results both for the developers, who were able to reclaim nights and weekends, and for Accenture, which was able to realize the promised productivity improvements. They also took a phased approach to their rollout, kicking off small, with innovators, before scaling.[7]

Copilot is only as effective as the skill set of the people using it and the readiness of the organization to roll it out. In the next chapter, we'll look at the clarity required to move at the right time when the organization is ready. First, it's worth understanding the common barriers to Copilot adoption before deciding how and when to approach the rollout.

Common barriers to Copilot adoption

The barriers to adopting AI, especially Copilot, blend old hurdles with new challenges. Spotting them isn't enough; leaders must dismantle them to realize the productivity and creativity gains Copilot can catalyze. The following are some key barriers to look out for:

- **Skills gap** AI access without AI literacy risks underuse. Leaders and employees alike need training in effective prompt engineering and critical thinking to evaluate and iteratively question outputs that might inform decision-making.

- **Data quality, quantity, and security** Copilot's unique value is the Microsoft Graph, which is fueled by your organization's digital exhaust, which includes emails, files, and chats. However, the value of that data source is diminished by human error, duplications, and privacy risks. Bad data doesn't just weaken Copilot's output; it kills trust.

---

[6] Boris Ewenstein, Wesley Smith, and Ashvin Sologar, "Changing Change Management," *McKinsey Quarterly*, July 1, 2015, https://www.mckinsey.com/featured-insights/leadership/changing-change-management.

[7] "Accenture and Avanade Are Reinventing the Way Forward with Microsoft Copilot Solutions," *Microsoft Partner – Success Stories*, July 26, 2024, https://partner.microsoft.com/en-US/case-studies/accenture-avanade-copilot.

- **Data siloes**   Copilot fits seamlessly into Microsoft 365, but often organizational data is siloed across many other legacy systems, old ERPs, or custom builds. Integration is doable, but it requires a robust data platform strategy.

- **Getting beyond cost**   At $30 per user per month, the price of Microsoft 365 Copilot can sting. Small firms flinch, and larger enterprises wrestle with murky ROI. Quantifying benefits—faster drafts and sharper insights—is tough when gains build subtly over time.

- **Lack of trust**   The black box effect of AI haunts Copilot, too. When it generates an insight or recommendation, users wonder, "How did it decide that?" Its inner workings and how it prioritizes data or avoids bias aren't always obvious. Doubt festers. Without trust, adoption sputters.

- **Resistance**   Change unnerves people. Familiar workflows feel untouchable; a new tool feels foreign. It takes time to change the way people work. Resistance is natural, and ignoring it invites trouble.

- **Failing to plan**   No plan, no payoff. Too many organizations fling Copilot at people, hoping for the best and calling it adoption. Result? Chaos. Efforts are frustrated without a focus on workloads and scenarios, phased steps, and success metrics.

Ways to bust the barriers

A strategic adoption plan can be the difference between falling at the first hurdle and leaping over those barriers. An effective adoption plan needs to include strategies to address the cultural, technical, and social barriers:

- **Launch a Center for Enablement**   Build an enablement hub blending a champions program (often made up of your innovators and early adopters) and a Center of Excellence. Champions spark excitement and share what they've learned with their peers. The Center of Excellence sets standards, curates wins, and tightens the rollout. It hits skills, culture, and strategy in one swing. See Chapter 7 for more about champions programs.

- **Train smart**   Plug the skills gap with focused sessions on prompt engineering and AI basics. Keep it hands-on and role-specific. Provide opportunities to reinforce learning over time.

- **Data governance**   Master the Microsoft Graph with audits and firm policies. Clean data fuels Copilot: tight rules build trust.

- **Integrate with care**   Map legacy and non-Microsoft tools early. Test pilots to fix hiccups before scaling.

- **Track real wins**   Tie Copilot to hard gains—faster drafts, fewer meetings, better insights. Measure usage and impact, not just logins.

- **Demystify to build trust**   People trust what they can understand. Explain how Copilot works—how it uses data, counters bias, and protects privacy.

- **Face the fear**   Copilot is an assistant, not a replacement. Acknowledge the fear and prove your commitment to your people with reskilling and opportunities to enable them to swap repetitive, busy work for innovation.

- **Encourage a learning mindset**   Weave continuous learning into your culture. Position Copilot as a thought partner and encourage people to learn how to be effective thought leaders when working with AI.

Try this prompt: Copilot for your industry

Developing an AI-enabled mindset and skill set requires daily practice. The goal is to get comfortable understanding how Copilot can help with different tasks so that you can grow your working knowledge of generative AI. At the end of each chapter, you will find a customizable prompt—like this one—that you can use with Copilot.

In this example, the prompt below is designed to help you brainstorm with Copilot specific applications of AI and the business value they can create for your organization in the industry that you operate. Replace [Your Industry] with the one that's most relevant for your organization:

Act as a [Your Industry] Copilot Coach. Help me identify 5-7 specific workloads where Copilot would deliver the most value in a [your industry] environment. For each workload:

1. *Describe the specific business challenge*
2. *Explain how Copilot addresses this challenge*
3. *Outline expected business outcomes (time savings, quality improvements, etc.)*
4. *Reference a relevant real-world example from the Microsoft Copilot Scenario Library (https://adoption.microsoft.com/copilot-scenario-library/)*

Focus on [Your Industry]-specific scenarios and include implementation complexity (low/medium/high) and potential ROI.

> **Tip**   Throughout this book, you'll see prompts like this to try in Copilot. You don't need to be on a paid Microsoft 365 Copilot per-seat license. These prompts will work in Copilot Chat as well. Go to *https://copilot.microsoft.com/* and log in with your work or personal account. (You also have the option to try Copilot without logging in.) Keep in mind that the results you get will be different in each experience because they are based on different data.

Next steps

In this chapter, we discussed why it's important to avoid rushing to roll out Copilot without first considering the context in which it will land in your organization. Understanding the unique psychological barriers AI presents enables you to develop a formal adoption plan that will work for the unique context of your people and organization. A key step in formulating an effective AI adoption plan is to get clarity on why your organization is adoption AI. Otherwise, you're risking more than wasted licenses; you're throwing away the competitive advantage Copilot offers.

- The gold in your Microsoft 365 environment stays buried when half of your team avoids another tool they don't trust or understand how to use effectively.

- Past technology adoption history, current data quality, and cultural readiness will influence whether you join the success stories or the cautionary tales.

- By addressing both technical fundamentals and human resistance, you'll convert that $30-per-user monthly investment into measurable efficiency gains and innovation opportunities.

CHAPTER 2

Clarity

With Copilot, it's not about replacing people—it's about empowering people by simplifying workflows and inspiring a forward-thinking mindset. It makes us faster, more productive, and easier to do business with.

—Ryan Asdourian, VP Lumen Technologies

In this chapter, you will:

- Explore why aligning Copilot capabilities with your strategic business objectives is fundamental for successful adoption

- Learn how to evaluate the readiness of your data and technology ecosystem for AI

- Discover how to build a compelling business case that demonstrates the value Copilot can add across your organization

The cost of confusion

Say you were starting a construction project, and your CEO bursts into the first planning meeting, shouting excitedly about new, innovative bricks. "They're better than traditional bricks because they are self-stacking and align automatically," she exclaims. The project manager flips through photos of buildings made from these amazing bricks; you're sold. "Let's start straight away," you say. It's a no-brainer. But even a house built with self-stacking bricks would require a blueprint—a strategy for building and a clear idea of the purpose that the structure will serve.

This scenario might feel farfetched, but a version of this conversation has been playing out in boardrooms around the world as AI hype inspires leaders to decree, "We must add AI to this project." Forging ahead without taking the time to get clarity on the problems you're solving with Copilot and the outcomes you want to achieve is likely to waste resources and ultimately delay progress. It's important to get the foundations right. Just as a house requires a strong foundation and a clear blueprint, Copilot's ability to help you get more stuff done is dependent on the quality of your data. The rate at which the building goes up and the condition of the building that stands in the end are still influenced by the skill set of the people involved.

Deep knowledge of how your organization operates and an understanding of the customers you serve are required to get value out of Copilot. Take the time to understand the current digital literacy of your staff; identify gaps in knowledge that could impact their ability to utilize Copilot effectively. And just as constructing a physical building requires permits and inspections, implementing AI like Copilot safely requires appropriate consideration of ethical, governance, and compliance implications.

Prioritizing creative and meaningful work

On average, knowledge workers spend 60 percent of their working day on repetitive tasks, in unnecessary meetings, or making sense of duplicated communications. That means that many organizations are losing hundreds of hours every week to "work about work," as one report phrases it.[1] That's time that could be spent on strategic initiatives, creative problem-solving, or proactive customer service. It can be hard to prioritize creativity and meaningful work when interruptions are constant.

The 2025 Work Trend Index report from Microsoft and LinkedIn highlights that employees are interrupted every two minutes, averaging 275 interruptions a day. This results in a workforce that is exhausted and overstimulated; the same study found that 80 percent of workers say they lack the time or energy to do their job.[2] Microsoft Copilot can help solve these challenges so that people can reclaim time in the day to prioritize what truly matters. As a leader or consultant, are you clear on what that means?

What would it mean if you could get several hours a week back? Do you know what you would do with the time saved? At a personal level, there's no shortage of ways to fill half an hour. Many workers already juggle more than a day's work, so that time could be spent getting ahead for the next day or recharging with family. But what about when those 30 minutes a day are aggregated across thousands of employees into perhaps weeks or months of time saved? How do you ensure that recovered time is reinvested wisely? Clarity on your organization's purpose and objectives means you can align the capabilities of Copilot with your organization's goals.

Copilot is so much more than just a shiny new tech too. It can be a partner that helps everyone get stuff done if you pinpoint the workloads where Copilot can make an immediate difference and then create a clear vision and adoption strategy. This allows your people to leverage Copilot in every area of their daily work. Clarity on the value your organization stands to gain by embracing Copilot will prevent it from becoming another failed technology adoption project.

Let's explore the capability, leadership, technology, and data readiness needed for your organization to realize value from Microsoft 365 Copilot and make the cost justification clear.

---

[1] Asana, *Anatomy of Work Global Index*, 5th ed. (San Francisco: Asana, 2025), https://asana.com/resources/anatomy-of-work.

[2] Microsoft Corporation and LinkedIn, *2025 Work Trend Index Annual Report: The Year the Frontier Firm is Born*. (Redmond, WA: Microsoft, April 23, 2025), *https://www.microsoft.com/en-us/worklab/work-trend-index/2025-the-year-the-frontier-firm-is-born*.

Caution   Studies show that people are bringing their own AI to work and engaging in Shadow AI within the organizations they work for. If you aren't already providing access to generative AI tools, talk openly about your intentions and make staff aware of the risks of using their own AI tools at work. Encourage your people to start experimenting with Microsoft 365 Copilot Chat if they don't have a paid license for Copilot yet. Copilot Chat offers a secure, trusted environment for experimentation that does not leak your IP or train models outside your organization's tenant.

The vital role of executive sponsorship

Cross-functional leadership—from the board and the CEO through to people managers and team leaders—acts as a compass guiding the organization through AI transformation. Leaders must set the direction and stay on the course to realize the benefits AI offers. Unlike traditional technology projects, where the drive often originates from the IT department, the pervasive impact AI will have across all business functions necessitates a top-down approach led by the C-suite. It's important to understand the pivotal role executive sponsorship plays in AI adoption and how leaders can effectively champion this change.

AI is not just another piece of technology but a transformative force that will significantly impact every person and process involved in an organization's operations. For many organizations, Copilot will be the first step in AI adoption at scale. Given its strategic importance, it is essential that the leadership team, including the CEO, CFO, CTO, and other department leaders, are active and visible sponsors of AI initiatives. This group of leaders is responsible for aligning the AI adoption goals with the organization's overall strategy and objectives. They don't necessarily need deep technical knowledge about how AI works, but they do need to be able to articulate why AI solutions will help the organization hit its targets. An Ipsos study found that all organizations that are realizing value from their AI investments had leader-driven AI strategies, with clear vision and commitment from senior leaders. By contrast, only 1 percent of organizations that were at the earliest stages of creating value with AI had buy-in from senior leaders.[3] When leaders are seen as the drivers of change, it reinforces the importance of AI and the strategic role it can play in achieving business targets.

A clear example of this is Lumen Technologies. When President and CEO Kate Johnson set a vision to evolve the company from a traditional telecom into a technology leader, she placed AI adoption at the heart of that strategy. Through the Microsoft 365 Copilot Early Access Program, Lumen deployed Copilot across several departments. Sales people saved an average of four hours a week in meeting preparation, unlocking an estimated $50 million in annual value through increased customer engagement

---

[3] Microsoft, *AI Strategy Roadmap: Navigating the Stages of AI Value Creation* (Redmond, WA: Microsoft Corporation, 2024), PDF, *https://info.microsoft.com/ww-landing-AI-Strategy-Roadmap-Navigating-the-stages-of-AI-value-creation.html*.

and productivity. Strong leadership and a clear vision for AI turned early adoption into real business outcomes.[4]

Trust is critical to the change process. A clear vision for AI, mapped to strategic goals, inspires trust in why it is being used. Employees also need to trust that the leadership has their best interests at heart and that AI is being used in a trustworthy manner. If they feel that AI is being brought in to increase surveillance or to extract more work from employees instead of increasing efficiency and creativity, it will erode trust and hinder adoption. Leaders inspire trust by communicating transparently about the purpose and benefits of AI, addressing any concerns, and demonstrating its positive impact on the organization.

Executive sponsors must be visible and active

Leaders who sponsor AI initiatives and actively model the use of generative AI tools have an outsized impact on their successful use across the organization. This involves integrating AI tools like Copilot into their daily workflows and demonstrating their practical applications, such as ensuring Copilot transcription is turned on for meetings when appropriate. Using Copilot live in board meetings and executive sessions to run data analysis to inform decision-making and aid with strategic planning is another way to be visible and active. By acquiring their own applied knowledge of how Copilot can assist in tasks throughout the workday, leaders will build belief and credibility, which will flow through to their communications about the vision for Copilot across the organization. As they lead by example, executives can inspire confidence and encourage wider adoption across the organization.

Given the impact executive sponsors have on the success or failure of Copilot adoption, a tailored training approach will help build their confidence and proficiency with AI tools. This may involve a white glove service with dedicated coaches who can provide personalized training sessions, practical advice for how executives would use Copilot, and ongoing support.

The goal of this training program is to turn executive sponsors into Copilot power users because doing so means their vocal endorsement will carry more weight. Alongside the executive rollout, it's a good idea to empower executive assistants and other business support roles to leverage AI effectively, enhancing their productivity and enabling them to better support the team. If they believe in Copilot, it will be easier to encourage widespread adoption among most employees.

> **Note** Executives use Copilot very differently from other workers, but their delegation skills can set them up to be excellent power users. It's important to customize the support and training approach to meet the unique needs of leaders who will become executive sponsors for your Copilot rollout. A coach who can support them one-to-one will help uncover how they can use Copilot as a strategic thought partner.

---

[4] Deborah Bach, "The only way: How Copilot is Helping Propel an Evolution at Lumen Technologies," *Microsoft Source — Digital Transformation*, July 25, 2024, *https://news.microsoft.com/source/features/digital-transformation/the-only-way-how-copilot-is-helping-propel-an-evolution-at-lumen-technologies/*.

For AI to be truly effective, it must be integrated into the organization's strategic operational framework. AI initiatives should not only support existing strategic objectives but also have the potential to reshape them. Leaders must continuously evaluate how AI can drive innovation, improve efficiency, and create new opportunities. To do that, they need to be using it daily so that they are making strategic decisions based on a practical, hands-on understanding of how generative AI works. Copilot improves constantly with advanced capabilities like Researcher and Analyst agents to help leaders make strategic data-driven decisions. Leaders can ensure that Copilot delivers maximum value by aligning AI with the organization's strategic goals.

Chapter 3, "Commitment," highlights the ongoing role leaders can play as drivers of change when it comes to reimagining their organization for an AI-powered future.

Technical readiness for Copilot

Evaluating the current state of your organization's technology ecosystem will help ensure your data, systems, and security posture are aligned to unlock business value from Copilot. Without access to the right data and the right governance around that data, Copilot can't deliver meaningful outcomes. Getting technical readiness right means Copilot has safe, targeted access to information that can drive productivity, insights, and innovation.

Data accessibility and integration

Start by assessing the current state of your data. This is a discussion that should be conducted with people in your IT department:

- How accessible is your organizational data, and have you restricted access to only what's needed?

- Are critical line-of-business systems integrated, or are data siloes limiting visibility?

- Are your users creating, duplicating, and storing content in ways that create noise or risk?

Achieving an ideal data estate through cleanliness, security, and structure is a constant moving target. Perfect data hygiene is unattainable. Content is constantly being created, copied, and shared. The goal is not perfection but control, ensuring that Copilot can access the data it needs—and nothing it shouldn't. One effective way to achieve this is to use Microsoft Purview, which allows content to be classified and accessed based on roles. It allows you to set up rules to continually classify data across the data estate. Combined with tools like Microsoft Entra, Defender, Intune, and Sentinel, organizations can maintain a Zero Trust posture while allowing Copilot to reason over high-quality, trusted content.

> **Note** Zero Trust in a Microsoft context refers to a security approach that assumes no one—inside or outside an organization—should be trusted by default. It continuously verifies identity and access at every step to protect sensitive data and systems from threats. Read more at *https://learn.microsoft.com/en-us/security/zero-trust/zero-trust-overview*.

As demonstrated in Figure 2-1, it can be helpful to reduce data from the total available artifacts to a refined subset of filtered artifacts so that Copilot is grounded on the most relevant and accurate data. Let's say an average-sized organization has 10 million digital artifacts—files, images, videos, and meeting recordings. It's beneficial to filter this number to a targeted amount for the specific scenarios it will be used for. This involves filtering out duplicates and errors to prevent hallucinations in the dataset, ultimately refining it to a smaller, more accurate set of records for use by Copilot.

Data reduction process

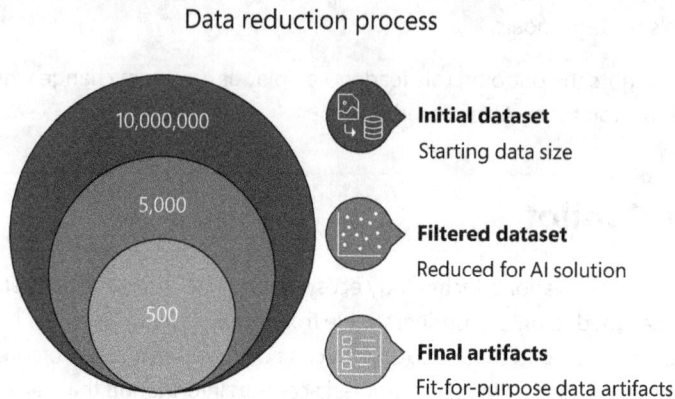

10,000,000

5,000

500

Initial dataset
Starting data size

Filtered dataset
Reduced for AI solution

Final artifacts
Fit-for-purpose data artifacts

FIGURE 2-1 Data reduction process

For a construction company that regularly responds to requests for proposals (RFPs), instead of Copilot reasoning across all the files they've collected on SharePoint, this type of refinement process could result in grounding Copilot with only the best quality, winning RFPs to learn from when generating a response to a new one. The key is to reduce and refine this to a targeted set of useful, well-governed information aligned to specific scenarios. That reduces hallucination risk, enhances output quality, and builds user confidence.

Another component is the organization of data within the data estate. Most organizations now operate across a sprawl of cloud platforms and apps. With hundreds of tools in play, data fragmentation is inevitable. Microsoft Fabric can act as a unifying layer, orchestrating data across systems like Google Cloud Platform, AWS (Amazon Web Services), Oracle, SAP, and Snowflake, helping maintain a clean, connected data estate for Copilot to work from.

The role of digital exhaust

Digital exhaust is the invisible trail of data from everyday digital work. Each email sent, meeting scheduled, chat message swapped, or document edited leaves signals and metadata such as timestamps, application IDs, and relationships. The Microsoft Graph exposes and aggregates these data points, giving a live insight into how applications are used. This "digital exhaust" becomes a powerful input for Copilot. It's what allows Copilot to tailor responses based on your context, calendar, projects, and team interactions—things no public large language model (LLM) could access. This differentiator means that Copilot isn't just smart when you get the technical foundations right; it's situationally aware, and because of that, it can turn that into valuable outputs.

Workloads and scenarios

Identifying typical workloads and their associated scenarios can help you work out how Copilot can have the most significant impact. For example, some workloads and scenarios apply broadly. Communication is a good example of a workload that applies to most knowledge workers. Copilot can assist in email management by summarizing long threads and generating draft responses. This can make communications more efficient and effective, thanks to the ability to specify the appropriate tone and language.

Say your usual email communication style is abrupt and straight to the point. Copilot can help you adapt your tone and soften your message while maintaining professional communication etiquette. Meeting preparation is another typical workload that Copilot can help with by compiling and summarizing relevant documents and even setting agendas, allowing knowledge workers to focus on strategic thinking rather than administrative details.

Note *Workloads* refer to specific tasks or groups of tasks that professionals routinely perform, such as drafting emails, preparing reports, or analyzing data. Scenarios are the contexts or situations where these workloads occur, like preparing for sales meetings with customers or conducting market research.

Then, there are workloads that will be specific to industry sectors. For example, in healthcare, Copilot can summarize patient data, draft clinical notes, and analyze research findings, enhancing patient care and operational efficiency. In a legal context, Copilot can review contracts, draft legal documents, and stay updated on regulatory changes, reducing time spent on routine tasks and focusing more on client advocacy.

Tip The Microsoft Scenario Library highlights examples of how you can use Copilot by Function and Industry. Explore workloads and use cases relevant to you at *https://adoption.microsoft.com/en-gb/scenario-library/*.

Start with high-value workloads

Organizations should identify their top three time-consuming tasks across priority functions and explore how Copilot can eliminate at least two. Each department will have a different view on which scenarios would deliver the most value, so it's a good idea to run this process within teams to get the most impactful ideas. Extending the legal example, one firm in the UK crafted a lengthy and detailed Copilot prompt that, once rolled out for use in document analysis across the firm, significantly reduced the time spent on legal matters. This prompt offered tremendous value to the organization in terms of accuracy and time saved.

Productivity is often the first area in which Copilot can deliver significant impact. Even your most productive employees have a more extensive to-do list than time in the day, so using Copilot with existing processes creates efficiency and allows people to get stuff done in less time. But the real value creation happens when that time saved on automating repetitive tasks is reinvested in more strategic and value-added activities.

Even if that reinvestment looks like enabling people to leave work on time, enhancing morale, and improving overall job satisfaction, it may be difficult to put a dollar value on improved employee morale. However, it's worth collecting quantitative feedback from staff about what extra time means to them as you factor in the value Copilot is adding to your organization. Copilot contributes to a more engaged and motivated workforce by freeing up time for more meaningful tasks.

> **Note** You don't need everything perfect to kick off. It's better to get started and iterate. Start with the capability, leadership support, and data you have available. Look at how Copilot can help with workloads that are repetitive and time-consuming.

Building a case for the value Copilot delivers

To get buy-in from senior leaders, you need to be able to pitch the payoff to decision-makers in a way that links what Copilot can do with what they care about—saving time, being more productive, reducing overheads, or creating the next big thing. Linking the impact of Copilot to key business goals such as productivity, innovation, and employee experience, and then outlining a comprehensive cost-benefit analysis, is an effective way to present the value to executives.

A detailed analysis of the financial return on investment (ROI) for adopting Copilot can silence the critics who might designate it as a cost to be cut. This should compare expected returns on initial implementation investment with potential cost savings from increased efficiency and productivity.

As people get good at delegating tasks to Copilot, a multiplication of time input to value output is created. However, it is equally important to explore the intangible benefits of Copilot, such as risk reduction, knowledge capture, and innovation. Copilot can help mitigate risks by ensuring consistent and accurate task execution and capturing valuable organizational knowledge that might otherwise be lost. Emphasizing a multi-lens approach to ROI, considering both financial and nonfinancial benefits, provides a more comprehensive understanding of the value Copilot can deliver for the organization.

Measuring and communicating the ROI of Copilot

Successfully adopting Copilot requires not just implementing technology but clearly demonstrating the tangible value it delivers. Stakeholders across the organization—from executives to frontline employees—must clearly see how Copilot improves business outcomes.

> **Tip** One way to track ROI is by building a custom solution on the Microsoft Power Platform to reflect this ROI framework. It can be an effective way to highlight the value to your leadership in real time.

Building your Copilot ROI framework

A robust return on investment (ROI) framework for Copilot should systematically address three core components:

- Strategic alignment

- Value measurement

- Impact communication

By structuring your ROI approach around these elements, you'll create compelling, data-driven narratives that resonate with stakeholders and drive continued support for Copilot adoption.

Step 1: Align Copilot with strategic goals

Start by identifying how specific Copilot capabilities align with your organization's strategic priorities. Strategic themes include operational efficiency, employee productivity, innovation acceleration, and enhancement of customer experience.

For each Copilot scenario, explicitly document the following:

- **The business challenge** Clearly state the problem, inefficiency, or opportunity you want to solve with Copilot.

- **The Copilot solution** Explain how Copilot resolves the challenge or capitalizes on the opportunity.

- **The strategic alignment** Articulate how the Copilot solution aligns with and contributes to broader organizational goals.

Step 2: Define and measure the value of Copilot

Use measurable Key Performance Indicators (KPIs) related to productivity, quality, efficiency, or innovation. Follow these steps to measure impact:

- **Establish baseline metrics** Gather current performance data before implementing Copilot, such as the average time spent drafting documents, response times to customer queries, or the number of tasks completed per day.

- **Capture post-adoption metrics** After Copilot adoption, remeasure these metrics. Ensure the period is sufficient to capture reliable data (typically, 30-90 days post-adoption).

- **Calculate the impact** Compare baseline and post-adoption data to quantify the impact of using Copilot. For example, reducing the time it takes to draft documents from 2 hours to 45 minutes is a clear, quantifiable improvement.

- **Convert metrics to value** To translate improvements into ROI, multiply productivity improvements by relevant average costs. For example, saving 1.25 hours per document, multiplied by the average employee's hourly rate, provides quantifiable value. Multiplying it by what your client pays for that document provides a clear opportunity to generate more revenue.

> **Note** This is just one way to demonstrate value through time saved. Ideally, you'll be able to quantify the impact beyond time saved by looking at the capacity Copilot creates. Perhaps that means being able to win and service more business with the same resources or demonstrate how the time saved has enabled the team to create a new offering.

Step 3: Continuously collect user feedback

Quantitative data alone is insufficient; capturing qualitative user insights strengthens your business case. Regularly collect user feedback on how they are using Copilot, using simple surveys or interviews, asking questions like:

- What is easier to do with the help of Copilot?

- How much time does Copilot save you for key tasks?

- How has Copilot improved the quality of your work?

- How much faster is it to prepare for client meetings when you get Copilot to help you?

- How would you feel if you lost your Copilot license?

This qualitative feedback enriches your ROI story, offering relatable examples of impact.

Step 4: Communicate Copilot impact with value cards

Create concise, visually appealing "value cards," summarizing key outcomes that can be published via Teams and SharePoint. Each value card should

- Highlight a clear metric improvement (such as "Document creation time reduced by 40 percent")

- Include monetary value estimates (such as "Annual productivity gain equivalent to $50,000")

- Provide a direct user testimonial (such as "Copilot helped me complete the quarterly report in half the time.")

- Include customer feedback if you have it (such as "We got our replacement order in record time.")

Distribute these Value Cards regularly through organization-wide communication channels, presentations, intranets, or internal newsletters.

Step 5: Aggregate and present data through dashboards

For ongoing transparency and impact tracking, consider creating a Copilot ROI dashboard using tools like Microsoft Power BI. Dashboards should visually aggregate

- KPI improvements

- Financial impact estimates

- User feedback trends

- Adoption rates across teams

This real-time visualization helps people see the cumulative and ongoing benefits of Copilot, fostering sustained support. Dashboards like this also make it easier to encourage friendly competition between teams and use gamification to accelerate the adoption process.

Step 6: Proactively evaluate and prioritize future Copilot use cases

Use this ROI framework proactively. Before implementing new Copilot scenarios, you should

- Evaluate potential Copilot use cases based on strategic alignment, projected impact, and uniqueness.

- Prioritize use cases demonstrating the greatest expected ROI and alignment with strategic objectives.

This disciplined approach ensures resources are invested effectively, increasing the overall value Copilot delivers for your organization.

Setting the vision builds momentum for Copilot adoption

By aligning Copilot initiatives with strategic objectives, rigorously measuring impact, capturing qualitative feedback, and communicating outcomes clearly and consistently, you can demonstrate the substantial value Copilot can deliver. This approach validates your Copilot investment and builds momentum for broader adoption, embedding AI innovation into your organizational culture.

Why is it important to know this framework at the start? Because you need to set your course. Determine where you're heading, and then you can evaluate whether you got where you intended to go. Clear goals aligned with your organization's mission will help you quantify the impact of adopting Copilot.

Try this prompt: Board meeting follow-up

Helping leaders find their a-ha moment with Copilot is an important step on their personal Copilot adoption journey. Effective executive sponsors need to use Copilot daily. This prompt is a good way to show how Copilot can be used to synthesize actions from meeting transcripts.

Because there is usually a person taking notes and recording actions, the AI outputs from this prompt could be evaluated against those notes for accuracy. It's also a quick way to see any actions that have been assigned to you if you have missed the meeting. Use this prompt with Copilot in Teams after your meeting has been transcribed:

As my Board-Meeting Action Assistant, analyze this meeting transcript to:

1. *Extract and itemize all follow-up actions explicitly mentioned*
2. *Compile a separate list of formal decisions approved during the meeting*
3. *Identify actions where ownership is unclear*

Present both lists in a structured format with clear, formal language. Group actions by discussion topic where applicable.
For each action item:

- *Include verbatim context from the transcript*
- *Note if timeframes were specified*
- *Flag items requiring clarification*

If multiple potential owners are mentioned for an action item, highlight this ambiguity for my review. When complete, ask me specifically about any actions requiring ownership clarification.

> **Tip**   Ask Microsoft 365 Copilot directly in the recap of the Teams meeting, or if you are using Chat, include a link to the meeting recording and transcript in your prompt.

Next steps

In this chapter, we discussed the importance of a clear, leader-driven vision for AI. Successful adoption relies on clarity of how AI transformation initiatives align with strategic organizational goals.

- Get clear on how Copilot can help achieve business goals by assessing the readiness of your people, leaders, data, and technology ecosystem.

- Prioritize meaningful work by reinvesting the time saved with Copilot on strategic and creative tasks, thereby improving productivity and job satisfaction.

- Secure strong, cross-functional executive sponsorship for Copilot by building a compelling business case for AI adoption and transformation.

Commitment

Trust is fundamental to driving change. We must authentically put earning and retaining our users' trust above all else if we are to help them along this journey and make up for the technology failures in their past.

—KARUANA GATIMU, DIRECTOR OF CUSTOMER ADVOCACY, MICROSOFT

In this chapter, you will:

■ Learn why moving beyond one-time sponsorship to sustained commitment from leaders across the organization directly influences the impact AI can have

■ Explore how an AI council can help build trust by aligning AI initiatives with organizational goals and ensuring responsible innovation

■ Discover the importance of a transparent and innovative culture and learn why fostering such a culture is essential for integrating Copilot into daily operations

From executive sponsorship to enduring commitment

Throughout the early 2010s, industry analysts repeatedly declared, "This is the year of the mobile." Yet despite these bold proclamations, user behavior didn't shift in a matter of months. The evolution from mobiles as secondary screens used for communication and gaming to a screen we can't live without seems inevitable now, but it didn't happen as quickly as pundits predicted. The notion that people wouldn't make significant purchases like airline tickets on their phones gradually gave way to data showing precisely that behavior became commonplace. This pace allowed digital strategists to postpone adaptation. Organizations that maintained their desktop-first approach missed significant opportunities as user behavior shifted, even as they annually acknowledged the growing importance of the mobile phone.

The AI transformation we face today shares similarities, but with one critical difference: The timeframe for adaptation has compressed dramatically. Unlike the mobile revolution's decade-long progression, it's difficult to keep pace with week-to-week changes in AI capabilities and applications. Organizations lack the luxury of the gradual commitment curve that characterizes mobile adoption.

In Chapter 2, "Clarity," we touched on the crucial role of executive sponsorship in successful AI adoption, where an executive actively endorses and assumes responsibility for an AI initiative. However, a project-by-project approach is insufficient; one-time sponsorship must be replaced with an ongoing commitment. Effective leadership means going beyond conveying messages to repeated, demonstrable actions that foster trust and create a cohesive approach to adoption across the organization. Executive vision and engagement should be unwavering, permeating the entire change implementation and adoption process and shaping the strategic direction for the future. As business leaders, we must recognize that our behaviors are observed more keenly than our words.

In this chapter, we examine why sustained organizational commitment directly influences AI implementation outcomes and explore practical approaches for establishing the necessary foundations for successful Copilot adoption in this accelerated environment.

Bringing everyone on the journey

Successful AI implementation requires a sustained commitment across at least one year, but this responsibility extends beyond any single executive. Like cybersecurity initiatives, AI adoption impacts every organizational function and should be positioned as a collective obligation across the entire leadership team. This shared accountability embeds Copilot in the organization's strategic foundation rather than functioning as an isolated initiative.

Organizations must develop differentiated approaches for various employee segments throughout the adoption process. Applying Rogers' Adoption Bell Curve helps identify and engage the innovators—individuals already experimenting with AI tools to enhance their productivity. However, strategies must evolve significantly when moving from early adopters to the late majority, with distinct considerations needed for different departments based on their unique workflows and priorities. Leadership teams face particularly important decisions regarding the final adoption segment—the laggards, representing approximately 16 percent of employees. Some enterprises take a definitive stance on this group, clearly communicating that resistance to core technological change may signal a misalignment with the organization's future direction. While bold, this approach exemplifies how executive commitment shapes adoption program outcomes and organizational culture.

The progression from initial executive sponsorship to enduring commitment plays a central role in determining AI adoption success. This journey requires coordinated leadership effort, strategically tailored approaches for different adoption phases, and decisive action to address resistance. By integrating Copilot adoption strategies into the organization's operational foundation, leaders create the conditions for meaningful digital transformation.

Establishing a cross-functional AI council

A cross-functional AI council serves as a cornerstone for successful AI adoption within your organization. This governance body does more than oversee AI initiatives—it aligns them with organizational goals, effectively manages risks, and creates the foundation for responsible innovation.

Purpose and scope of the AI council

The AI council should establish a governance framework that addresses technical, ethical, and operational aspects of AI implementation. Beyond risk management, this group creates a shared vision for how AI will transform your organization's capabilities and culture. The council demonstrates commitment by connecting AI adoption to core business strategies and values, transforming AI from a technology initiative into an organizational priority.

Composition of the AI council

When forming your AI council, create a diverse team representing various functional perspectives. Each member must bring active leadership and domain expertise with a genuine commitment to collaborative governance. Passive attendance is not an option; every member should be well-researched in their area of value and maintain connected relationships throughout the organization to gather feedback and insights.

As shown in Figure 3-1, key stakeholders should include:

- IT and technology leadership

- Data science and AI specialists

- Business unit leadership

- Legal and compliance representatives

- HR and organizational development

- Ethics and risk management

- Executive leadership

- End-user advocates from various departments

Because AI impacts every part of the organization, this representative mix enables comprehensive decision-making that considers diverse user needs, technical capabilities, and business outcomes. The council should reflect the full breadth of stakeholders involved in or affected by the AI adoption process.

Roles and responsibilities

The AI council should develop a rigorous evaluation process for reviewing and approving AI workloads. As shown in Figure 3-2, the key questions should assess the following:

- Technical feasibility—Can we do it?

- Desirability—Will people value it?

- Viability—Do we have the resources and business case?

- Ethical considerations—Should we do it?

Key stakeholders in AI council

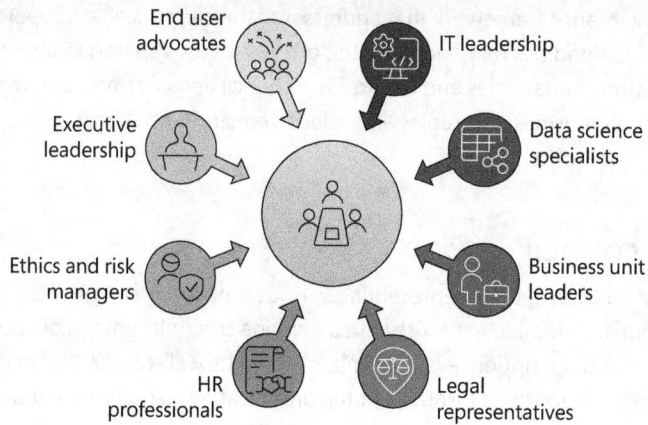

FIGURE 3-1 Key stakeholders to include in your AI council

Pathways to AI innovation

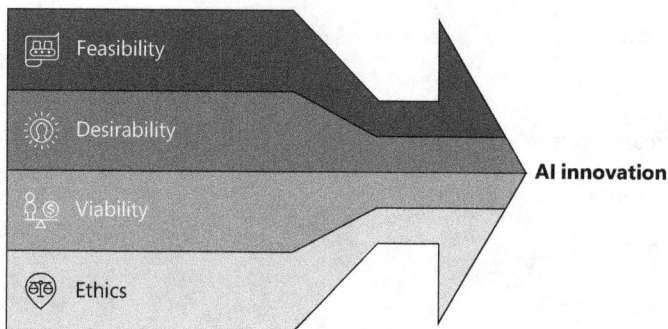

FIGURE 3-2 Pathways to innovation with AI

Regular assessment of deployed solutions should measure both performance metrics and adherence to ethical standards. The council should

- Define and communicate the organization's AI vision and principles

- Review and approve proposed AI initiatives based on established criteria

- Monitor AI solutions for performance, impact, and potential risks

- Guide teams that are implementing AI capabilities

- Foster innovation with responsible development practices

- Engage with external stakeholders on AI governance matters

Building trust through transparency

An effective AI council creates trust through transparent decision-making processes and clear communication. By documenting and sharing its evaluation criteria, review procedures, and oversight mechanisms, the council demonstrates accountability to all stakeholders. This transparency extends to how the organization handles data, trains users, and measures AI impact. The council should establish transparent processes for testing and approval before any AI initiative goes into production. This could include conducting red-teaming exercises to identify and mitigate potential risks.

> **Note**   Red-teaming means testing AI systems by simulating attacks to find weaknesses. Read more about it at *https://learn.microsoft.com/en-us/azure/ai-services/openai/concepts/red-teaming.*

More than technology governance

The AI council transcends traditional IT governance by addressing the multidimensional nature of AI adoption. Unlike standard technology initiatives, AI implementation touches on organizational culture, workforce transformation, customer relationships, and business models. The council serves as the organization's lighthouse for navigating these interconnected changes. Adoption and use of Copilot is just one of the initiatives that the AI council would oversee. It's important that this council acts as a central governance body for AI strategy across the organization. That way, they have the context and visibility to avoid duplication of efforts or the building of custom functionality that exists in platforms that have already been adopted.

The council ensures that technological capabilities align with human needs and organizational values. By establishing this cross-functional governance structure, your organization signals its commitment to responsible innovation and creates the foundation for sustainable AI transformation. The council becomes both a steering mechanism for current initiatives and a visionary body that anticipates future opportunities and challenges in your AI journey.

> **Tip**   If you're involved in an AI council or planning to establish one, see the whitepaper "Creating an AI Council—An Exercise in Transparent Leadership" in the Copilot Success Kit. You can download the kit at *https://adoption.microsoft.com/en-gb/copilot/success-kit/*

Clarifying roles and cascading leadership

Establishing clear roles and cascading leadership is important if you want to scale the adoption of Copilot to every employee. Set clear expectations around roles and responsibilities and define what is expected at each level of the organization. This clarity ensures that everyone understands their part in championing the adoption of Copilot and identifying areas to create more value.

Cascading leadership

Leadership should cascade from the top down, ensuring that directives from the executive team flow through various departments and ultimately reach the teams on the ground. This approach creates a unified direction and commitment across the organization. It also facilitates a two-way feedback loop, where outcomes and challenges are communicated back up the chain, enabling quick decision-making and responsiveness. Research highlights that people are most likely to respond positively to change when it comes from their direct managers.[1]

Agile and responsive culture

Adopting an agile methodology like Scrum can enhance the organization's responsiveness and effectiveness. Regular stand-ups and feedback loops help identify what has been accomplished, what is next, and any blockers that need to be addressed. This agile nature fosters a culture of action and getting things done, which is vital for AI adoption. It sets your organization up to benefit from iterative improvements, stacking skills, and new habits so that you can move forward a little each day.

Identifying Copilot champions

Your AI council and team leaders can help identify people who will make impactful Copilot champions and change agents. Champions are AI-curious, enthusiastic, and ready to drive AI adoption through peer-to-peer learning. These individuals will be instrumental in supporting the implementation and scaling of Copilot workloads and scenarios across various departments and teams.

Chapter 7, "Champions," covers how to build a champions program in more detail.

Role of the AI council

The AI council is pivotal in setting guardrails, methodologies, and a vision for Copilot implementation. Rather than being a bottleneck for approvals, the council should focus on enabling quick decision-making and providing the necessary support for Copilot champions and change agents within the organization. The council and champions should meet on alternating weeks , so that there is a constant feedback loop, allowing ideas raised by the champions to be vetted by the council for implementation approval.

By clarifying roles and cascading leadership effectively, organizations can embed Microsoft Copilot into every department and use it to reimagine every business process, developing an AI-powered culture of innovation and responsiveness.

---

[1] Prosci. Best Practices in Change Management. 12th ed. Fort Collins, CO: Prosci Inc., 2025.

Commit to a culture shift

Trust is often earned very slowly but can be lost quickly. When creating a culture that supports sustained AI adoption, people's trust in how the organization plans to use AI is crucial. Establish a clear purpose early, communicate it with intention, and regularly check in on your organization's AI sentiment. The AI council can play a key role in fostering trust. It should formulate a plan for measuring that sentiment, particularly focused on the level of trust that people have in regard to the use of Copilot within the organization. Trust extends to data as well. The data supporting AI initiatives must be trustworthy.

Be open about the capabilities and limitations of AI, demonstrating an understanding of how it is being used to evolve your processes. Build continuous learning, experimentation, and a culture of transparency into your approach. Creating an environment where innovation can thrive means allowing people to fail without consequence. Enable people to experiment and innovate without the risk of negative implications if they don't get to a valuable outcome straight away, because failure is a necessary step in learning. Corporate culture, especially in relation to performance and promotion cycles, has established patterns of communication that encourage people to shout about their successes and say nothing of their failures. It can feel like a risk to personal reputation to open oneself up to criticism by sharing a strategy that didn't work.

In one organization with a highly competitive, results-driven culture, the leadership introduced awards to recognize both successful sales strategies and valuable lessons from failed initiatives. Despite even offering greater rewards for "failure" stories, submissions remained overwhelmingly focused on wins. The risk to personal reputation outweighed the incentive, highlighting how deeply ingrained cultural norms can resist efforts to normalize failure. Creating a true culture of trust requires more than incentives; it demands visible leadership behaviors that model openness and vulnerability. When senior leaders publicly iterate through their own Copilot use, improving steadily rather than expecting immediate mastery, they create psychological safety for people across the organization to do the same.

Another critical element is the creation of channels where people can express concerns without fear. Trust flourishes when organizations encourage constructive dissent and provide clear mechanisms for raising issues about AI use. These might include anonymous feedback systems, regular listening sessions with the AI council, or designated "AI ethics ambassadors" who can amplify concerns from various departments. When people feel their apprehensions about AI tools are acknowledged rather than dismissed, they become more willing to engage meaningfully with the technology. Organizations should treat expressions of mistrust not as resistance to be overcome but as valuable intelligence that can strengthen implementation approaches.

Innovation inherently involves experimentation. Toyota's production system offers a valuable approach through the "five whys" technique—a method that focuses on fixing processes rather than finding someone to blame when mistakes occur. By repeatedly asking "why," the root cause of the issue can be identified and corrected.[2] This systematic approach improves the ability to validate hypotheses, test assumptions, innovate, and uncover new potential. It transforms "failures" into organizational learning that benefits everyone.

---

[2] Taiichi Ohno, *Toyota Production System: Beyond LargeScale Production* (Portland, OR: Productivity Press, 1988).

Embedding Copilot into daily work

To realize value from Copilot, it must become seamlessly integrated into daily operations and business processes. The goal of an effective adoption program would be to help employees get to the point where they turn to Copilot first to ask, 'How can Copilot help me here?' as the starting point for any task. This approach means Copilot becomes ingrained in workplace thinking and routines, maximizing its benefits. Let's look at two key elements that help embed Copilot into daily work:

- **Continuous improvement and adaptation** Regular feedback loops are important to maintaining Copilot's effectiveness and relevance. Update training and governance policies based on user feedback to enable people.

- **Robust governance and guardrails** Effective integration requires robust governance and clear guardrails, creating a secure and trustworthy environment. These measures help employees confidently use Copilot, reinforcing a culture of safety and support.

Sustaining momentum through continuous improvement

By committing to regular assessment and enhancement of Copilot adoption efforts, your organization can be agile and responsive to new opportunities and challenges.

Continuous communication

Regular updates and feedback loops are essential to keep everyone informed and engaged. One study revealed that while 85 percent of leaders believe their organization communicates consistently during change, only 55 percent of individual contributors agree, highlighting that leaders need to be overcommunicating in order to land that message with their people.[3] Updates in newsletters or regular internal communications can help share wins and breakthroughs across different parts of the organization. Allocate time in regular meetings for leaders and team members to share how they are using Copilot and what they are learning. Sharing successes can spark new ideas for innovative uses of Copilot, so make it an important part of your regular communications.

Reinforce behaviors with rewards

Celebrating success helps maintain enthusiasm and resilience in the Copilot adoption journey. Recognizing and rewarding new scenarios that have tangible business impacts and intangible benefits within the organization can foster a culture of innovation. As successes are celebrated, more ideas will emerge, and people will iterate on the ideas provided by their colleagues, creating a continuous cycle of improvement.

---

[3] Microsoft Viva People Science, *The State of AI Change Readiness: Accelerating AI Transformation through the Employee Experience* (Redmond, WA: Microsoft Corporation, August 2024), PDF, https://adoption.microsoft.com/files/viva/The-state-of-AI-change-readiness-eBook.pdf.

Using Microsoft Teams for Copilot conversations

One practical example is to use Microsoft Teams to converse with Copilot so that you can clarify your thoughts and practice effective communication:

1. Create a meeting with yourself in Microsoft Teams and turn on Copilot transcription.

2. To avoid distractions, turn off the camera. (We know you're really good-looking.) This setup allows you to have a focused conversation and lay out your thinking on whatever you're working on. The transcription captures what you say, and then Copilot summarizes it.

3. Next, open Copilot as part of the Teams session. Now, you can chat with Copilot to summarize your ideas, query your thinking, or identify gaps and opportunities for improvement. For instance, say you were preparing for a presentation.

4. You could use this approach to do a practice run and then engage in a conversational feedback session with Copilot.

5. Use the summary to determine if you've effectively communicated the points you wanted to make or if there are gaps in your thinking.

This approach to conversing with Copilot in Teams is a good example of using AI as a thought partner to help you improve the quality of your work.

> **Tip** Ask Copilot to summarize any document or presentation so that you can check whether the key messages you wanted to communicate are clear. Keep in mind that your intended audience might use Copilot or another AI to summarize your work, so interrogating it in this way can help ensure that your key messages, themes, and points come through strongly.

Iterate and adapt

Continuous improvement drives innovation within the organization. As people use Copilot more in their daily actions, they discover new ways it can benefit them. Because its capabilities are being updated all the time, how we learn to use it needs to be iterative and adaptive as well. Innovation will naturally bubble out of the organization through the continuous use of Copilot, and celebrating new use cases and workload scenarios will spark further ideas and improvements.

Commitment to governance and social responsibility

Adopting Copilot demands a steadfast commitment to governance and social responsibility, permeating every level of the organization, from executives to employees. This is not a mere checkbox exercise but a core principle that guarantees the ethical and responsible use of AI. Leaders who champion the cause set a tone that underscores the importance of ethical AI practices. Every organization will have a different approach according to its unique values and purpose. The role of the AI council also includes aligning your AI policies and governance approach with organizational values and regulatory responsibilities.

Responsible AI (RAI) framework

Responsible AI, often called RAI, refers to AI systems that are reliable, safe, fair, inclusive, transparent, and accountable. These principles should be non-negotiable in the adoption of Copilot. Organizations can achieve ethically sound AI adoption by integrating Environmental, Social, and Governance (ESG) considerations into the governance framework. While organizations have increasingly focused on the environmental aspect of ESG, the social and governance components are equally important in using AI ethically.

Social responsibility in AI adoption

Using AI should not be solely about cost-cutting or revenue generation at the expense of people. AI can add tremendous value, but it must be harnessed to benefit everyone. The advantages of AI should be distributed equitably across the organization rather than only benefiting shareholders. Social responsibility in AI adoption involves looking beyond immediate financial gains and considering the broader impact on employees and society.

Governance and inclusion

Effective AI governance involves creating policies and frameworks that promote inclusivity and fairness. This includes transparent decision-making processes and accountability mechanisms to ensure AI systems are used responsibly. By fostering an inclusive approach, organizations can drive a balanced and beneficial adoption of AI that supports all staff members.

Practical implications

In practice, this commitment to governance and social responsibility means

- Establishing clear guidelines and policies for AI use

- Regularly reviewing and updating these policies to keep pace with technological advancements

- Providing training and resources for employees so they understand and can adhere to these guidelines

- Engaging with external stakeholders, including regulators and the public, to maintain transparency and trust

With a firm commitment to trustworthy AI practices, organizations can lead the way in ethical AI adoption, ensuring that the benefits of AI are realized without compromising on social responsibility and governance.

Try this prompt: Keeping up

One of the most common questions we hear from leaders is "How am I supposed to keep up? The AI landscape is changing so quickly." One strategy is to use AI to help you make sense of how the latest Copilot news relates to your role. Try this prompt to help you stay up to date on the latest features and continuously improve your use of Copilot:

I'd like to stay updated on how to use Copilot more effectively in my leadership role. Please:

1. *Share 2-3 recent updates or features added to Microsoft Copilot for M365 in the past month that could help me be more productive.*
2. *Based on my role as a leader, suggest one specific way I could use you this week to have more impact in my work. Please provide a clear example of how to implement this suggestion.*
3. *Recommend one simple skill I can practice with you this week to build my AI literacy.*

Next steps

In this chapter, we explored the importance of sustained commitment from leadership in driving the successful adoption of both AI broadly and Copilot specifically. This commitment extends to demonstrable acknowledgment of collective responsibility across the organization through establishing governance structures like an AI council.

- Trust is foundational for effective AI implementation. Leaders can influence this by prioritizing user confidence and transparency.

- Clear roles and responsibilities must cascade from executives to team leaders to facilitate effective Copilot adoption throughout the organization.

- Tailored strategies are necessary to engage various employee segments in the adoption process, focusing on their unique needs and workflows.

- Embed governance and social responsibility principles into your AI practices to ensure the ethical and equitable use of AI technologies.

PART 2

Driving change and adoption

Once you have clarity on the vision for AI in your organization and the commitment of your executive team and board, the next part of Copilot adoption focuses on how to drive change. Part One focused on the "why" of Copilot adoption. In Part Two, we explore the how. Learning from the success of organizations that have enabled their people and processes with Copilot, we share strategies and tactics to manage change, build capability, prepare for evolving compliance requirements, and foster a thriving community of champions.

- In Chapter 4, "Change management," we look at the people side of change, highlighting the need for an intentional approach to help people adopt Copilot and embed it into their daily work.

- In Chapter 5, "Capability," we discuss how to build digital and AI literacy among your teams with modern training approaches that help people develop the confidence and competence to use Copilot.

- In Chapter 6, "Compliance," we cover the important and evolving topic of compliance and regulation when it comes to AI and Copilot. This chapter is designed as a roadmap to help you make a plan that can be adapted as the regulatory environment continues to evolve. We examine the role of an AI council and highlight how an enduring commitment to transparency and innovation with AI creates trust.

- In Chapter 7, "Champions," we highlight how you can support the motivated and AI-curious people in your teams to be the heroes who help drive effective Copilot adoption amongst their peers. Champions communities—or communities of practice—are as essential to your Copilot adoption plan as executive sponsors.

These chapters involve a lot of tips and practical advice on steps you can take to support adoption and proficiency, rather than just access to Copilot. That's where you'll realize the true value of empowering your teams with Copilot.

> **Tip** "Microsoft 365 Copilot has completely transformed the way I work. Repetitive, manual tasks have been replaced by intelligent, natural, and contextual interactions with the tools I already use every day. It understands the full picture—documents, emails, meetings—and delivers answers, summaries, and ideas as if it already knew my thought process. I rarely start anything from scratch anymore. Today, I focus my energy where it matters most: strategic decisions. And with the rise of Agents, I'm taking it even further—automating entire workflows that once demanded constant attention. What used to feel like effort now feels like flow."–**Danilo Nogueira** is a Microsoft MVP for M365 Copilot, a Microsoft Certified Trainer, and leads Cloud Target's Modern Work practice in Brazil.

CHAPTER 4

Change management

*The secret to successful change lies beyond the visible and busy activities that surround change. Successful change, at its core, is rooted in something much simpler: how to facilitate change with **one** person.*

—*Jeff Hiatt, Prosci Founder*

In this chapter, you will:

■ Learn about change management and understand why a formal approach to change management is necessary to drive impactful Copilot adoption

■ Discover proven change management frameworks to support the people aspect of change that delivers results

■ Recognize the unique challenges and barriers that can cause resistance to change for people who are learning how to incorporate Copilot into their daily workflow

Introduction to change management

Change is a constant in both work and life, but it doesn't come naturally to most people. For change to be successful, you need to provide the right conditions. When the scope of change is as broad as that required to reimagine work with the help of AI and Copilot, it's even more important to create an intentional plan to manage the transition. That's where change management comes in.

What is change management?

According to Prosci, a leading research firm in change management, change management is "the process, tools, and techniques to manage the people side of change to achieve a required business outcome."[1] While technology implementation focuses on technical aspects, change management addresses the human elements necessary for successful adoption. It seeks to provide the support each person needs to transition from their current state to a desired future state. Without change management, adoption won't happen.

---

[1] Prosci. "What Is Change Management?" Accessed May 6, 2025. *https://www.prosci.com/resources/articles/what-is-change-management*.

The need for formal change management

While the critical role project managers play in technology rollout is now commonly acknowledged, people often struggle to understand the important role of change management. Here's a simple yet effective exercise:

1. Take out a piece of paper.

2. Hold a pen in your dominant hand.

3. Sign your name.

How did that feel? You probably completed the task without thinking about it.

Now, switch the pen to your nondominant hand and try to sign your name. How did that feel? You likely noticed the difference immediately. That probably felt uncomfortable. You might be thinking, why on earth would I do it that way when the way I usually do it works so much better?

That's because our brains develop neural pathways or muscle memory through instruction and repetition, enabling us to complete familiar tasks without much cognitive effort because they become part of our subconscious behaviors. You don't have to think about how you sign your name; you do it on autopilot. By contrast, new tasks feel awkward and inefficient, and it's natural to resist because the new process is uncomfortable compared to what we're used to.

A well-thought-out change management process can help people overcome that resistance and other barriers to adoption and move from discomfort to proficiency. The goal is to help people transition from the initial awkwardness of new tasks to the muscle memory of doing them instinctively.

The role of change management in AI adoption

When it comes to adopting AI tools like Copilot, we have discussed some of the unique challenges that can create resistance: constantly evolving technical capabilities and noisy headlines that make people feel like everyone else is already using AI, which stokes a fear of becoming obsolete. The familiarity of a search box often leads people to treat Copilot and other AI tools as simple Q&A tools rather than sophisticated dialogue partners. In fact, to counter this, the Copilot Chat user interface (UI) has evolved to include a separate search area so that it's easier for users to differentiate between searching and conversing. Learning how Copilot can help you get stuff done requires a curious mindset and a new focus on essential skills like critical thinking and delegation. Using Copilot effectively, as a true thought partner and assistant, requires a shift in your thinking and a change to the way you are used to working.

Issuing Copilot licenses and activating the service constitute merely "deployment." Without a deliberate change management plan, most organizations experience an immediate performance dip and settle for slow, surface-level usage—where employees interact with the tool but only realize a fraction of the promised business benefits. When change is strategically facilitated through executive sponsorship, targeted enablement, and consistent reinforcement, usage evolves into genuine adoption based on proficiency. Focusing on supporting those habitual behaviors elevates organizational performance much faster than reporting on the usage of Copilot. Prosci's 2024 research highlights that projects with an intentional approach to change management are seven times more likely to meet or exceed objectives.[2] Change management isn't an optional extra for Copilot implementation; change management is necessary for converting AI access into measurable business value.

The Prosci change methodology

Prosci's change management methodology, which has been around since 1994, offers a practical framework that is based on extensive research and insights from real-world projects. The Prosci 3-Phase Process approaches change management in three core phases:

1. **Preparing for change**   This involves defining the change management strategy, preparing the change management team, and developing a sponsorship model. Key questions to answer in this phase include:

   - What are we trying to achieve?
   - Who has to do their jobs differently now?
   - What will it take to achieve success?

2. **Managing change**   Focuses on executing change management plans while engaging, educating, and enabling all stakeholders. Key questions to answer in this phase include:

   - What will we do to prepare, equip, and support people?
   - How are we doing?
   - What adjustments do we need to make?

3. **Reinforcing change**   Includes collecting and analyzing feedback, diagnosing gaps, managing resistance, and implementing corrective actions to sustain the change. Key questions to answer in this phase include:

   - Now, where are we? Are we done yet?
   - What is needed to ensure the change sticks?
   - Who will assume ownership and sustain outcomes?

Change management can facilitate a transition to a new way of working so that the organization can maximize the benefits of AI-enabled people and processes. Applying and adapting change management frameworks like this one allow you to effectively prepare and support people. The individual experience of change is what drives organizational value in adopting Copilot.

---

[2] Prosci, "The Correlation Between Change Management and Project Success," Prosci Blog, July 31, 2024, *https://www.prosci.com/blog/the-correlation-between-change-management-and-project-success.*

Prosci ADKAR model for individual change

Often, you'll hear people talk about "organizational change," but one of the insights from over two decades of Prosci's research is that change happens at the individual level. Organizational change happens when many people in an organization transition to a new way of working. Prosci's ADKAR model describes the process a person goes through, which is especially relevant to the change required to build Copilot into the way you work every day. The ADKAR model outlines five essential steps for change to happen: Awareness, Desire, Knowledge, Ability, and Reinforcement. Each step must happen in order before people will change how they work. Let's look at this process in the context of Copilot.

- **Awareness**   Creating awareness involves communicating the need for change. It requires clear messaging on why the organization is adopting Copilot, transparently outlining the thinking behind the strategy, and emphasizing benefits, such as freeing up time for innovation, improving productivity, and getting stuff done. Leaders who can explain the broader context of AI-driven work and how Copilot fits this vision will inspire trust in this phase.

- **Desire**   Generating desire means fostering a willingness to support and participate in change. Highlight the personal benefits of Copilot so people can go from surviving to thriving. Sometimes described as an a-ha moment, desire happens when a person can connect how they could use Copilot to a compelling vision for the organization.

- **Knowledge**   Providing knowledge involves equipping employees with the information and skills to use Copilot effectively, including training sessions that explain how Copilot works, its functionalities, and practical applications in daily tasks. Clear explanations that are easily understood by nontechnical employees are vital to ensure everyone understands how to leverage Copilot to get stuff done.

- **Ability**   Developing ability means ensuring employees demonstrate the skills and behaviors required to use Copilot proficiently. This step often involves hands-on training and practice sessions where employees can apply what they've learned in real scenarios. Continuous support and feedback will help them build confidence and competence.

- **Reinforcement**   Reinforcement sustains change by embedding new behaviors into the organizational culture. This step is arguably the most important when it comes to adopting a new way of getting work done with Copilot. Over 90 days, regular refreshers and follow-up sessions can reinforce key learning points. This ongoing support ensures that using Copilot becomes second nature, leading to long-term adoption and success. One of the challenges with Copilot adoption is to build constant learning and experimentation into how people use it because Copilot's capabilities are changing week to week. Equally, as their skills develop, people will learn new ways to use Copilot to help them with their work.

The ADKAR model outlines the journey people need to go through to transition from the current state to the desired future state. Leaders can use insights from these phases to design a tailored approach to change management that caters to people wherever they are on the change journey. Too often, the rollout of new technology starts with training—but the research behind ADKAR shows that before people are ready to learn how to use new tools, they first need to know why the shift to AI-enabled work is happening (awareness) and what's in it for them (desire). Each person needs to have their own a-ha moment.

> **Note** It's important to tailor your change approach based on the needs of the people you are working with. Where awareness and desire for Copilot are high amongst the AI-curious, focus on enabling them with the knowledge to use it effectively.

Activities at each stage

While frameworks like Prosci's 3-Phase Process and ADKAR[3] provide a solid foundation, with Copilot adoption it's important to extend these frameworks with practical hands-on activities that allow people to experience how Copilot works. This includes defining specific actions, communication patterns, and engagement strategies, as well as visibly using Copilot in Microsoft 365 apps to facilitate the change management process.

As shown in Table 4-1, there are communications and team engagement activities that work well at each phase.

TABLE 4-1 Ideas to use Copilot to support change management activities

ADKAR Phase	Activities	How Copilot can help
Awareness	Town halls, team meetings, and email announcements	Record, transcribe, and summarize
Desire	Surveys, case studies, awards, and incentives	Analyze results, draft communications
Knowledge	Microsoft Learn, workshops, and certification paths	Tailor Learning plans
Ability	Lunch-and-learns, hackathons, promptathons, and innovation challenges	Scheduling, brainstorming and ideation, and evaluation
Reinforcement	Quarterly awards and refresher training	Audio summaries and quality checks

Start by raising awareness through a series of announcements that explain the need for change and the benefits of Copilot. Share success stories to generate desire and demonstrate how Copilot can help with daily tasks. Then, provide comprehensive training to build knowledge and conduct hands-on

---

3 Prosci. "Prosci 3-Phase Process" Accessed May 7, 2025. *https://www.prosci.com/methodology/3-phase-process*

sessions to develop ability. Finally, reinforce the change with regular follow-ups and refreshers, ensuring Copilot remains firmly embedded in your work culture.

> **Tip** Run a waitlist of people who want a paid Copilot license because they have an idea of how they would use it in their work. This highlights the people who have moved from awareness to desire and are ready for knowledge. Regularly asking people how losing their Copilot license would impact their work can help reinforce the value to people in that phase of change, and create awareness and desire among people who are earlier on their change journey.

Roles in the change team

In any successful change management initiative, it's important to first assemble the right team. The change team needs to be able to anticipate frustrations, fears, and resistance. They are responsible for devising ways to overcome challenges and courageously empower people. For Copilot adoption, the people in these roles must be competent and confident Copilot users. They should know what it functionally does and be practically using it themselves to facilitate the change management processes. The change team includes these three core roles:

- **Change manager**

  - **Role** The change manager oversees and guides the entire change project. They are responsible for ensuring that the change management process is aligned with the organization's goals and is progressing smoothly.

  - **Skills** They need to be familiar with how Copilot works, have practical hands-on experience, and have strong interpersonal skills. Perhaps they have a change management certification or experience. They also need high emotional intelligence (EQ) to understand how messaging is landing and address organizational frustrations and fears.

- **Communications specialist**

  - **Role** The communications specialist manages the communications plan, ensuring that information is rolled out effectively across the organization. They coordinate how the executive layer communicates with the rest of the organization, matching the channel and the stakeholders to deliver messages effectively.

  - **Skills** Expertise in communication strategies, ability to coordinate timely and frequent communications, and proficiency in using internal channels that people in the organization are familiar with.

- **Training coordinator**

  - **Role** The training coordinator manages the training plan and facilitation to ensure that all team members have an opportunity to learn how to use Copilot. The training coordinator needs to consider frequency and modality so that people can learn in the way that suits them best.

- **Skills** Familiarity with training tools and templates, ability to facilitate training sessions, and strong organizational skills. Applied understanding of using and extending Copilot. Depending on the organization, the role might be combined with the Change Manager and Communications Specialist roles.

Depending on the scale of the rollout, these roles might be done by several adoption practitioners, perhaps dedicated to these roles or as champions for smaller-scale implementations. For best results, dedicated adoption specialists will facilitate Copilot adoption sessions. When people with applied Copilot experience carry out these roles, the change process will empower transformation across the organization.

Stakeholder analysis and engagement

Implementing change within an organization requires a deep understanding of the people involved and empathy for how the change will impact them. Spending time on stakeholder analysis and engagement, and using those insights to adapt the change management approach for different roles and departments, will increase your chances of success. The goal is to identify, engage, and support the key stakeholders throughout the change process.

As shown in Figure 4-1, it's important to first identify the core stakeholders. These are the people who are most engaged in the change process, from executive sponsors to the AI council, the project team, and the change team. Next, map the direct stakeholders. This group is actively involved and connected with the Copilot rollout but doesn't have decision-making authority. It could include department leaders, managers, and end users. Finally, map the indirect stakeholders. This might include customers or suppliers.

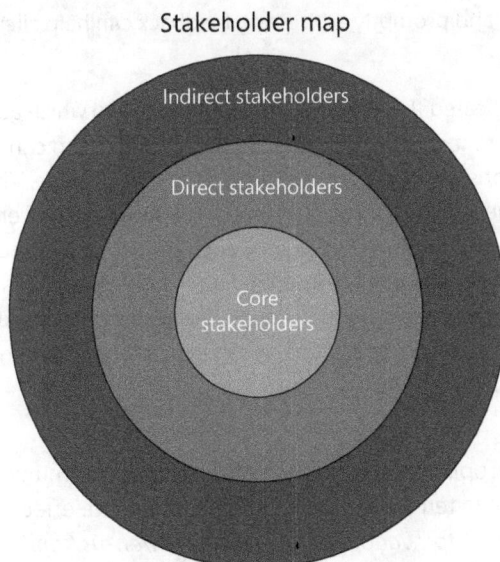

Stakeholder map

Indirect stakeholders

Direct stakeholders

Core stakeholders

FIGURE 4-1 An example of a stakeholder map

You might find it beneficial to complete several stakeholder maps, depending on how you structure your change plan. For example, you might have one for each department if your Copilot adoption plan focuses on one function at a time.

> **Tip** As you complete your stakeholder map, ask Copilot to analyze and provide feedback. Who have you missed? How might you tailor your communications for different stakeholders based on which circle they fall into?

Different stakeholder groups require different engagement strategies. For example, innovators and early adopters can be engaged through pilot programs and early access to Copilot features, allowing them to provide feedback and become advocates. The early and late majority may need more structured training and clear demonstrations of how to use Copilot. Laggards might require additional support and reassurance to overcome their resistance. Engaging stakeholders effectively can create a positive culture around Copilot adoption.

Communication strategy

The stakeholder map informs the frequency and detail of communications. For example, core stakeholders need the most frequent and detailed communication, while direct stakeholders require less frequent updates and opportunities for input. Be prepared to adjust your communication strategy as you progress through the adoption curve. This flexibility will help maintain engagement and address any emerging challenges. Leverage the enthusiasm of innovators and early adopters to build momentum that encourages the early and late majority to follow suit. Sharing success stories can help address concerns and showcase the tangible benefits of Copilot. Each stakeholder group will have different concerns regarding the use of Copilot. It is important to address these concerns transparently to build trust. Regular communication, open discussions, and promptly addressing feedback can help alleviate fears and build confidence in the new technology.

Clearly define what messages will be communicated through specific channels and to which audience. Tailor your communication to address different stakeholder groups' specific needs and concerns. Document the frequency of communications and the channels you will use, for example, Viva Engage. This could include town hall meetings, newsletters, interactive webinars, and other stakeholder engagement tactics. Regularly evaluate your communication plan at least once a month to ensure it is meeting its objectives. Ask questions like: Is the plan reaching the intended audience? Is it delivering the expected results? Are the stories being shared resonating with the audience? Use storytelling techniques to make your communications more relatable and impactful. This can help address concerns and build a positive narrative around the adoption of Copilot.

> **Tip** Leverage resources from Microsoft's Copilot Success Kit to enhance your communication strategy. These resources provide valuable templates and guidelines to ensure effective and comprehensive communication. See *https://adoption.microsoft.com/en-us/copilot/success-kit/*.

Training and support

Copilot adoption requires modern training approaches, moving away from traditional classroom formats to microlearning experiences that deliver focused, practical skills. Organizations should create bite-sized content demonstrating task-specific applications across Word, PowerPoint, Excel, Outlook, Teams, and SharePoint, teaching employees how to delegate tasks, engage in specific scenarios, and craft effective prompts. This application-specific guidance ensures employees learn exactly what they need for their roles without unnecessary technical complexity.

Support mechanisms must include feedback channels through help desks, user groups, and communities of practice, complemented by champion networks across departments to facilitate peer learning and cross-functional knowledge sharing. Training should emphasize business outcomes rather than technical functionalities—positioning prompt engineering as a conversational skill for achieving results, not a technical exercise. By incorporating real-world scenarios that demonstrate productivity gains and business benefits, organizations can ensure smooth adoption and empower employees to maximize Copilot's potential. Champions from different departments should coordinate their efforts, creating a unified support system that drives organization-wide success.

Chapter 5, "Capability," covers training strategies in more detail.

Measuring and reporting change impact

Understanding the impact of adopting Copilot and demonstrating that value to stakeholders will help you maintain buy-in. You can only manage what you can measure. Tracking both adoption rates and user satisfaction provides a comprehensive view of success. While tools like Viva Insights offer valuable data, complement them with regular user satisfaction surveys and feedback requests to understand what's working and what needs refinement. It's important to align the qualitative and quantitative feedback you collect with the strategic objectives for the adoption of Copilot. The Microsoft Copilot Dashboard tracks readiness, adoption, impact, and learning, though you might find that creating custom Power BI dashboards can capture deeper insights about who uses Copilot, how they use it, and the benefits that are specific to your organization.

Make it easy for users to share experiences and provide feedback. They will be more motivated to keep sharing as long as they can see how their input drives continuous improvement. Beyond quantitative metrics, collect and share "stories from the field" that showcase successful Copilot scenarios across the organization. These qualitative insights build a culture of innovation and encourage wider adoption by demonstrating tangible benefits in daily work. Formal processes for capturing and distributing success stories transform individual wins into organizational momentum, highlighting the need to make measurement and reporting an ongoing commitment rather than a one-time activity.

> **Note** You can access the Microsoft Copilot Dashboard at *https://insights.cloud.microsoft/#/CopilotDashboard/.*

Sustaining outcomes

Sustaining outcomes requires tracking performance and regularly adapting your action plan to address gaps and resistance areas. By understanding where challenges exist, you can develop targeted strategies for ongoing reinforcement and upskilling, allowing employees to learn new Copilot skills at their own pace. Regular reinforcement through bite-sized learning materials, Teams "Did you know?" cards, or weekly prompts in newsletters keeps skills fresh and encourages continuous learning. These incremental gains must be reinforced consistently to ensure lasting adoption.

An effective Copilot change program equips people with the adaptable skills and mindset they need to iterate and evolve how they use it to help them get stuff done. The change management process for Copilot is continuous due to constant platform updates and improvements, requiring leaders to maintain momentum beyond the initial rollout. It's not a one-time process. Done right, it will change the way every process in your organization operates. This includes creating sustainable models for onboarding new employees from diverse backgrounds with varying experience levels. Building a community of champions who share knowledge and help others creates a culture of continuous improvement where Copilot becomes integral to daily work. These champions foster peer learning and ensure the organization maintains its commitment to innovation and efficiency long after the initial implementation phase.

In Chapter 7, "Champions," we explore how to create and foster a thriving champions community.

Try this prompt: The best next step

Intentional change management requires a focused effort. If the frameworks discussed in this chapter are new to you, it can be hard to know where to start, but Copilot can help you work out what to do next. Use this prompt to deepen your understanding of change management by providing Copilot with context on your current state and the change you want to facilitate. The output will help you prioritize the best next step in your Copilot adoption journey, taking into account the unique context of your organization.

Act as my organizational change strategist to help me determine the best next step for preparing my organization for Copilot adoption.

Please interview me by asking one question at a time about:

- *My organization's current state*
- *Existing change readiness*
- *Previous technology adoption experiences*
- *Key stakeholders and decision-makers*
- *Timeline and constraints*

After gathering sufficient context through your questions, recommend:

1. *The single most impactful next step I should take.*
2. *Who I need to involve in this step.*
3. *What resources I'll need to execute this step.*
4. *How this step will set up future phases.*

Begin with your first question.

Next steps

In this chapter, we covered what change management is and the vital role it plays in driving successful Copilot adoption. Successful change starts with an a-ha moment and requires a structured approach to overcome resistance.

- A formal change management plan is essential to ensure smooth transitions, as people often resist new processes due to discomfort with change.

- The Prosci methodology consists of three phases: preparing for change, managing change, and reinforcing change, each addressing different aspects of the transition process.

- Effective change management requires understanding stakeholder dynamics and tailoring engagement strategies to different groups, ensuring that communication is clear and addresses specific concerns.

Capability

If you take two people, one of them is a learn-it-all, and the other one is a know-it-all, the learn-it-all will always trump the know-it-all in the long run, even if they start with less innate capability.

—Satya Nadella

In this chapter, you will:

- Understand why it's important to design training programs that will raise AI literacy for everyone in your organization to enable Copilot adoption

- Explore foundational AI concepts that underpin AI literacy and allow the organization to develop a shared language when discussing AI and Copilot

- Discover how to design and implement tailored training programs and lift the Copilot capability of your teams

Building AI literacy across your organization

Imagine it's your first day as a forestry apprentice. You're handed a powerful chainsaw, pointed towards the forest, and told, "Off you go!" No training, no safety briefing—just a tool capable of both incredible productivity and serious harm. Sounds reckless, doesn't it? Yet, that's how many organizations are approaching Copilot adoption. We equip employees with powerful AI tools capable of revolutionizing their productivity without proper training or guidance. Just like a chainsaw, Copilot requires skill, understanding, and careful handling to maximize benefits and avoid unintended consequences.

Building capability includes establishing a shared AI vocabulary that enables clear communication across the organization. When training frameworks are tailored to specific roles, the entire organization advances together. This deliberate approach to capability building doesn't just enhance individual performance; it acts as a foundation for innovation.

Defining AI literacy

Start by defining what AI literacy means for the organization. At its core, AI literacy involves understanding foundational AI concepts such as natural language processing (NLP), generative AI, and large language models (LLMs). These concepts, while technical, need to be made accessible to all employees.

Move beyond jargon to teach people how AI practically impacts their daily tasks and how it broadly is reshaping your industry. The definition may differ slightly by department or role. For instance, AI literacy in your IT department might require a technical understanding of how large language models work and an applied knowledge of building solutions around them. By contrast, AI literacy for a salesperson might mean knowing how to prompt Copilot to effectively prepare for an upcoming meeting with a customer. The foundational element of AI literacy aims to demystify the technology and make it more relatable.

When everyone is on the same page about what AI is and how it can be used, it reduces the risk of miscommunication and ensures that efforts are aligned toward common goals. A shared language encourages collaboration that helps address questions about trust. When people understand how AI systems, like Copilot, generate answers based on the data they rely on, their experience of those systems improves significantly.

Developing a shared language

Analogies serve as bridges to understanding complex AI concepts by connecting them to familiar experiences. When people struggle with abstract AI terminology, well-crafted comparisons create immediate clarity. For example, explaining machine learning as a process where AI learns from data, much like humans learn from experiences, can make the concept more tangible. Compare pattern recognition to how you instinctively recognize a friend's face, or automated decision-making to how you can roll through the steps of your morning routine on autopilot. These concrete parallels not only demystify AI capabilities but also build confidence in our ability to work alongside these tools effectively.

A refresher on foundational AI concepts

As shown in Table 5-1, there are several key foundational AI concepts everyone needs to understand as a technical baseline.

TABLE 5-1 Foundational AI terms and definitions

Term	Definition
Natural language processing (NLP)	Natural language processing (NLP) allows AI to understand, interpret, and generate human language. It powers technologies like chatbots, virtual assistants, and language translation services, enhancing communication and automating tasks. By understanding NLP, people can appreciate how AI is able to understand spoken and written instructions.
Machine learning (ML)	Machine learning involves AI learning from data to improve its performance over time without explicit programming. It is the backbone of many AI applications, from recommendation systems to predictive analytics. People should understand how data quality directly impacts the effectiveness of machine learning models.
Deep learning	A subset of machine learning, deep learning uses neural networks with multiple layers to process complex patterns in data. It is used in applications such as image and speech recognition. Understanding deep learning helps people grasp how AI can handle intricate tasks requiring high accuracy.
Speech recognition and synthesis	Speech recognition and synthesis technologies allow AI to understand spoken language and generate speech. They are used in virtual assistants and voice-controlled devices. By understanding this concept, people can explore how AI can improve accessibility and user interaction through voice commands.

Term	Definition
Knowledge representation and reasoning	Knowledge representation and reasoning is the structuring of information so that AI can use it for problem-solving and decision-making. It is crucial for applications that require understanding and reasoning, such as expert systems. It's important to understand these concepts to know how AI can assist in making informed decisions based on structured knowledge.
Large language models (LLMs)	Large language models (LLMs) are AI models primarily trained on vast amounts of text data to understand and generate human language. They often power chatbots and content creation. Some advanced versions, known as multimodal models, also incorporate images or videos, expanding the ability of AI to interpret and respond to multiple data types.
Small language models (SLMs)	Small language models (SLMs) are compact, specialized AI models that are smaller and typically more focused than LLMs. Due to their reduced size, they can efficiently run locally on smaller devices like phones and tablets. They're often applied to targeted tasks or specific organizational needs. Knowing about SLM helps people consider how customized, efficient AI solutions can be built to address certain requirements.
Hallucination	A hallucination occurs when AI generates plausible-sounding yet entirely fabricated or unsupported information rather than directly replicating inaccuracies already present in source documents. Errors found within employees' digital artifacts (such as incorrect data within the Microsoft Graph) can propagate misinformation in AI outputs. Still, this scenario is generally considered a data quality issue rather than a true hallucination.
Deterministic AI	Deterministic AI systems produce identical outputs when given the same inputs and conditions, following algorithmic, rule-based processes where the output behavior is entirely predictable and repeatable.
Nondeterministic AI	Nondeterministic AI systems can produce different outputs from identical inputs. This is due to elements of randomness, probabilistic processes, or sampling methods, making their responses variable and less predictable even under the same conditions. Copilot is primarily a nondeterministic system, though it can perform deterministic tasks like mathematical equations.
Retrieval-augmented generation (RAG)	Retrieval-augmented generation (RAG) is like having an assistant who, rather than guessing answers from memory, consults trusted reference documents before responding. This approach ensures that the information is accurate, relevant, and backed by reliable sources. Understanding RAG helps people use AI tools that can deliver more precise, informed, and trustworthy responses.
Chat (in the context of Copilot's chatbot interface)	Chat interacts with AI through a conversational interface. Understanding this concept helps employees leverage chatbots for efficient communication and task automation.
Agents	Agents are AI systems designed to perform specific tasks autonomously. They can be used for various applications, from customer service to data analysis. Knowing about agents helps people understand how AI can automate and optimize different organizational processes.
Prompting	Prompting refers to interacting with AI systems through thoughtfully crafted questions or instructions called "prompts." Unlike static searches on search engines, prompting is an iterative, conversational process, often requiring multiple attempts and adjustments to achieve optimal results. Understanding prompting helps people engage effectively with AI by continuously refining their inputs, leading to more precise, accurate, and valuable responses.
Microsoft 365 Copilot	Microsoft 365 Copilot is an AI-powered assistant embedded directly into core Microsoft 365 applications, including Word, Excel, PowerPoint, Outlook, Teams, and many more. It assists users in drafting emails, generating presentations, summarizing documents, and analyzing data. Awareness of M365 Copilot enables employees to leverage AI effectively, significantly enhancing productivity and efficiency in their daily work.
Microsoft 365 Copilot Chat	Microsoft 365 Copilot Chat is a free conversational interface built directly within your organization's Microsoft 365 tenant and also into personal and school Microsoft accounts. It allows users to interact easily with Copilot using natural language commands. This integrated approach not only streamlines workflows and provides quick assistance across various applications but also provides a secure alternative to external or unapproved AI tools (BYOAI or Shadow AI). Keeping interactions within your organization's governed environment significantly reduces the risk of sensitive organizational data leakage. It is used as an incremental AI solution.

Term	Definition
Agent Builder	Agent Builder allows people to build customized agents in either the Microsoft 365 Copilot or Teams apps. This experience is designed to allow people without coding or developer experience to describe and configure how they want their personalized agents to work.
Copilot Studio	Copilot Studio is a low-code tool that enables people to build custom AI copilots and specialized AI agents tailored to their unique business needs. It empowers low-code makers to design, test, and deploy targeted AI assistants that can perform specialized tasks, significantly enhancing the functionality and relevance of AI within the organization. By understanding Copilot Studio, employees can see how tailored AI solutions like customer service agents or internal process automation bots can drive productivity, efficiency, and innovation. It is used when creating extensible AI solutions.
Azure AI Foundry	Azure AI Foundry provides developers with a comprehensive suite of AI tools and services within Microsoft Azure. It allows advanced customization abilities so that organizations can efficiently create, deploy, and manage AI solutions on a large scale. Understanding Azure AI Foundry helps people recognize how cloud-based AI services can be leveraged to foster innovation, improve operational efficiency, and deliver impactful business outcomes. It is used when creating differential AI solutions.

Building AI literacy establishes a foundation of shared understanding across your organization. Tailored training programs and practical tools detailed in the next section transform this foundational knowledge into role-specific capabilities that drive measurable business outcomes.

> **Tip**   To develop your foundational AI literacy further, take the Microsoft Learn course Azure AI Fundamentals at *https://learn.microsoft.com/en-us/training/courses/ai-900t00*.

Designing effective Microsoft 365 Copilot training

Effective Copilot training aligns learning outcomes with organizational objectives and employee roles. When training programs directly support strategic goals, they maximize productivity gains and foster innovation. A scalable training structure includes developing an adaptable framework that will support capability building across all organizational levels—from tailored executive leadership sessions to frontline staff onboarding. This framework ensures all employees develop appropriate Copilot proficiency for their position, creating a cohesive organizational capability rather than isolated pockets of expertise.

> **Note**   Consider the impact that raising the AI literacy of all your staff by 30 percent would have on your organization. The goal isn't necessarily to build every person's capability to the same level; Rather, it's to create momentum with incremental improvements.

Training should be role-specific and adapted to address the unique workflows of different departments. Customizing the training content ensures that the training is practical and relevant. For instance, the IT department might need in-depth technical training on how to build agents, while the HR department could benefit from learning how to use Copilot to streamline recruitment processes.

The method and modality of training also play a significant role in its effectiveness. Workshops, for example, provide rich, interactive learning experiences. These hands-on sessions require a considerable time investment but offer deep learning opportunities. On the other hand, self-paced learning modules and short videos can be easily incorporated into busy schedules, while just-in-time learning, enabled by Copilot, provides on-demand resources and contextual assistance that reinforces skills through immediate application.

Take a modern approach to Copilot training

Shift from traditional classroom sessions to microlearning experiences—short, focused learning moments that improve retention and fit into busy schedules. These training methods emphasize active learning, encouraging people to try Copilot features. The goal is to deliver practical skills when needed rather than overwhelming users with comprehensive training as a one-off. A modern approach includes

- **Bite-sized content**   Create concise training videos (90 seconds to 4 minutes) that employees can easily consume between tasks. This format increases engagement while respecting time constraints, making continuous learning sustainable.

- **Self-paced e-learning**   Structured online courses that people can complete at their own pace. Tiered learning paths build Copilot knowledge and skills cumulatively, from the fundamentals to the advanced. Modules should include interactive tutorials and simulations of use cases that are relevant to their role in your organization. This allows people to practice in a safe environment.

- **Practical skill development**   Focus on task-specific training that directly impacts job performance. Instead of general overviews, demonstrate how to use Copilot to delegate tasks, draft communications, or analyze data. Provide clear guidance for application-specific functionality across Word, PowerPoint, Excel, Outlook, Teams, and SharePoint.

> **Tip**   The "Create and draft with Microsoft 365 Copilot" module in Microsoft Learn's Copilot Fundamentals learning path includes guidance on using Copilot in Word, PowerPoint, Outlook, and Chat at *https://learn.microsoft.com/en-gb/training/modules/create-draft-content-with-microsoft-copilot-microsoft-365/*.

- **Support networks**   Establish feedback mechanisms through help desks, user groups, or communities of practice where employees share experiences and learn collaboratively. Develop Copilot champions across departments that provide peer support and drive adoption.

> **Note**   Chapter 7, "Champions," explores establishing successful champions programs in more detail.

- **Business-focused learning**   Avoid technical training in favor of business skills. Teach prompt engineering as a conversational skill for achieving business outcomes rather than a technical procedure. Use relevant scenarios that demonstrate how Copilot enhances productivity and supports strategic goals, helping employees understand the value proposition and prioritize skill development.

Practical training techniques

Hands-on activities help embed learning into everyday work. These training approaches highlight practical ways to use Copilot, encourage peer-to-peer learning, and foster innovation across the organization:

- **Scenario-based learning**   Create realistic workplace scenarios for employees to practice using Copilot. For instance, simulate managing an overflowing inbox using Copilot in Outlook to prioritize emails, capture action items, and set reminders, as well as draft quick, effective replies.

- **Role-specific task demonstrations**   Provide targeted examples showing how specific roles can leverage Copilot effectively. For example, demonstrate how to quickly generate professional client proposals using Copilot in Word to sales staff.

- **Microlearning modules**   Develop short, focused videos (up to 4 minutes in length) that employees can access anytime. For example, "How to use Copilot in Excel to analyze quarterly sales data and visualize it instantly."

- **Interactive "Ask Copilot" sessions**   Host live Q&A webinars where employees interact directly with Copilot, solving real-time business issues. For example, when brainstorming ideas in Teams, they use Copilot to structure the ideas based on the discussion and identify patterns and gaps in thinking.

- **On-the-job Copilot shadowing**   Pair employees proficient in Copilot with new learners for short, practical shadowing sessions. For example, have new users observe and mirror experienced colleagues as they effectively leverage Copilot in Outlook to manage calendar scheduling, task assignments, or inbox management, providing real-world, observational learning opportunities.

- **Gamified learning challenges**   Set weekly Copilot skill-building challenges with incentives. For example, employees compete to efficiently manage a simulated project in Microsoft Planner using Copilot, showcasing how it can automate task assignments and status updates. Give away an Amazon gift card for the winning ideas.

- **Hands-on hackathons**   Run an internal event in which teams use Copilot to develop creative solutions to departmental problems, such as automating monthly HR report generation. See Appendix A for a framework to run hackathons.

- **Lunch-and-learn sessions**   Facilitate informal group training sessions over lunch, where small teams explore practical Copilot applications together. For example, using Copilot in Teams to summarize key meeting points and action items.

- **Step-by-step Copilot playbooks**   Provide clear, printable playbooks or digital cheat sheets outlining step-by-step instructions for frequent tasks. For example, create a playbook for using Copilot to generate drafts of routine legal documents or policies for review.

- **Real-time feedback loops**   Encourage employees to share immediate feedback on Copilot's suggestions via quick polls or forms integrated within their workflows. For example, embedding a short feedback survey after Copilot helps draft an email or document, ensuring continuous improvement and relevance.

- **Workload showcase**   Schedule regular sessions where team members demonstrate specific examples of successfully integrating Copilot into their daily work tasks, highlighting measurable improvements. For instance, an HR team member could present how they've streamlined the candidate interview scheduling process using Copilot in Outlook and Teams, significantly reducing administrative workload and increasing candidate response times. Collect these in a team prompt or scenario library that is coauthored and updated as people learn which prompts support specific workloads.

Encouraging experimentation and continuous learning

Cultivating an experimental mindset begins with creating a safe space where employees feel empowered to explore and innovate without fear of failure. Leaders play a crucial role in this by visibly supporting learning through doing and celebrating productive failures. This approach boosts morale and drives a culture of continuous improvement and innovation.

Another key aspect is encouraging teams to share and learn from their early Copilot experiences. Organizations can build a repository of best practices and insights by documenting and scaling successful Copilot experiments across the team. This collective knowledge becomes valuable, enabling teams to learn from each other's successes and challenges. Providing guidelines for documenting these experiences ensures consistency and facilitates easy access to this shared knowledge.

Use Microsoft 365 to help build Copilot capability

People often overlook the comprehensive toolkit already available within their Microsoft 365 environment. The native integration of Copilot across the Microsoft ecosystem creates natural opportunities to embed learning directly into daily workflows, accelerating adoption through contextual application rather than isolated training events. There are many ways to leverage this advantage while building sustainable Copilot proficiency in your team.

- **Microsoft Teams**

  - **Innovation channel**   Create dedicated channels in Teams to share insights, Copilot experimentation stories, and lessons learned.

  - **Live learning sessions**   Schedule regular Teams meetings to showcase wins and lessons with Copilot, fostering open discussion and collective learning.

- **SharePoint**
  - **Copilot knowledge hub** Develop a centralized SharePoint site to store Copilot documentation, templates, and best practices based on experiments within the organization.
  - **Lessons learned library** Implement document libraries with tagging and metadata to help employees easily find insights and guidance.
- **Viva Engage**
  - **Innovation community** Launch communities based on role type or department to share questions, tips, and discussions around Copilot use cases, creating a culture of openness and collaboration.
  - **Recognition posts** Encourage leaders to publicly acknowledge productive failures and innovative efforts, reinforcing psychological safety.
- **Microsoft Forms**
  - **Feedback surveys** Distribute feedback forms regularly to capture employees' experiences, successes, and challenges with Copilot. Use these insights to refine your approach to both training and task scenarios.
- **Stream**
  - **Video showcases** Document Copilot success stories and experimentation walkthroughs through short, accessible videos, making learning engaging and practical.
- **Viva Learning**
  - **Curated learning paths** Develop custom learning pathways highlighting relevant Copilot Microsoft Learn courses, case studies, and resources gathered from internal experiments, creating structured yet flexible learning opportunities.
- **Planner**
  - **Experimentation tracker** Use Planner boards to visualize, track, and collaboratively manage Copilot experimentation projects, helping teams monitor progress and share outcomes transparently.
- **Power BI**
  - **Insight dashboards** Build dashboards to visualize engagement metrics, successful practices, and learning outcomes from Copilot experimentation, supporting data-driven continuous improvement.
- **Viva Insights**
  - **Reflection reminders** Utilize Viva Insights to encourage regular reflection on learning experiences, reinforcing continuous development and self-improvement habits.

Offer people engaging learning experiences

Boost engagement and creativity amongst your teams by running Copilot events, such as innovation challenges and hackathons, and regular peer-to-peer learning sessions. These events provide structured opportunities for people to experiment with Copilot and develop innovative solutions to real-world problems. By facilitating these events and groups, organizations can create a supportive learning environment that encourages continuous skill development.

Chapter 12, "Culture," covers innovation challenges and hackathons in detail; however, high-level explanations are included here to introduce the concepts and key activities.

Copilot innovation challenges

A Copilot innovation challenge is a structured competition run over one or two days that allows your organization to crowd-source novel ways to use Copilot to create value. It can involve employees from all departments, partner representatives, and Microsoft technical experts. For instance, a Copilot innovation challenge might invite employees to submit ideas for how Copilot could solve specific business challenges, like reducing the time it takes to process a customer order. This generates a wealth of creative ideas and fosters a sense of ownership and involvement among employees.

Innovation challenge checklist

- **Define objectives and scope**   Establish clear objectives, success metrics, and specific business challenges for employees to address through Copilot innovation.

  - **Recommended tools**   Microsoft Planner and Word.

- **Plan and schedule the event**   Develop a structured event timeline, setting key dates, submission deadlines, and milestones.

  - **Recommended tools**   Microsoft Planner and Outlook Calendar.

- **Design idea submission process**   Set up transparent, structured processes to collect employee submissions of ideas and solutions.

  - **Recommended tools**   Microsoft Forms and SharePoint Lists.

- **Event communication**   Communicate regularly before, during, and after the event to maximize employee participation and engagement.

  - **Recommended tools**   Microsoft Teams and Viva Engage.

- **Document and share results**   Create a centralized location to share results, winning submissions, and insights gathered from the event, making them accessible to all employees.

  - **Recommended tools**   SharePoint Knowledge Hub and Microsoft Stream (for video content).

Copilot hackathons

Hackathons are more intensive events where power users and innovators can get hands-on with Microsoft's AI tools, including Copilot, exploring advanced functionalities and developing sophisticated solutions. These events often result in breakthrough innovations that can be scaled across the organization, driving significant value.

Hackathon checklist

- **Prepare event framework**   Clearly outline the goals, themes, and the specific Copilot functionalities to be explored in the hackathon.

  - **Recommended tools**   Microsoft Planner and Word.

- **Manage registration and form teams**   Coordinate registration and team formation for participants, highlighting the need for cross-functional collaboration when forming a team.

  - **Recommended tools**   Microsoft Forms and Microsoft Teams (channels and groups).

- **Facilitate live event collaboration**   Provide participants with collaboration spaces and resources needed for real-time interaction and teamwork during the hackathon.

  - **Recommended tools**   Microsoft Teams Meetings, Breakout Rooms, and Microsoft Whiteboard.

- **Provide support and resources**   Ensure teams access relevant Copilot documentation, guidelines, and examples to maximize productivity and innovation.

  - **Recommended tools**   SharePoint Document Libraries and Viva Learning.

- **Manage presentations and judging**   Coordinate presentations, facilitate judging panels, and streamline the voting and evaluation processes.

  - **Recommended tools**   Microsoft Teams, Microsoft Forms, PowerPoint Live.

- **Post-event communication**   Publish outcomes, recognize outstanding solutions, and broadly communicate successes and innovations developed during the hackathon.

  - **Recommended tools**   Viva Engage, SharePoint News, and Microsoft Stream.

Peer learning groups

Establishing peer learning groups is another effective strategy to build Copilot capability. These groups bring together employees with similar roles or interests to share their Copilot experiences and learn from each other. For example, a peer learning group in the finance department might focus on using Copilot in Excel to streamline financial analysis and reporting.

Peer learning group checklist

- **Identify and set up peer groups** Create groups based on shared roles, departments, or interests to encourage mutual learning and sharing of experiences with Copilot.
  - **Recommended tools** Microsoft Teams channels and Planner.
- **Schedule regular learning sessions** Establish a consistent meeting schedule to maintain momentum and continuous learning.
  - **Recommended tools** Outlook Calendar and Microsoft Teams meetings.
- **Share practical insights and resources** Encourage participants to exchange practical Copilot tips, templates, examples, and lessons learned within the group.
  - **Recommended tools** SharePoint Document Libraries and Viva Learning.
- **Facilitate ongoing discussions** Support informal communication and knowledge sharing between scheduled sessions to maintain engagement.
  - **Recommended tools** Microsoft Teams and Viva Engage communities.
- **Gather feedback and measure impact** Regularly evaluate group effectiveness and participant satisfaction to improve the peer learning experience.
  - **Recommended tools** Microsoft Forms (surveys) and Power BI (analysis and reporting).

Sample agenda: Peer learning group session

As shown in Figure 5-1, facilitated sessions for peer-to-peer learning can include group discussions, case study showcases from members, and collaborative learning activities.

The power of learning in a community

At IBM, a peer-to-peer learning program called "IBMaking" emerged to leverage employees' collective knowledge and creativity worldwide. This initiative created a community where individuals shared innovative solutions and technology applications for the Microsoft Power Platform, fostering a culture of continuous learning and experimentation.

The program began with a small group of recent graduates tasked with developing a brand name that resonated with the spirit of innovation and collaboration. They coined the term "IBMaking," which quickly gained traction throughout the company. The community grew organically, attracting participants from various departments and regions, eventually reaching a membership of over 2,000 employees.

Each month, the IBMaking community would hold regular check-ins where members could share their latest projects, insights, and successes. These sessions became a platform for storytelling, where employees could showcase how they had used the Microsoft Power Platform to solve real-world problems, improve processes, or create new opportunities for IBM's customers.

The impact proved profound. IBMaking facilitated the cross-pollination of ideas and knowledge, enabling employees to learn from each other's experiences. This grassroots movement empowered individual innovation while driving a broader cultural shift within IBM that emphasized collaboration, experimentation, and continuous improvement. The success demonstrated the power of community-driven learning and the value of creating spaces where employees feel encouraged to experiment. It highlighted how a well-supported initiative could scale across a large organization, driving significant value and fostering a culture of innovation.

Peer Learning Group
Session Agenda

Duration: 60 minutes
Frequency: Bi-weekly or monthly
Audience: Employees grouped by department, role, or share interests

1. Welcome and introductions (5 minutes)
- Brief welcome to attendees
- Quick introductions for new group members (if applicable)

2. Session objectives and focus area (5 minutes)
- Outline this session's purpose and specific learning goals (e.g., exploring Copilot in Excel for financial analysis)

3. Member showcase: Sharing experiences (15 minutes)
- One or two members share practical Copilot use cases or recently completed experiments
- Focus on successes, challenges, and key insigts

4. Group discussion and Q&A (15 minutes)
- Open discussion where group members ask questions, provide input, and discuss presented use cases
- Facilitator encourages participation from all members

5. Collaborative learning activity (10 minutes)
- Short practical exercises or demos where participants explore or apply new Copilot features or concepts together

6. Action planning and takeaways (5 minutes)
- Members briefly outline actions or experiments they will attempt before the next session
- Define clear next steps and accountability partners, if relevant

7. Closing and feedback (5 minutes)
- Summarize key learning points from the session
- Collect brief feedback from participants on the session's effectiveness

FIGURE 5-1 Sample agenda with time allocated for each item

Training tactics, templates, and tools

Providing templates for setting up and running Copilot events ensures consistency and ease of implementation. These templates might include agendas, facilitation guides, and evaluation criteria, making it easy for employees to organize and participate in these events. AI skill assessment templates and surveys can help identify gaps and track progress. By regularly assessing employees' Copilot skills, you can design tailored learning programs to address specific needs and measure the impact of your training efforts. Use case study snapshots showcasing the successful use of Copilot to inspire and provide practical insights.

> **Tip** Check out Microsoft Learn and *https://adoption.microsoft.com/copilot* for comprehensive training materials, templates, and suggested learning paths to include in your training plans.

Create templates for Copilot events

Templates will help you run Copilot training events like innovation challenges and hackathons at scale. As you run events, make sure you keep evolving these templates based on what you learn about running effective and engaging events.

- **Agenda templates**
  - Develop standard event agendas, including introductions, objectives, practical exercises, Q&A sessions, and wrap-up reflections.
  - Include clearly defined time slots to ensure events run efficiently.
- **Facilitation guides**
  - Provide detailed scripts or talking points to facilitators to maintain consistency and ease pressure on organizers.
  - Offer guidance on how to manage group dynamics, handle challenging discussions, and encourage participation.
- **Evaluation criteria**
  - Define clear, measurable criteria for evaluating event success (e.g., participant engagement, practical skills demonstrated, satisfaction surveys).
  - Provide prebuilt forms (such as Microsoft Forms) to easily capture participant feedback.

AI skill assessment and survey templates

To show the impact of your training efforts, it's necessary to establish a capability baseline so that you can understand how different initiatives are working together to build capability. Tracking your progress over time helps sustain buy-in for Copilot.

- **Baseline assessment templates**

  - Develop an initial skills survey to gauge employees' current proficiency levels in Copilot.
  - Include self-assessment questions with clearly defined skill-level descriptions (e.g., novice, intermediate, expert).

- **Ongoing progress surveys**

  - Schedule quarterly assessments using identical formats to track progress over time.
  - Compare results to demonstrate tangible skill growth, identify skill gaps, and target follow-up training appropriately.
  - Use Microsoft Forms assessments to automate distribution and data collection.
  - Integrate results into a Power BI dashboard to visually track skill progression and training effectiveness.

Case Study snapshots for inspiration

People learn from real-life stories. Make sure you are capturing and sharing case studies from your organization as you adopt Copilot. It's a powerful way to enable learning.

- **Curated case studies**

  - Regularly collect short, impactful case studies (one-page snapshots) highlighting practical Copilot successes within the organization.
  - Include specific insights like implementation challenges, how they were overcome, and measurable outcomes (productivity gains, return on investment [ROI], and employee satisfaction).

- **Case study library**

  - Build an easily searchable digital library of case studies, prompts, and scenarios (such as a SharePoint site or Microsoft Teams channel) that is accessible to all employees.
  - Categorize by department, Copilot product (M365 Copilot or Copilot Studio), or business outcome.

- **Bring the stories to life**

  - Assign responsibility to someone to regularly source, format, and publish new snapshots. Ideally, this could be someone in the core change team, perhaps working in collaboration with an internal communications expert.
  - Feature monthly highlights through internal newsletters or Announcement channels on Microsoft Teams and Viva Engage. Include short videos, making successes visible and relatable.

Fostering future-ready capabilities

Copilot enhances efficiency and creates opportunities for employees to refocus their time on new tasks. By encouraging employees to consider how their roles will evolve with Copilot you're help-ing them build adaptability into their approach to work.. Providing a framework for structuring their thoughts on how Copilot can empower them individually, enhance team processes, and impact the organization helps them envision the future. Supporting employees in reimagining their job descrip-tions in an AI-enabled world ensures they are prepared to embrace new roles and responsibilities. Learning opportunities like those discussed in this chapter give people the environment to develop transferable skills.

Try this prompt: Ideas to raise AI literacy

We've outlined several approaches to building capability when it comes to Copilot. To come up with a strategy tailored to your organization, spend some time brainstorming ideas with Copilot. You can paste this prompt directly into Copilot in Word, Copilot Chat, or in Loop or Teams if working collabora-tively. Replace the details in brackets with information that is relevant to your organization.

I'm leading a company-wide initiative to increase AI literacy by 30% over the next 12 months, using Microsoft 365 Copilot. We have [insert number] employees across [insert number] locations in various roles (e.g., HR, IT, sales, finance).

I need a clear, research-based training and adoption strategy that includes modern learning formats, phased rollout, tools to support delivery, ways to tailor content by role, and how to measure progress.

Please create a structured plan (like a report or roadmap) that I can use to brief stakeholders and guide implementation. Make it actionable, professional, and grounded in current best practices for enterprise learning and AI adoption.

Next steps

In this chapter, we discussed the need to develop AI literacy programs that build the capability of every person in your organization. This structured approach not only boosts individual performance but also creates a collective understanding that supports Copilot adoption.

- Fostering a shared understanding of AI concepts among employees is crucial for effective communication and collaboration, ultimately leading to improved productivity and innovation as Copilot becomes part of every process.

- Designing effective training programs aligns learning outcomes with organizational objectives. Training should be role-specific and incorporate modern learning techniques, such as microlearning and scenario-based learning.

- Rewarding those who adopt a learn-it-all mindset encourages them to share what they learn as they experiment with Copilot, contributing to collective knowledge and encouraging ongoing learning.

CHAPTER 6

Compliance

AI needs competition, but AI also needs collaboration, and AI needs the confidence of the people and has to be safe.

—Ursula von der Leyen, European Commission President

In this chapter, you will:

- Learn how to transform compliance from a potential barrier into a strategic advantage that builds trust in your Copilot implementation

- Discover practical tools and frameworks for managing data governance, regulatory requirements, and ethical AI considerations

- Develop an actionable compliance strategy that protects your organization while enabling innovation through responsible AI adoption

Compliance as a competitive advantage

Remember those self-stacking bricks from Chapter 2, "Clarity"? Even the most innovative construction materials require building codes, permits, and regular inspections to ensure the structure remains safe and sound. Similarly, implementing Copilot without robust compliance frameworks creates a digital infrastructure that may appear functional but harbors significant vulnerabilities. The blueprint that guides your AI implementation must consider compliance policies from the outset. Compliance isn't a one-off box to check as part of your Copilot rollout; it's the foundation upon which responsible AI adoption stands.

As regulations around AI evolve at unprecedented speed across global markets, organizations must build resilience and adaptability into their compliance approaches. The chief information security officer (CISO), legal counsel, and data protection officer become essential partners in this journey, bringing specialized expertise to navigate complex requirements around data governance, customer information protection, and emerging AI regulations. Their involvement and leadership role on the AI council transform compliance from a potential barrier into a strategic advantage, enabling your organization to move forward with confidence while competitors may remain paralyzed by regulatory uncertainty. Compliance is a team sport. This chapter provides the framework you need to facilitate these critical conversations and establish a compliance strategy that evolves alongside both your use of Copilot and the regulatory landscape.

Trustworthy and responsible AI

The business case for responsible AI hinges on ethical compliance and trust, which can serve as significant competitive differentiators. Responsible AI principles include transparency, accountability, fairness, and reliability. These principles guide the ethical use of AI and underpin the success of your Copilot adoption program. By examining real-world examples of compliance missteps and ethical challenges, we can better understand the consequences and the importance of adhering to these principles.

As we explore this topic, we'll reference some technical concepts, but you don't need in-depth technical knowledge to become an advocate for responsible AI in your organization. Familiarity with these terms and tools acts as a starting point for discussions that you should have with your IT and security teams, executive stakeholders, and technology partners. These conversations will help you collectively establish a compliance strategy based on existing safeguards and identify what you need to do to maintain ongoing compliance.

Copilot's incredible ability to find and summarize information across Microsoft 365 apps has become a catalyst for security conversations that organizations have often deprioritized. A practical example of this is data governance: an employee could potentially use Copilot to access sensitive information, such as executive salary details. Many organizations have been relying on what security professionals call "security by obscurity"—the information wasn't secure before Copilot; it was just harder to find. This highlights the need for stringent role-based access controls (RBAC) to ensure that only authorized personnel can access specific data.

As AI has uncovered this challenge, it also offers solutions. With Microsoft Purview, an organization can classify HR documents containing sensitive employee details. The system proactively blocks or alerts administrators if Copilot or other AI tools attempt to access or process this labeled data by applying the "Confidential" sensitivity label linked to a data loss prevention (DLP) policy.

> **Note** Microsoft's Restricted SharePoint Search (RSS) switch can act as an "air-gap" for Copilot and Microsoft Graph. When enabled, only content from a curated list of SharePoint Online sites (plus each user's own OneDrive and explicitly shared items) is searchable by Copilot, keeping sensitive or messy sites out of AI reach. This gives organizations breathing room to audit permissions and apply proper governance—such as sensitivity labels or Purview—without delaying a broader Copilot rollout. Direct access to the blocked sites still follows normal SharePoint permissions, so RSS is best viewed as an initial discovery-layer circuit-breaker rather than a substitute for long-term data-protection controls.

Regulatory compliance is another critical aspect of responsible AI. Governments and states increasingly enact legislation to govern AI usage, from the European Union's AI Act to state-level regulations in the United States and more than 200 other legislative changes currently being considered worldwide. Regulation when it comes to AI is only expected to grow, so organizations must make it an ongoing priority to stay ahead of these developments. Transparency is essential to mitigate concerns about AI being a "black box" and to ensure that AI systems are explainable and accountable.

An ethical approach to AI also encompasses workforce impact. As organizations incorporate tools like Copilot, we'll continue to see a shift toward teams that include both human and digital workers. Balancing technological advancement with human considerations is part of ethical commitments, ensuring, wherever possible, that employees are redeployed to add value in innovative ways rather than being displaced. Establishing a process that strategically handles reinvestment and redeployment of human talent to maximise the value of deep organizational knowledge will be key. Managers and individual contributors alike will need to learn how to make compelling recommendations on new ways to add value as AI and human collaboration increase. Committing to responsible AI principles and demonstrating how they inform your compliance strategies will help build trust in your AI initiatives. This trust becomes the foundation upon which successful adoption is built.

> **Tip** Read the "Crafting your Future-Ready Enterprise AI Strategy" authored by AI thought leaders from Microsoft and Cloud Lighthouse to gain a deeper understanding of the pillars and dimensions that underpin a trustworthy approach to AI. Download the paper at *https://cloudlight.house/blog/wp-crafting-your-future-ready-enterprise-ai-strategy-e2*.

Implementing ethical AI decision-making

Implementing ethical AI decision-making requires embedding these responsible AI principles into daily business operations. Microsoft's Responsible AI (RAI) Framework provides practical guidance for this process, emphasizing transparency, accountability, and explainability in how AI systems operate. This framework gives you a structured approach to move from abstract principles to concrete practices. Educating staff about responsible AI practices is crucial to ensure these principles are understood and followed throughout the organization. When employees understand why certain guardrails exist and how they protect both the organization and its customers, compliance becomes a shared value rather than an imposed restriction.

> **Tip** The Microsoft Responsible AI Toolkit provides resources and guidelines to help organizations identify, measure, and mitigate risks in AI systems, ensuring ethical and transparent AI practices. See *https://www.microsoft.com/en-us/ai/tools-practices*.

Data governance and customer data protection

Data governance involves identifying, managing, and protecting personally identifiable information (PII) and personal information (PI) on an organization's networks. With the introduction of Copilot, there is a risk that this data could be inadvertently exposed or misused. Therefore, robust data governance practices are paramount to mitigate these risks.

Microsoft Purview stands out as an effective tool for proactive data governance. This comprehensive solution helps organizations classify, label, and discover sensitive data across their digital estate.

For instance, data that has been sitting on networks for years—such as onboarding surveys containing next-of-kin information—must be protected to prevent unauthorized access, especially as Copilot makes information discovery more efficient.

By integrating Purview's sensitivity labels with data loss prevention (DLP) policies and role-based access control (RBAC), organizations create a comprehensive protection system. Implementing RBAC helps manage access to sensitive data within AI solutions. Organizations must define and manage precise Azure Entra ID roles, delegated permissions, and application permissions for Microsoft Graph APIs.

Leveraging Azure Entra ID conditional access policies allows organizations to finely control how Copilot interacts with sensitive organizational data, significantly reducing exposure risk. These technical controls ensure that even if someone asks Copilot for information they shouldn't access, the system will respect existing security boundaries. The system works in real time, classifying documents as they're created or modified to maintain ongoing compliance rather than relying on periodic audits.

To implement these protections effectively, organizations should follow a structured approach using Purview Compliance Manager. This tool provides a centralized dashboard for managing compliance activities, offering visibility into your compliance posture and recommended actions. Meanwhile, the DLP components prevent data leaks by monitoring and controlling data transfers based on the sensitivity labels applied to content. When discussing data governance with your IT and security teams, ask specifically about how Microsoft Purview is being utilized to secure SharePoint sites and Microsoft Graph data, key information sources that Copilot accesses. Understanding these protections will allow you to confidently address stakeholder concerns about data security in your Copilot adoption strategy.

Implementing Microsoft's Zero Trust security principles, including rigorous identity verification, enforcing least-privilege access, and continuous monitoring and verification, is a core step in securing Copilot environments and mitigating data breach risks.

Regulatory compliance

While data governance focuses on protecting information within your organization's control, regulatory compliance addresses how you meet external requirements that govern AI usage. These two areas are deeply interconnected: effective data governance enables regulatory compliance, while regulatory requirements often inform your governance approach. Your Copilot adoption strategy needs to be able to adapt to evolving regulations. Foundational legislation, such as the General Data Protection Regulation (GDPR) in Europe and the California Consumer Privacy Act (CCPA) in the United States, has established high standards for data protection. These regulations impact how Copilot can be deployed and used within your organization.

Requirements differ by country, so understanding the legislation and data residency requirements you need to comply with is an important step. The EU AI Act represents a significant development in AI regulation, with notable implications for organizations worldwide—not just those based in Europe. One of its key requirements focuses on AI literacy among staff who work with AI systems. To address this requirement, consider these practical steps:

- **Assess your employees' current AI literacy levels through baseline evaluations** Simple surveys or quizzes can help identify knowledge gaps across your organization. This assessment serves two purposes: it provides documentation of your compliance efforts and highlights specific areas where training resources should be directed.

- **Develop role-specific training modules that go beyond generic AI awareness** Business analysts need different AI literacy skills than sales representatives or customer service teams. Tailoring your training approach ensures that employees receive practical guidance relevant to their daily work with Copilot.

Documentation is necessary to demonstrate compliance should you be audited. Maintain detailed records of all training activities, including attendance, completion rates, and assessment results. These records serve as evidence during compliance audits and help you track progress over time. Finally, implement a regular update cycle for all training materials. AI technology and the regulations governing it evolve rapidly, making static training programs quickly obsolete. Schedule quarterly reviews to incorporate new Copilot features, emerging best practices, and regulatory changes into your training materials. Include a process for retiring and removing content that is out of date or no longer valuable in response to the evolving Copilot and regulatory landscape. By taking a structured approach to regulatory compliance, you transform what could be a burdensome requirement into an opportunity to build organizational capability and confidence with Copilot.

Practical compliance guidance

To align Copilot initiatives with legal, ethical, and security standards, organizations should implement a structured approach across several key areas. The following framework provides a comprehensive roadmap for ensuring compliance while enabling innovation:

- **Develop and implement an Ethical AI Decision-Making Framework**
  - Define clear ethical AI principles aligned with organizational values (fairness, transparency, accountability).
  - Establish an AI ethics review board responsible for overseeing ethical considerations.
  - Document decision-making protocols for ethical dilemmas, including scenario analysis.
  - Implement accountability measures with clear roles and responsibilities.
  - Regularly review frameworks against emerging ethical challenges and stakeholder feedback.

- **Leverage Microsoft's Responsible AI (RAI) Framework**
  - Perform a gap analysis to identify current adherence levels to Microsoft's RAI principles.
  - Create a strategic roadmap integrating RAI tools, including interpretability and fairness assessments.
  - Conduct regular staff training sessions on Microsoft's RAI toolkit and guidelines
  - Establish ongoing assessment mechanisms and periodic reporting to measure progress.

- Update organizational practices continuously in response to evolving Microsoft recommendations.

■ **Adopt Zero Trust principles for AI security**

- Document a Zero Trust strategy tailored to your Copilot implementation.
- Create a detailed inventory of AI resources and identify protection priorities.
- Enforce strict identity verification, multifactor authentication, and continuous validation.
- Implement network segmentation to isolate sensitive AI and data resources.
- Perform regular reviews and adjust security measures based on usage analytics.

■ **Implement Role-Based Access Control (RBAC)**

- Clearly define organizational roles specific to AI tasks and Copilot usage.
- Develop detailed permission matrices aligned precisely with defined roles.
- Regularly audit and revise roles and permissions at least quarterly.
- Automate audit processes using security management tools for continuous compliance.
- Train administrators thoroughly in RBAC best practices and tools.

■ **Educate staff on Responsible AI practices**

- Create targeted training modules covering responsible AI concepts and ethical use cases.
- Provide clear guidelines on AI transparency, explainability, and shared responsibility between the organization, the user, and vendors like Microsoft. Every user needs to be able to articulate their personal responsibilities and how they contribute to the overall approach.
- More advanced training on trustworthy AI should be developed for people who are building agents in Copilot Studio or Azure AI Foundry for broad deployment.
- Schedule mandatory training refreshers periodically to ensure sustained awareness.
- Develop accessible resources like FAQs and scenario-based training materials.
- Implement regular assessments to measure understanding and awareness levels.

■ **Develop a comprehensive AI Compliance Action Plan**

- Form a cross-functional compliance team involving compliance officers, IT experts, and business leaders.
- Develop a comprehensive compliance checklist addressing privacy, security, ethics, and regulatory requirements.
- Assign clear accountability, detailed tasks, and timelines for all compliance-related actions.
- Regularly review and update compliance actions based on regulatory and technological changes.
- Conduct quarterly assessments and adjustments to reflect progress and compliance status.

■ **Configure security boundaries for Copilot and Microsoft Graph**

- Document clearly defined security boundaries for your implementation.

- Configure strict API permissions for Microsoft Graph based on the minimum necessary data access.
- Precisely define and implement data access controls for Copilot.
- Regularly test, review, and adjust access control configurations.
- Set up automated alerts and monitoring to detect unauthorized access attempts.

- **Conduct regular data audits**

  - Schedule comprehensive quarterly data audits.
  - Identify and classify sensitive data within SharePoint and other repositories.
  - Apply effective data sanitization practices (anonymization, encryption, or removal).
  - Document audit findings, issues, and corrective actions.
  - Track and monitor the implementation of corrective actions through structured follow-up.

- **Implement best practices for managing permissions and sensitive data**

  - Establish and enforce strict data classification and management protocols.
  - Limit access to sensitive data strictly to essential personnel.
  - Deploy automatic monitoring tools to detect and respond to permission anomalies.
  - Provide explicit guidelines for secure data sharing and handling.
  - Conduct regular training sessions to reinforce security awareness among all staff.

This framework transforms compliance from a reactive requirement into a proactive strategy that supports trustworthy AI adoption while protecting your organization from potential risks. By addressing each of these areas systematically, you create a foundation for sustainable Copilot implementation that builds trust with both internal and external stakeholders.

> **Caution** This guide is not comprehensive, and compliance considerations are subject to change, but it gives you practical steps that should be a starting point you can take to your IT leadership to formulate a joint approach based on your organization's unique needs.

Tools and resources for managing AI compliance

To support your Copilot compliance efforts, Microsoft provides several practical and accessible tools you can leverage.

Foundational security and identity management

Your organization likely already has an existing approach to security and identity management. Start by understanding the current state and work with your security and IT leaders to evolve that approach for Copilot.

- **Microsoft Entra ID**   A cloud-based identity and access management solution (formerly Azure Active Directory) that securely manages user identities, enabling protected access across applications, devices, and services. See *https://www.microsoft.com/en-us/security/business/identity-access/microsoft-entra-id*.

- **Zero Trust guidance center**   Offers comprehensive guidance and practical resources to help businesses implement a Zero Trust security approach, minimizing risks through strict identity and access management. See *https://learn.microsoft.com/en-us/security/zero-trust/*.

Data protection, governance, and compliance

We've discussed the importance of data quality and protection, governance, and compliance in the context of AI and Copilot. Microsoft provides several tools within Microsoft Purview and the Microsoft Trust Center to help.

- **Microsoft Purview**   A unified data governance solution designed to help organizations manage, protect, and ensure compliance of sensitive data across multiple environments and platforms. See *https://www.microsoft.com/en-us/security/business/microsoft-purview*.

- **Microsoft Purview Data Loss Prevention (DLP)**   A set of tools within Microsoft 365 designed to identify, monitor, and automatically protect sensitive information from accidental sharing or unauthorized access. See *https://www.microsoft.com/en-us/security/business/information-protection/microsoft-purview-data-loss-prevention*.

- **Microsoft Purview Compliance Manager**   Reduce risk by translating complex regulatory requirements into specific improvement actions that help you raise your score and track progress. See *https://www.microsoft.com/en-us/security/business/risk-management/microsoft-purview-compliance-manager*.

- **Microsoft Purview Data Security Posture Management for AI (DSPM)**   Provides recommendations, reports, and data assessments to help organizations secure, monitor, and govern their use of AI applications, especially in environments where sensitive data is involved. See *https://learn.microsoft.com/en-us/purview/dspm-for-ai-considerations*.

- **Microsoft Trust Center**   Acts as a central hub outlining Microsoft's commitments and approaches to privacy, security, compliance, and transparency across all products and services. See *https://www.microsoft.com/en-us/trust-center*.

Regulatory framework and compliance training

Regulatory requirements differ by region and country, so it's important to familiarize yourself with the compliance training that's relevant for your organization. These examples are included to support references to specific legislation mentioned in this chapter.

- **General Data Protection Regulation (GDPR)**   A comprehensive EU regulation is designed to enhance privacy rights and ensure the secure handling of personal data for EU citizens, impacting global data management. See *https://gdpr-info.eu/*.

- **EU Artificial Intelligence Act (EU AI Act)**   Proposed legislation aimed at regulating AI systems within the EU, ensuring transparency, safety, and accountability, particularly addressing high-risk AI applications. See *https://artificialintelligenceact.eu/*.

- **Microsoft Learn compliance training modules**   Provides resources and guidelines to help organizations identify, measure, and mitigate risks in AI systems, ensuring ethical and transparent AI practices. See *https://www.microsoft.com/en-us/ai/tools-practices*. These resources provide practical support for your compliance journey. Remember that compliance tools and requirements evolve rapidly. Maintain regular contact with Microsoft and regulatory experts to ensure your approach remains current and effective.

Try this prompt: Monitor AI regulations

As there are currently hundreds of pieces of legislation related to AI regulation under consideration by governments around the world, it's important for AI leaders to stay across those that might impact your use of Copilot. Run this prompt regularly to keep up to date on changes in regulations and new compliance requirements. Replace the details in brackets with the specific regions, timing, and industry relevant to your organization.

> *I need to stay updated on AI regulations that might impact our business.*
> *Please help me by:*
>
> 1. *Summarizing the latest developments in AI regulations globally, with special focus on [specific regions: e.g., EU, US, UK] in the past [timeframe: e.g., 3 months]*
> 2. *Highlighting any recent changes to:*
>   - *Data protection requirements*
>   - *AI transparency and explainability rules*
>   - *Compliance documentation needs*
>   - *Industry-specific AI regulations in [your industry: e.g., healthcare, finance]*
> 3. *Creating a brief analysis of how these developments might impact our:*
>   - *Current AI implementation strategy*
>   - *Data governance policies*
>   - *Risk management approach*
>   - *Staff training requirements*
> 4. *Suggesting 3-5 proactive steps we could take to prepare for these regulatory changes*
> 5. *Recommending reliable sources I should follow to stay informed about AI regulation trends*

Next steps

In this chapter, we explored how compliance forms a critical pillar in successful Copilot adoption. It ensures that your AI implementation builds trust, protects sensitive information, and adheres to evolving regulatory requirements. By embedding compliance considerations from the beginning of your Copilot journey, you transform what could be perceived as a limitation into a strategic advantage. As you progress through your Copilot implementation, the compliance foundation laid in this chapter enables you to confidently embrace the opportunities that AI presents.

- The tools, frameworks, and practical guidance in this chapter provide a foundation for implementing Copilot in a manner that aligns with both internal policies and external regulations.

- As regulations continue to evolve, the structured approach outlined here will help you adapt quickly while maintaining confidence in your compliance posture.

- This adaptable approach not only boosts individual performance but also creates a collective understanding that supports Copilot adoption.

CHAPTER 7

Champions

Give our crew a dozen rockstars and we'll super-charge the whole enterprise, learning and adoption will rocket amazingly faster than any top-down mandate ever could! Tools might crack the door open, but it's those courageous champions who rally the folks and lead everyone across the threshold.

—CHRIS HUNTINGFORD, DIRECTOR OF AI, CLOUD LIGHTHOUSE

In this chapter, you will:

- Learn about the central role champions communities play in successfully scaling Copilot adoption across your organization

- Understand how to identify and recruit the right people to champion AI and Copilot

- Discover practical tools and strategies to develop and empower a champions community that people want to listen to and be part of

Champions as catalysts for cultural transformation

Champions can play a pivotal role in driving and scaling the use of Copilot in your organization. Champions, also known as *ambassadors*, *advocates*, or *influencers*, are people who combine technical knowledge and interpersonal influence to accelerate Copilot adoption through peer-to-peer connections. These champions can be found at all levels of the organization and are distinguished by their genuine enthusiasm for AI and the impact it can have on people at work and at home.

The power of champions stems from their ability to influence skeptical but interested colleagues to start using Copilot confidently. A well-structured champions network extends this influence beyond immediate peers to teams and departments throughout the organization. Champions uniquely accelerate Copilot adoption through two critical functions: sharing personal experiences with peers and elevating emerging ideas to the AI council for strategic consideration. By systematically identifying and empowering these champions, organizations begin to shift their culture toward continuous learning and innovation.

Identifying potential Copilot champions begins with recognizing AI-curious individuals who independently explore the technology. Look for people who use AI for personal projects, for example, creating personalized children's stories or generating custom meal plans for specific dietary needs.

Effective champions often have experience with consumer AI tools like ChatGPT from OpenAI, Claude from Anthropic, or Gemini from Google in their personal lives. This helps them develop fundamental prompting skills and build AI literacy that transfers directly to their use of Copilot at work.

> **Tip** One way to discover who on your team is already passionate about AI is by running internal competitions or creating opportunities in regular team meetings so that people can share how they are using AI.

Once you've identified your champions, create dedicated platforms for them to share knowledge and influence others. Combine structured support mechanisms with opportunities for organic peer learning through Microsoft Viva Engage and Teams. Amplify champion visibility by recognizing their achievements through internal events, showcases, newsletters, and podcasts. Each celebration reinforces their credibility and extends their impact.

Malcolm Gladwell's concept of "mavens," as described in *The Tipping Point*, provides a valuable framework for understanding the influence champions can have. Mavens act as information brokers, sharing their knowledge and expertise with others. They influence trends and ideas through their recommendations and guidance. The Microsoft Most Valuable Professional (MVP) program is a prime example of a maven program, where individuals passionate about technology share their knowledge to benefit the entire community. When MVPs share their valuable expertise and resources with Microsoft's global user community, they help Microsoft scale the adoption of their solutions. Similarly, Copilot champions who embody these maven qualities serve as knowledgeable advisors who accelerate adoption through their credibility and enthusiasm.

Embedding champions in the organizational culture and formally acknowledging their contributions accelerates Copilot adoption and reinforces a sustainable culture of innovation. Their contribution should be recognized by allocating time out of their core work tasks to fulfill this important role. This chapter explores strategies for identifying, empowering, and scaling a champion network, along with the tools, resources, and incentives necessary for champion growth and success.

SLB's champion strategy: The three Hs approach

Examining successful champion programs provides valuable insights for forming your own community. A standout example comes from SLB (formerly Schlumberger), where Alan Chai developed an innovative "agent" network that embedded champions within business units. This strategic placement enabled agents to understand the unique challenges of their respective units and deliver tailored solutions.

Under Chai's leadership, the selection process for this champion community prioritized three core traits, which became known as "The Three Hs":

- Hunger to learn
- Hunger to teach
- Humility

More important than technical ability, these traits ensured that the agents were motivated by curiosity and a desire to share their experiences to help their colleagues. Using unique identifiers, such as agent numbers (such as Agent 001), fostered a strong sense of community and professional pride among the agents. This sense of belonging extended beyond the organization, as evidenced by agents proudly displaying their agent numbers on their LinkedIn profiles.

The centralized leadership role played by Chai proved instrumental to the program's success. He actively contacted potential agents, even during their initial interviews, to invite them to join the program. His focus was not on technical skills alone but on their willingness to learn, remain humble, and teach others. This approach helped establish credibility and scale the champions program effectively across a large organization in multiple geographies.

The SLB case demonstrates two critical success factors for champion communities: the strategic value of embedding champions within business units and the powerful community effect created when champions share a distinctive identity and mission.

Finding your champions

Identify and empower the innovators and early adopters who will form the foundation of your Copilot champions community. These individuals often emerge naturally as they experiment with new technologies before formal adoption programs begin. Citizen developers (also known as makers, power users, or business developers) make particularly strong champions, as they've already demonstrated initiative in solving business problems with technology. Citizen developers are people who create applications using low-code/no-code platforms, such as Microsoft's Power Platform, despite having no formal development role. They are often businesspeople who understand how technology can help solve the challenges they are currently facing in their roles. Rather than waiting for IT to provide and authorize an official solution, they are the people who are motivated to find their own solutions that will support the business outcome they are responsible for delivering. They have a bias to action and get stuff done. Selecting and empowering these people will accelerate Copilot adoption across your organization.

Selection criteria

When identifying the right individuals to form your champions community, look for people with these key attributes:

- **Demonstrated technical expertise** Champions should have proven, hands-on experience with AI tools, not limited to Copilot but also other AI tools like Grammarly, which uses AI to help people edit and improve their writing, or Midjourney, an AI art generator. These people are often already using AI and consider themselves prompt experts or prompt engineers.

- **Motivation and enthusiasm** Champions must be motivated to participate in a peer-to-peer community; they are eager to share their knowledge and excited about the impact AI can have. They should be actively using Copilot and driven by a desire to help others adopt it.

- **Interpersonal skills** Effective champions possess strong interpersonal skills, which enable them to influence and mentor their colleagues. They can make complex concepts easy to understand. They can empathize with people whose reactions to AI aren't as positive as their own, and they can inspire a change in attitude through sharing their own experiences.

- **Impact on productivity and innovation** Look for individuals who have demonstrated a measurable impact on productivity, innovation, and organizational outcomes through the innovative use of technology. These champions should be recognized as heroes within the organization for their contributions and technical prowess.

- **Curiosity and willingness to experiment** Champions should be AI-curious, constantly exploring new ways to leverage AI in their work and personal lives.

> **Tip** Direct managers are often able to spot potential champions first because they are familiar with how their teams approach their work. Note that while managers can help identify potential champions, it's important that champions are willing participants in the program.

Once identified, find out whether the people who have demonstrated these traits are interested in becoming Copilot champions. Do they have a desire to share their knowledge and experiences with others? How motivated are they to be part of a peer-to-peer community? For many people, the answers to those questions will depend on the support and incentives you offer to your champion community.

Empowering champions

Providing a platform that empowers Copilot champions with the necessary support and resources will make the program more appealing. This platform might include:

- **Training and development** Offer exclusive training sessions and beta testing opportunities to keep champions at the forefront of AI advancements. This ensures they have the latest knowledge and skills to promote Copilot adoption effectively. This first access to knowledge also creates a network of "Copilot Coaches" who are well-positioned to provide one-on-one mentoring to executives, an opportunity that also offers champions the benefit of interacting with senior leaders.

- **Recognition and incentives** Recognize and celebrate champions' achievements through internal events, showcases, newsletters, and podcasts. Highlight opportunities to grow their internal profile by presenting Copilot scenarios to the AI council. Provide formal recognition through performance reviews and recommendations so that champions see how being a champion benefits their career advancement.

- **Community building** Foster a sense of belonging and community among champions by organizing regular meetups, social gatherings, and informal interactions. Show that you value your champion community by allocating a budget for refreshments as part of their meetups. Doing so helps maintain a strong engagement and reinforces the community spirit.

- **Structured support**   Utilize structured platforms like Microsoft Viva Engage and Teams for knowledge sharing and collaboration. Tools like the Microsoft Champion Management Platform can facilitate communication, track impact, and ensure the visibility of champions' contributions.

By carefully selecting and empowering champions, organizations can create a network of motivated people who drive Copilot adoption and organically support a creative and adaptable culture.

Structuring and scaling champion communities

When champion communities are well structured and supported, the result is accelerated adoption. Copilot champions programs have had a measurable impact on productivity, innovation, and organizational outcomes and are, therefore, worth investing in. Microsoft, for example, uses the concept of making champions the organization's heroes, celebrating their achievements and contributions.

Clear roles and responsibilities

Structuring and scaling a champions network involves defining clear roles and responsibilities for the champions so that they understand what they are signing up for.

Define clear roles and responsibilities for champions based on:

- **Engagement and evangelism**   Champions will actively engage with their colleagues, evangelize the benefits of Copilot, and mentor others. They provide critical feedback between business units, project teams, and the AI council to ensure Copilot is having the best possible impact.

- **Embedded resources**   Position champions within business units to better understand specific challenges and uncover helpful Copilot solutions. This embedded approach allows champions to tailor their support to each department's unique needs.

Creating buzz, belonging, and belief

One key aspect of scaling a champion community is creating a sense of identity and pride among the champions. In the SLB example Alan Chai did this with an agent numbering system (like James Bond's) that designated champions 'Agent 001' or 'Agent 002'. A community name like the 'IBMakers' mentioned in Chapter 5 fosters a sense of belonging and pride that encourages champions to take ownership of their roles and responsibilities. Build community and excitement around your champion program and you'll have people lining up to join.

Do this by cultivating

- **Buzz**   Create a buzz about the champion community by recognizing and celebrating achievements. Highlighting successful Copilot scenarios and sharing impact stories can generate interest and enthusiasm.

- **Belonging** Implement distinctive identifying markers, such as agent numbering systems or exclusive community language (for example, AI Black Ops), to foster a sense of belonging. Being a champion should be fun.

- **Belief** Demonstrate a belief that champions are integral to the organization's success. This belief builds on belonging and can significantly influence the organization's culture and drive Copilot adoption.

Continuous recruitment and development

Maintaining a continuous pipeline of potential champions is essential for sustaining the community's recruitment and development:

- **Recruitment** Identify individuals who exemplify curiosity, capability, and a collaborative spirit. Allow champions to nominate others and provide opportunities for self-nomination. If we refer to the Rogers adoption curve, the champions will be identified from the segment before the one you are entering. For example, the champions for the late majority will be found in the early majority.

- **Development** Establish structured but flexible check-ins, meetings, and social interactions to maintain strong engagement and community spirit. Regularly track champion-driven metrics, adoption rates, user satisfaction, and productivity gains to measure impact and adjust strategies accordingly.

By structuring and scaling the community effectively, organizations can leverage the power of internal influence to champion Copilot adoption and help the organization remain agile and responsive as Copilot evolves.

Blending structured support and organic peer learning

Provide ongoing support and resources to ensure the champions community remains effective, including access to exclusive training, beta testing opportunities, and structured platforms for knowledge sharing and collaboration.

Support structures

Provide structured support through formal organizational channels. Use platforms like Microsoft Viva Engage or Teams for knowledge sharing and collaboration among champions. Select the platform that is most loved and used by your organization so that it becomes the go-to place for Copilot champions to connect. As part of their adoption resources, Microsoft offers the Champions Management Platform toolkit that integrates with Teams, providing leaderboards, digital badges, and a tournament of teams to manage and scale the champions program effectively. This tool offers bragging rights for champions and fosters a sense of competition and achievement.

> **Tip**   The Microsoft 365 Champion Management Platform is a toolkit designed to help you manage and scale your champion community. See *https://adoption.microsoft.com/en-us/microsoft-teams/app-templates/champion-management-platform/*.

Regular showcases or town halls are another helpful component of structured support. These events highlight impactful Copilot use, focusing on specific workloads and scenarios. For example, the manufacturing team might showcase how they use Copilot to streamline production processes. In contrast, the sales team might demonstrate how they leverage Copilot to analyze financial reports and gain strategic insights. By sharing these success stories, organizations can inspire other teams to adopt similar practices and drive broader Copilot adoption.

Informal and peer-driven initiatives

In addition to structured support, champion-led informal and organic peer learning opportunities can help drive Copilot adoption. Encouraging informal meetups, social gatherings, and casual interactions can reinforce community bonds and engagement. Promoting a culture of safe experimentation, where people feel comfortable innovating and sharing without fear of failure or being observed by managers, is also a core part of a thriving champion community. These social interactions help build relationships and create a supportive environment for champions.

Storytelling and sharing successes

Encouraging champions to tell their stories is another powerful approach. Real people inspire us. Compelling storytelling highlights real-life experiences and can help make the benefits of Copilot more tangible. Showing the tension between challenges and outcomes creates interest and relatability. Champions can inspire others to care about and adopt Copilot by sharing these stories. This collaborative spirit can inspire others to join the champion community and contribute to its success.

Involving internal communications personnel in champions meetings can help identify and amplify success stories. These stories can benefit the champions community and the organization's external reputation. Champions can become voices for the organization, demonstrating innovation and sharing their experiences in public forums.

Engage and grow your champions

Make sure your champions have access to exclusive Copilot training and testing opportunities. For instance, Microsoft uses deployment rings in Microsoft 365 to gradually release new features and updates to users. These rings allow organizations to test and validate new features with a smaller group of users before rolling them out to a larger audience. Also, they allow champions to preview and test new features before they are widely available. With this early access, champions can stay ahead of the curve and share their insights with the broader organization to help drive adoption.

Incentives people care about

Don't underestimate the significant role incentives and recognition play in motivating champions. Organizations can celebrate champions through event invitations, external visibility, and storytelling opportunities. For example, champions might be invited to speak at conferences, participate in podcasts, or be featured in internal and external communications. This recognition boosts their morale and highlights their contributions to the organization's success. Increase their impact in these moments by actively helping your champions shine. You could do this by providing speaker or media training and amplifying their profile through your organization's public social media channels.

Swag is another powerful motivational tool. Branded merchandise such as shirts, hoodies, mugs, stickers, and laptop decals can create a sense of pride and belonging among champions. Special limited-edition items like custom jackets, backpacks, or tech gear can be reserved for top-performing champions, further incentivizing their efforts. Providing useful and desirable swag, such as laptop sleeves, drink bottles, or backpacks, ensures champions feel valued and appreciated. Personalized swag can boost individual pride and identity, such as items with agent numbers or notable achievements.

Offering to fund certifications and courses as part of the training process can give champions a tangible reward to add to their resumes, further enhancing their professional development.

> **Caution**   Everyone is motivated by different things; take the time to find out what motivates each of your champions so that you can provide incentives, recognition, and support that will mean the most to them. Make sure your champions have the bandwidth to take on the role, as often the people who want to help are already overburdened at work.

Future-proofing your champions community

Maintaining the momentum of a champion's community requires continuous recruitment and development. A champions program is not a one-time setup; it needs ongoing attention to keep it vibrant and effective. Organizations should continuously identify individuals who exemplify curiosity, capability, and a collaborative spirit as potential champions.

It is also important to have a straightforward offboarding process for champions who wish to leave the program. This ensures that participation remains voluntary and that champions are not obligated to stay longer than they desire. Setting clear expectations during recruitment, such as defining a minimum commitment period, helps manage this process effectively.

Executive sponsors play a vital role in sustaining the champion community. Their visible and active support can significantly influence employees' willingness to participate. When managers and senior leaders celebrate the achievements of the champions community and show up to meetings, it reinforces the program's importance and aligns it with the organization's broader goals.

Try this prompt: Community brainstorm

Champions programs that people want to join need a compelling name. You may choose to crowd-source this with your first group of Copilot champions. Another option is to brainstorm with Copilot as a first step. You can use this multipart prompt that asks Copilot to do several tasks based on the information you provide. Make a cup of tea and prepare to spend some time chatting with Copilot to generate some quality ideas.

Goal:

Generate 5–10 creative, on-brand names for an internal community of Copilot evangelists. Each name should include a short rationale, a suggested member title, and a tagline.

Instructions:

> *1. Greet the user briefly and ask for the nine inputs below in a single numbered list.*
> *2. If any input is missing or unclear, ask only the necessary follow-up questions.*
> *3. Once all inputs are provided, generate a table with these columns:*
> > *- Program Name*
> > *- 1-Sentence Rationale*
> > *- Member Title*
> > *- Tagline (5–8 words)*
> *4. Provide at least the requested number of options. Vary tone, wordplay, and length to offer real choice.*
> *5. End wlith a short paragraph suggesting how to test and select the final name.*

Inputs (please complete and return as a list):

> *1. Organization name:*
> *2. Industry and size (e.g., "global law firm, 8,000 staff"):*
> *3. Culture keywords (3–5, e.g., innovative, playful, trusted):*
> *4. Preferred tone (e.g., Professional, Heroic, Playful, Secret-Agent, or other):*
> *5. Words/phrases to include (optional):*
> *6. Words/phrases to avoid (optional):*
> *7. Maximum length for the program name (e.g., "≤ 3 words" or "≤ 25 characters"; optional):*
> *8. Existing internal programs to echo or avoid (optional):*
> *9. Number of options wanted (default = 7):*

Guidelines:

Keep names brand-safe and tasteful.
Avoid trademark issues beyond "Copilot" and Microsoft ecosystem terms.
If multiple tones are selected, include at least one name in each.
Double-check spelling, acronyms, and cultural sensitivity.

> **Tip** Once you have narrowed down the ideas Copilot helps you come up with, run a quick stakeholder poll or A/B test in Teams or Viva Engage to choose the final name.

Next steps

In this chapter, we highlighted the important role champions play in driving cultural transformation within an organization; they become central change agents who fundamentally shape the innovative culture necessary to accelerate AI transformation.

- Training and recognizing champions empowers them to become advocates for Copilot adoption and enablers of sustainable cultural transformation.

- A well-structured champions program nurtures and rewards innovators, providing them with a platform to share their knowledge and experiences.

- By creating a sense of belonging and community, champions feel valued and motivated to contribute to the organization's success.

- As champions share their stories and successes, they inspire others to embrace Copilot and drive innovation within their teams.

PART 3

Essential skills to win with AI

The constantly evolving nature of work, thanks to continuing advancements in AI technology, requires a different personal leadership development approach. Professionals are asked to build on shifting ground to develop skills that will prepare them for the AI-enabled future of work. While the capabilities of Copilot and the application of AI will continue to expand, there are uniquely human skills that all professionals can focus on to add value in their roles at work and at home. These skills are important when collaborating with other people and AI tools.

- In Chapter 8, "Conversation," we discuss how a conversational approach to collaborating with Copilot produces significantly higher-quality outputs than treating it like a search engine. We also highlight the importance of creating space to connect as a team about how Copilot is changing the way we work.

- In Chapter 9, "Critical thinking," we explore the thinking models that support constructive skepticism and iterative questioning processes when evaluating AI outputs.

- In Chapter 10, "Communication," we talk about the importance of storytelling and tailoring your message for the intended audience. We also cover three frameworks you can use to level up your communications.

These skills will help you stand out as a leader in whatever role you take on, even if you're collaborating with a hybrid team that includes both people and AI agents.

> **Tip** "My absolute favorite Copilot use case is automatically transforming team meeting recaps directly into meeting notes. A recorded meeting with Teams Premium and Copilot generates AI notes that can be instantly imported into OneNote to keep track of important information, action items, and ongoing knowledge sharing. Copilot has become an indispensable assistant. From drafting client proposals to helping me find specific information from complex meetings and prepping content for workshops, it saves me many hours and truly elevates the quality of my output overall."–**Sharon Weaver** is a Microsoft MVP for Microsoft 365 Copilot, Microsoft Regional Director, and productivity expert who leads Smarter Consulting in Davenport, Florida.

CHAPTER 8

Conversation

I've learned that people will forget what you said, people will forget what you did, but people will never forget how you made them feel.

—Maya Angelou

In this chapter, you will:

- Discover the ingredients of a great conversation and why it's important to improve our conversation skills to get better outputs from Copilot

- Explore frameworks to structure conversations that facilitate collaboration and counter biases

- Understand the department-specific and cross-functional conversations required to scale the adoption of Copilot across the organization

Connection through conversations

As society increasingly moves online, traditional face-to-face conversations are giving way to email and chat exchanges. This shift has diminished the quality of our interactions. Conversation remains an essential skill for anyone who wants to stay relevant in our technology-driven world. Revisiting this fundamental skill can help us reconnect with others, develop shared thinking, and collaborate more effectively with generative AI tools like Copilot. There's an instinct to treat Copilot like a search engine; after all, the user interfaces look similar. However, generative AI tools like Copilot are designed for conversation, which requires a more open and curious mindset. When it comes to conversations between people, or between you and Copilot, we need to relearn what distinguishes great conversations from ineffective interactions.

This chapter explores both the opportunities for meaningful dialogue and the costs of silence—including misalignment, resistance, and decreased productivity when conversations are insufficient or poorly managed. Unspoken concerns and fears require regular, intentional conversations to address. When dialogue is avoided, people often fill information gaps with assumptions, fueling misinformation and resistance. Organizations that foster transparency and proactive communication can surface these issues effectively, reducing adoption risks and enhancing the successful integration of Copilot into how work gets done.

The ingredients of a great conversation

Great conversations require three essential elements: intention, attention, and trust. Intention clarifies the purpose and goals, ensuring meaningful and productive dialogue. Attention means being fully present, considering timing and context. Trust enables both parties to rely on each other's positive intent and shared information. These elements are crucial for both human-to-human and human-to-AI interactions, helping create effective, clear, and goal-oriented exchanges. Successful conversations with Copilot depend on all three ingredients.

- **Intention** Before engaging in any conversation, it's important to clarify why you are having it. What are you trying to achieve? Why is this conversation happening now, and are you speaking with the right person or entity? Setting a clear intention helps in aligning your mindset towards a productive engagement. This is especially true when interacting with AI. For instance, when using Copilot, think about the specific outcome you want to achieve and provide a clear context to guide the AI in delivering a relevant response.

- **Attention** Effective conversations require undivided focus. This means putting aside distractions, such as closing your laptop or putting down your phone, and giving the other party your full attention. Timing is equally important. Ensure that both parties are in a state where they can fully engage in the conversation. For example, if someone is busy or preoccupied, it might not be the best time to have an in-depth discussion. Similarly, when interacting with Copilot, allocate sufficient time to engage with the tool, provide detailed context, and refine your queries to get the best possible output.

- **Trust** Trust forms the foundation of conversations with humans and AI alike. In human interactions, this means trusting others' intentions and information. With AI, trust involves understanding how the AI generates its responses, the data sources it uses, and the mechanisms in place to ensure accuracy and reliability. For instance, knowing that Copilot draws on data from your organization's Teams, Outlook, and SharePoint helps build confidence in its outputs. You can request source links to verify information. Being transparent about AI's limitations and potential biases further strengthens trust.

Focusing on these three ingredients, intention, attention, and trust, can significantly improve the quality of your conversations, whether with colleagues or Copilot.

> **Tip** Understand your audience and tailor your conversations to highlight what they care about, at the level of detail that's most relevant to their role and personality. For example, some managers prefer updates in concise points while others require detailed context.

Strategic conversations

Strategic conversations align the vision and ensure all organizational levels share an understanding of Copilot use and adoption. These include leadership alignment, cross-functional collaboration, and effective communication with Microsoft and partners.

Leadership alignment

Strategic alignment begins with executive commitment, as discussed in Chapter 2, "Clarity". Leaders across departments must engage in structured discussions to harmonize their visions and strategies. This may involve dedicated workshops where leaders openly discuss goals, challenges, and expectations. Consistent messaging across executive teams ensures everyone is "singing from the same hymn sheet," creating a unified approach to Copilot adoption. Since individuals interpret terms differently based on their context, establishing agreed-upon definitions for key phrases and concepts ensures everyone is talking about the same thing when addressing Copilot adoption.

Cross-functional alignment

Departments must communicate and collaborate to share insights about what works and lessons learned as they prototype Copilot integration into organizational processes. Structured roundtables or Copilot alignment forums facilitate these conversations. For example, if IT successfully integrates Copilot with ServiceNow to improve ticket resolution times, this knowledge should be shared with HR, which might benefit from similar integrations. Cross-functional alignment sparks new ideas and innovations as departments can learn from each other's successes and challenges.

Microsoft and partner conversations

When evaluating potential partners or Microsoft, develop a standard set of questions and a checklist to ensure they meet your organization's needs. For instance, when working with Microsoft as the vendor for Copilot, it's beneficial to establish a feedback loop for feature requests and improvements. Engaging in ongoing dialogue with Microsoft can lead to mutual benefits, such as participating in Advisory Councils or case studies.

Assess Microsoft partners' maturity and expertise in Copilot adoption, as they will significantly contribute to your implementation. Key evaluation areas include their ability to align with your organization's strategy and vision, their understanding of ecosystem architecture, their experience with developing and deploying workloads, their approach to responsible AI, and their capability to scale AI solutions. Ask for examples of how they've driven and supported Copilot adoption amongst their own teams, including how they've improved their processes with agents. They should also be able to share their practical approaches to the data governance and compliance considerations raised in Chapter 6, "Compliance." Prioritize conversations that clarify expectations and responsibilities between your organization and the partner to ensure strong collaboration and successful Copilot implementation.

Operational conversations

Operational conversations serve as the practical foundation for successful Copilot adoption. These discussions ensure teams maximize Copilot's capabilities while addressing challenges promptly. By establishing a regular cadence for discussions, maintaining transparency across all levels, and implementing effective troubleshooting processes, organizations create an environment where Copilot becomes a seamlessly integrated tool rather than a disconnected technology. Operational conversations transform abstract strategies into tangible workflows.

Establishing regular cadence

To support the effective use of Copilot, establish a regular cadence for team check-ins and reviews. This can include

- **Structured team check-ins**   These are daily standups or Scrum meetings in which team members discuss what Copilot helped them with yesterday, how they plan to use it today, and any obstacles they face. This approach ensures continuous feedback and improvement.

- **Weekly reviews**   Regular reviews to assess Copilot's use and impact, using tools like the Copilot Dashboard to gather insights and metrics. This helps identify areas for improvement and ensures the tool is used effectively.

Ensuring transparency

Transparency in operational discussions about Copilot usage builds trust and ensures everyone is on the same page:

- **Sharing metrics**   Regularly sharing metrics and insights from the Copilot Dashboard and other qualitative and quantitative adoption metrics you are tracking with the team. This includes discussing which metrics are being tracked and why and gathering feedback on whether these are the right metrics to focus on.

- **Decision-making**   Using the insights gathered to make informed decisions about Copilot usage, such as determining which departments should receive licenses next or identifying areas that need additional support.

> **Note** As part of Microsoft Viva Insights, the Copilot Dashboard is prebuilt for business leaders to prepare for their Copilot rollout, understand how it is being used, and measure the return on investment. Access it at *https://aka.ms/copilotdashboard*.

Troubleshooting conversations

Effective troubleshooting requires a structured approach to diagnosing and resolving operational issues when it comes to Copilot adoption, including the following:

- **Step-by-step frameworks** Develop conversation frameworks for handling resistance, confusion, and misinformation. For example, create a library of responses to common issues and provide training for champions or mentors who can assist team members.

- **Multiple modalities** Offer various ways for team members to seek help, such as one-on-one conversations with champions, dedicated Teams channels for support, and FAQs that can eventually be turned into AI agents for self-service.

> **Tip** Make learning fun and engaging by asking Copilot to help create music, images, or quizzes for your team meetings.

User experience and feedback mechanisms

Establish a robust feedback mechanism to improve Copilot usage:

- **Frequent feedback** Encouraging team members to provide feedback regularly, using simple and friction-free methods like one-question surveys or recording their screen and talking through their feedback.

- **Timely responses** Ensure feedback is reviewed and addressed promptly, and that team members see their input being acted upon. This builds on your culture of trust and continuous improvement.

Sharing lessons and successes

Encouraging the sharing of lessons learned and success stories helps build a positive culture around Copilot usage. This can be achieved through forums and open mic sessions, where team members can share their experiences, challenges, and successes with Copilot. These peer-to-peer conversations create a sense of community and connection.

Structuring effective AI conversations

Let's explore practical techniques and methodologies you can experiment with to ensure that conversations with Copilot are effective, productive, and aligned with organizational goals.

Conversations with Copilot

Apply these techniques for clear, concise, and productive prompting to enhance productivity and accuracy.

- **Effective prompting techniques**

  - **Clear and concise prompts**   Start with a clear goal, add context, provide a source, and specify the desired response format. For example, bullet points, a Word document, or an Excel chart.

  - **Role assignment**   Assign Copilot a specific role to guide its responses. For example, "You are a communications expert. Please help me draft an engaging speech to clearly explain this complex concept."

  - **Ask for clarification**   "Ask me any questions before you respond" or specify, "Don't respond until you're 98 percent sure you understand what I'm asking for." This helps ensure that Copilot provides more accurate and relevant answers.

- **Optimizing Copilot responses**

  - **Iterative engagement**   Treat interactions with Copilot as a conversation. If the initial response is unsatisfactory, continue the dialogue to refine the output.

  - **Sample outputs**   Provide examples of the desired output to guide Copilot's responses.

  - **Feedback mechanism**   Use Copilot to conduct self-interviews on complex topics, asking it to interview you to draw out your knowledge and identify gaps.

- **Leveraging Copilot as a thought partner**

  - **Simplifying complex concepts**   Use Copilot to explain complex topics in simpler terms or to specific audiences. For example, "Explain this concept with an analogy that would make sense to a 15-year-old."

  - **Challenging ideas**   Ask Copilot to critique or evaluate your strategic plans or ideas, provide critical feedback, and identify potential gaps. For example, say you're creating a learning pathway for people in your customer service department to raise their AI literacy. You can ask Copilot to identify any key topics that are missing from your course content.

  - **Creative assistance**   Use Copilot to generate analogies, metaphors, or creative content to enhance communication and engagement.

Tip Play 20 Questions with Copilot to test your knowledge on a topic and summarize the information. This interactive approach helps reinforce learning while revealing knowledge gaps.

Active listening and constructive dialogue

Active listening is a conversational skill that requires intentional development. In the context of Copilot adoption, it is necessary to build trust and psychological safety when introducing significant technological change. By demonstrating genuine curiosity and respect for concerns, leaders create an environment where team members feel comfortable expressing concerns about AI. This approach transforms potential resistance into valuable feedback that strengthens implementation strategies and accelerates adoption across the organization.

Techniques tailored to AI adoption include

- **Acknowledging uncertainty** Recognize and validate concerns about AI usage without dismissing them. This means creating space for team members to express their anxieties about Copilot replacing their jobs. For example, respond with, "I understand your concern about how Copilot might change your role. Many people share this uncertainty, and it's important we address it together," rather than "You don't need to worry about that."

- **Validating concerns** Ensure team members feel heard by reflecting their concerns back to them and taking meaningful action. This involves summarizing what you've heard, confirming your understanding, and communicating specific steps being taken to address these concerns. For instance, "I hear that you're worried about data privacy with Copilot. We've developed comprehensive security protocols and will be conducting a special session next week to walk through exactly how your information is protected."

- **Checking assumptions** Regularly revisit and validate assumptions made during AI implementation through structured conversations. Schedule dedicated sessions to review initial assumptions about how Copilot would be used, what benefits it would deliver, and what challenges might arise. For example, "We initially assumed sales teams would primarily use Copilot for customer research, but our usage data shows they're finding more value in email drafting. Let's discuss how we might adjust our training to better support this unexpected use case."

These techniques transform potentially difficult conversations about AI adoption into productive dialogues that strengthen organizational alignment and accelerate Copilot integration.

Six Thinking Hats framework

As shown in Figure 8-1, the Six Thinking Hats framework, developed by Edward de Bono, is a powerful tool that can be applied to help you structure conversations around AI use and Copilot adoption.

Edward de Bono's Six Thinking Hats Framework

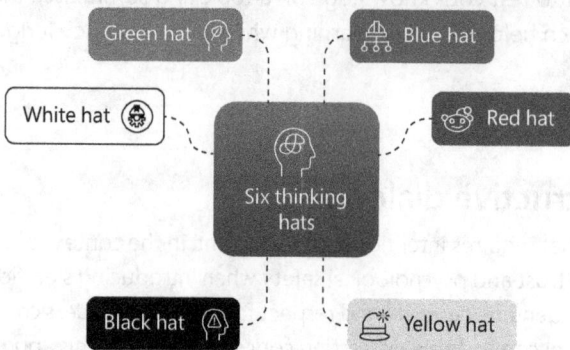

FIGURE 8-1 Edward de Bono's Six Thinking Hats framework can be used to structure conversations

This approach assigns different roles or "hats" to participants, enabling teams to explore ideas from diverse perspectives:

- **White hat (facts)**   This approach focuses on data and objective facts. Participants state what is known and identify missing information, such as examining Copilot's integration capabilities with existing Microsoft infrastructure or third-party systems like ServiceNow, SAP, or Oracle.

- **Red hat (emotions)**   Provides space for expressing feelings, fears, intuitions, and hunches without justification. This helps us understand emotional barriers, such as anxiety about job security or fears around AI mistakes. Creating this safe space allows concerns to surface rather than remaining hidden obstacles to adoption.

- **Black hat (caution)**   This approach highlights potential risks, pitfalls, and concerns. It ensures preparedness and mitigates risks, such as compliance risks or unintended biases that Copilot might introduce. This perspective prevents overly optimistic planning and strengthens implementation strategies.

- **Yellow hat (optimism)**   Identifies opportunities, benefits, and positive aspects. Leaders can highlight productivity gains and time savings Copilot provides, showcasing successful case studies from similar organizations. This perspective builds enthusiasm and motivation for adoption efforts.

- **Green hat (creativity)**   This hat encourages innovative thinking, brainstorming new use cases or scenarios, and exploring unconventional possibilities, such as developing custom prompts to solve specific business challenges or processes. The creative perspective helps organizations maximize Copilot's potential beyond standard applications.

- **Blue hat (process control)**   This role manages the overall process, ensures structured thinking, and keeps discussions productive and goal-oriented. Like an orchestra conductor guiding musicians into harmony, the Blue hat perspective maintains focus and moves the conversation toward actionable outcomes.

By rotating through these perspectives, teams can develop more comprehensive and balanced approaches to Copilot adoption, addressing both technical and human aspects of implementation.

> **Tip** You can also ask Copilot to wear these "hats" in conversations with you so that you can analyze a project or idea from a different perspective.

Conversations by department

Different departments require tailored conversations about Copilot adoption to address their unique needs, challenges, and opportunities. Strategic dialogue should reflect departmental priorities while maintaining alignment with broader organizational goals.

The following examples highlight specific conversations that drive successful adoption across key business functions:

- **Legal department**
  - Structured dialogues address compliance, data privacy, and regulatory requirements related to Copilot use, such as ensuring alignment with the European Union (EU) AI Act.
  - Regular updates and briefings on evolving AI legislation to ensure continuous alignment and risk mitigation. This includes understanding the implications of new regulations and how they affect the organization's legal framework.

- **IT department**
  - Frameworks for discussing infrastructure readiness, system integration, and technical support requirements. This includes evaluating the technical ecosystem and ensuring secure and scalable Copilot adoption.
  - Scheduled check-ins on security concerns, data governance, and system performance specific to Copilot use. For instance, ensuring that data governance policies are in place and that security measures are robust.
  - Dedicated forums for people to share how the IT department can use Copilot in their own work processes. For example, to reduce the time it takes to resolve support tickets. Avoid the common pitfall of the IT team being too busy helping others use Copilot that their own workloads aren't updated to include AI help.

- **Finance department**
  - Discuss budgeting, forecasting, and financial reporting with finance leaders. This includes evaluating the cost-benefit analysis to justify investment in Copilot licenses.
  - Conversations about specific tools that make the most sense for the finance department, such as Copilot for Finance and Operations within the Dynamics space, or using Copilot within Excel for data analysis and insights.

> **Note** The finance department may be strong advocates for adopting Copilot organization-wide due to the significant potential for cost savings and efficiency gains; they may be involved in conversations about reducing headcount, streamlining processes, and maximizing the financial benefits of the innovations Copilot can enable.

- **Customer service department**

  - Conversations around improving customer service by delivering higher-quality answers quickly. For example, using Copilot to draft emails based on approved responses and providing support through self-service portals.

  - Discussions on how Copilot can enhance the customer service experience by integrating existing knowledge bases and updating them in real time based on customer interactions.

By tailoring conversations to departmental contexts while maintaining a consistent message about Copilot's organizational value, leaders can accelerate adoption and maximize returns across diverse business functions.

Cross-departmental conversations

Effective Copilot adoption requires strategic dialogue that crosses traditional departmental boundaries. Cross-functional conversations about how Copilot can be used to transform end-to-end processes require curiosity beyond just the scope of your current job role or department. These interdisciplinary conversations create an environment for collaborative use of Copilot while addressing interconnected challenges and opportunities.

Here are a few specific examples of cross-departmental conversations that might be part of your Copilot rollout:

- Legal and IT departments collaborate to ensure that Copilot implementations comply with data privacy and security regulations

- Finance and IT departments work together to understand the financial implications of Copilot adoption and ensure the necessary technical infrastructure is in place

- Customer service and legal departments align on the potential risks and benefits of using Copilot for customer interactions, ensuring that responses are accurate and compliant with regulations

A specific example is the discussion around enabling the free version of M365 Copilot Chat. The legal department may push for its activation to ensure that data remains within the organization's boundaries, reducing the risk of data leakage to external platforms like Claude or ChatGPT as a byproduct of shadow AI. They would work with IT and department leads to make people aware of how they can use Copilot Chat for their work. This collaboration provides a safer environment for experimentation and usage before rolling out premium licenses.

Strategic cross-departmental conversations create an alignment that transcends functional silos, enabling more cohesive and effective Copilot adoption across the organization. These dialogues help transform potential points of friction into opportunities for collaborative innovation.

Try this prompt: 20 questions with Copilot

Switching from a question-and-answer mindset to a conversational mindset when interacting with Copilot takes practice. This prompt offers a fun way to have a conversation with Copilot to draw out and organize your ideas. It has many potential applications, from drafting blog posts to preparing a presentation on a topic to forming the start of a strategic plan. Customize this prompt with your own unique goal.

> *I'd like to play a 20 Questions-style game with you to help me draw out and organize my thoughts on [insert a specific topic].*
>
> *Please interview me one question at a time, and once we've completed all 20, create a cohesive summary or output based on my answers.*
>
> *My goal is to use this for [insert purpose: e.g., drafting a blog post, preparing a presentation, shaping a strategic plan, etc.]. Let's begin with your first question.*

> **Tip** Be clear about your topic or goal and answer each question thoughtfully. This is about depth, not speed. Specify the output you want and ask Copilot to adapt the tone for your audience.

Next steps

In this chapter, we discussed the importance of intentional conversations as a necessary skill to enable collaboration with Copilot as well as cross-functional teams across your organization. The techniques and frameworks outlined in this chapter provide practical tools for leaders who recognize that Copilot adoption is ultimately a human challenge requiring human solutions.

- Intention, attention, and trust are crucial for meaningful conversation. Intention clarifies the purpose, attention ensures focus, and trust builds reliability in exchanges with both humans and AI.

- Regular discussions help teams maximize Copilot's capabilities and address challenges. Establishing a cadence for check-ins and maintaining transparency fosters effective use of AI.

- Tailored discussions within departments like Legal, IT, Finance, and Customer Service ensure that Copilot adoption meets unique needs while aligning with organizational goals.

CHAPTER 9

Critical thinking

We are incentivized not to think.

—BRENÉ BROWN

In this chapter, you will:

- Learn why it's important to develop constructive skepticism to evaluate AI-generated content with the right balance of openness and scrutiny

- Discover how to master practical frameworks, including source triangulation, iterative prompting, and scenario planning, to enhance your interactions with Copilot

- Understand how to build organizational capability by recognizing cognitive biases, avoiding common pitfalls, and fostering a culture where critical thinking strengthens AI adoption

The need for constructive skepticism

In an AI-enabled workplace, thoughtful analysis and sound judgment are fundamental to success. As artificial intelligence becomes deeply integrated into our decision-making processes, the ability to analyze information objectively and form rational judgments has never been more important. Everyone can benefit from developing a personal practice of questioning and curiosity, but AI leaders especially must cultivate a habit of skepticism that's constructive rather than dismissive.

Consider the serious consequences when critical thinking is absent. Facial recognition technology used in law enforcement can match faces to databases of wanted individuals, but it's not infallible. There have been instances where individuals were wrongfully detained based on AI-generated matches. This highlights why human judgment and critical assessment must work in conjunction with AI outputs; the responsibility for decisions cannot be abdicated to technology.

From passive consumption to active questioning

This shift to critical thinking starts with recognizing how modern technology encourages passive consumption of content. Social media and news platforms serve information in ways that require little active thinking from audiences. Personalized algorithms deliver content designed for passive engagement, keeping us scrolling for the next dopamine hit. The winners in this scenario are platform owners who retain our attention and content creators who benefit from their ability to influence viewers. To interpret AI-generated information effectively, we must break this pattern and adopt an active questioning approach.

Generative AI has revolutionized content generation, but it brings distinct challenges. AI tools, including Copilot, generate outputs based on vast datasets that may contain biases or errors. One notable limitation is AI's tendency to "hallucinate"- providing confidently incorrect information. Imagine relying on AI to find a quote for a blog post, only to discover the quote was inaccurately attributed or entirely fabricated. When this happens, the consequences can range from inconvenient to catastrophic, depending on the context. Unquestioningly trusting AI without verification can lead to misinformation and damage credibility.

We need to question information presented to us, especially from AI-generated content. This means considering whether it's accurate, trustworthy, and whether the interests it serves align with our own or our organization's objectives. Not every interaction with AI requires exhaustive verification, but it's essential to decide when and how to apply constructive skepticism. The extent of verification needed relates directly to how the information will be used and the potential impact if that information proves incorrect or biased.

Cases like wrongful detention based on faulty AI highlight why critical thinking skills must be a focus for anyone developing future-ready capabilities in an AI-enabled world. When used with these thinking skills, AI enhances rather than replaces human judgment.

Practical critical thinking with Copilot

Working effectively with Copilot requires moving beyond simply accepting its first response. As a tool deeply integrated into Microsoft 365 applications, Copilot has access to your organization's data and can generate content that feels authoritative because it incorporates familiar information. This integration makes it even more important to apply the same verification standards you would to any business-critical information. Developing practical strategies to assess and verify outputs ensures you benefit from Copilot's capabilities while maintaining the quality and reliability your work demands.

Source verification and triangulation

Consider this scenario: you're using Copilot to determine visa requirements for an upcoming business trip. The response seems comprehensive and includes specific details about the documentation needed. However, relying solely on this information could result in being denied entry at the border—a costly mistake that could have been avoided with proper verification.

This example illustrates why developing a source verification and triangulation habit is one of the most effective strategies for working with AI. Cross-reference Copilot's outputs with multiple reputable sources, especially for high-stakes decisions. In the visa example, verify the information through official government immigration websites and at least one additional authoritative source. Make it standard practice to ask Copilot for its sources, then independently verify key information using search engines, official websites, or subject matter experts.

This triangulation approach, as shown in Figure 9-1, encourages you to confirm information through multiple independent sources and enables confident decision-making based on accurate information.

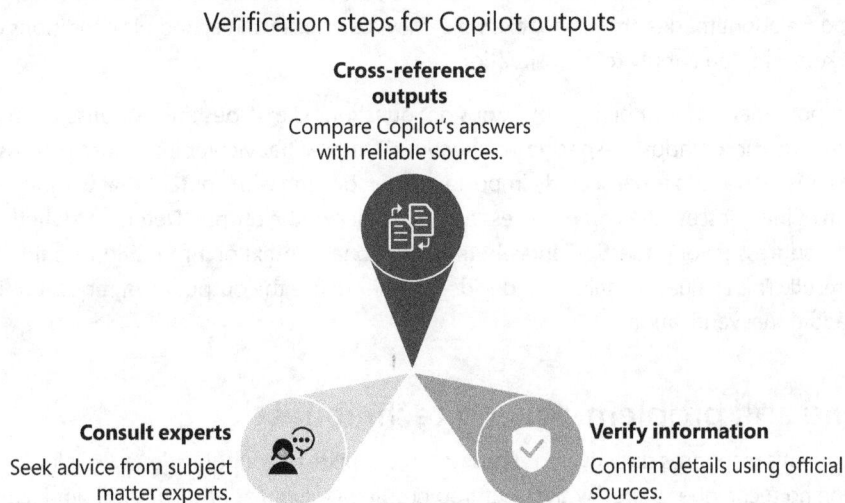

Verification steps for Copilot outputs

Cross-reference outputs
Compare Copilot's answers with reliable sources.

Consult experts
Seek advice from subject matter experts.

Verify information
Confirm details using official sources.

FIGURE 9-1 Source triangulation is the process by which you can cross-reference information from multiple sources to ensure accuracy.

> **Note** The definition of "reputable source" may differ between departments and applications in your organization. Encourage the creation of specific definitions with examples to help people analyze outputs and cross-reference with reputable sources.

Iterative prompt engineering

Effective prompting with Copilot is rarely a one-and-done process. Rather than spending excessive time crafting the perfect initial prompt, focus on refining your approach through iteration. This strategic back-and-forth improves both the accuracy and relevance of Copilot's responses. Start with prompts that encourage dialogue. Add phrases like "Before you answer, ask clarifying questions one at a time until you have all the context you need" to your initial request. This shifts Copilot from providing immediate answers to gathering the information it needs to give you better results.

Use follow-up prompts to refine outputs. If Copilot's first response is too general, ask it to "provide more specific examples." If it's too detailed, request a "high-level summary for executives." Each iteration builds on the previous response, creating a more targeted final output. Challenge your own thinking by asking Copilot to play devil's advocate. For instance, if you're developing a new product strategy, ask: "What are the strongest arguments against this approach?" or "What risks am I not considering?" This technique helps uncover blind spots and strengthens your decision-making process.

Post-output analysis

Don't accept Copilot's responses immediately; pause to evaluate what you've received. Post-output analysis involves systematically reviewing AI-generated content for assumptions, limitations, and potential biases before using it in your work. Begin by examining the underlying assumptions. Ask yourself: "What premises is this response built on?" and "Are these assumptions valid for my specific context?" A response about market trends, for example, may assume certain economic conditions or geographic markets that don't apply to your situation.

Next, look for potential biases or blind spots. Consider questions like: "Does this response reflect any cultural, demographic, or industry-specific perspectives?" and "What viewpoints might be missing from this analysis?" This step is particularly important when dealing with content that will influence strategic decisions. Finally, assess the completeness and relevance of the output. Determine whether the response fully addresses your question and whether additional context or information would strengthen the result. This evaluation helps you decide whether to use the output as-is, request refinements, or seek additional verification.

Questioning and problem-solving techniques

The quality of Copilot's responses directly correlates with the quality of your questions. Developing effective questioning techniques paired with structured problem-solving approaches will significantly improve your results. Use open-ended questions to encourage comprehensive responses. Instead of asking, "Should we launch this product?" try "What factors should we consider when evaluating this product launch?" This approach invites Copilot to explore multiple dimensions rather than providing a simple yes-or-no answer.

Incorporate reflective questioning to uncover blind spots and new perspectives. Ask questions like "What have I missed?" or "What assumptions am I making that might be incorrect?" These prompts push beyond your initial thinking and can reveal valuable insights you hadn't considered. Apply structured frameworks to guide your inquiry. The "How might we?" approach from design thinking is particularly effective because it opens possibilities without constraining solutions.

For example, instead of asking, "How might we create a better mobile app experience?" ask, "How might we create better user experiences?" This broader framing prevents you from limiting potential solutions to mobile platforms alone. Provide context and ask Copilot to challenge your ideas. Share your current thinking, then request alternative viewpoints: "Here's my current strategy—what are the strongest counterarguments?" or "Given this approach, what risks should I be most concerned about?" This technique transforms Copilot into a strategic thinking partner rather than just an information provider.

> **Tip** Providing Copilot with access to specific data sources or content that is relevant to what you are asking it to do reduces the risk of hallucination. This process grounds the model and tethers outputs to the provided data.

Critical thinking frameworks

Developing structured approaches to critical thinking transforms how leaders evaluate and implement AI-generated insights. While cultivating general curiosity by using phrases like "I'm curious about..." or "Tell me more about..." is valuable for encouraging deeper exploration, systematic frameworks provide the rigor needed for high-stakes decisions. The following four frameworks offer practical tools for incorporating critical thinking into your Copilot interactions, whether you're analyzing outputs individually or working with teams to evaluate AI-driven recommendations.

The "five whys" root cause analysis

Building on the concept introduced in Chapter 3, "Commitment", the five whys technique can be applied directly to Copilot interactions when outputs seem questionable or incomplete. This iterative questioning framework helps uncover the deeper reasoning behind AI-generated responses, moving beyond surface acceptance to understand underlying factors. When Copilot produces an unexpected or seemingly flawed output, guide your team through the iterative "why" process. For instance, if Copilot's quarterly report misses a key market insight, ask the following questions:

- Why did Copilot overlook this insight? (The prompt may have been too narrow.)

- Why was the prompt narrow? (We didn't include all relevant context.)

- Why didn't we provide full context? (We assumed Copilot had access to our prior discussions.)

- Why did we make that assumption? (We're unclear about Copilot's knowledge boundaries.)

- Why are we unclear about these boundaries? (We need better training on Copilot's capabilities.)

This process reveals that the root issue isn't Copilot's failure but rather an unclear understanding of how to effectively interact with the tool. By training teams to practice the five whys with AI outputs, leaders instill a habit of inquiry that improves both problem-solving rigor and future Copilot interactions.

The ORID framework

The ORID (Objective, Reflective, Interpretive, Decisional) framework provides a structured four-step process for analyzing Copilot outputs and turning raw information into actionable decisions. Developed by the Institute of Cultural Affairs in Canada, this approach ensures you consider both factual content and emotional responses before determining the next steps. Apply ORID whenever you receive complex outputs from Copilot that require careful evaluation. For example, when reviewing Copilot's analysis of your organization's AI adoption progress:

- **Objective (what): Identify the facts**   "Attendance reports show that 45 percent of our 1,500 staff members attended the initial Copilot training sessions."

- **Reflective (gut reaction): Explore emotional responses**   "I feel concerned about the low engagement and frustrated by the apparent lack of enthusiasm."

- **Interpretive (so what): Analyze implications** "This low attendance likely signals resistance or anxiety around Copilot adoption, suggesting our communication strategy isn't resonating."

- **Decisional (now what): Determine specific actions** "We could launch targeted listening sessions to understand barriers, then redesign our awareness campaign based on those insights."

This systematic progression from facts to feelings to analysis to action prevents rushed decisions based on incomplete evaluation. Regular use of ORID with Copilot interactions builds a habit of thorough assessment that strengthens both individual and team decision-making.

> **Tip** Ask Copilot to step you through this ORID framework when evaluating reports to determine next steps.

Devil's Advocate exercises

This involves deliberately challenging Copilot's outputs to identify weaknesses before implementing recommendations. This structured approach assigns team members to act as skeptics, questioning assumptions and exploring potential failure points in AI-generated analysis. Use this framework when evaluating high-stakes Copilot recommendations that could significantly impact your organization. For instance, when Copilot suggests a new market expansion strategy, consider

- **Question data quality** "What if the market data Copilot used is outdated or biased toward certain demographics?"

- **Challenge assumptions** "Has Copilot considered regulatory differences in these new markets?"

- **Explore alternatives** "What other expansion strategies weren't evaluated, and why might they be better?"

- **Test failure scenarios** "If this strategy fails, what would be the most likely causes?"

Rotate a "Copilot challenger" role among team members for major decisions. Set up regular scenario drills where the goal is to critique AI-generated proposals constructively. This approach exposes blind spots, prevents groupthink, and ensures thorough evaluation before execution. Regular devil's advocate exercises normalize healthy dissent and build organizational capability to evaluate AI recommendations rigorously. The result is more robust, well-vetted decisions that leverage Copilot's insights while maintaining critical oversight.

Premortem scenario planning

A premortem is a proactive decision-making exercise where a team imagines a future failure and works backwards to determine what went wrong. In contrast to a post-mortem (after failure), this forward-thinking exercise helps teams identify risks and build appropriate safeguards before implementation.

Use premortems when evaluating significant Copilot-informed decisions or processes. For example, before relying on Copilot to generate an important client presentation:

- **Assume the outcome** "The presentation didn't achieve our objectives." Explore possible reasons: "Perhaps Copilot's data wasn't current," or "The messaging didn't align with the client's priorities."

- **Identify contributing factors** "We may not have provided sufficient context about the client's preferences."

- **Develop preventive measures** "Add extra review steps for data accuracy and tone; include detailed client briefings in our process."

This "prospective hindsight" technique forces teams to surface risks and vulnerabilities in advance that could jeopardize the client relationship. By identifying these pitfalls upfront, teams can put safeguards in place or adjust the approach before any harm is done. Premortems strengthen critical thinking by helping people actively anticipate what could go wrong with AI outputs, thereby reducing overconfidence. While you can use Copilot to run a premortem, it's important not to rely on it to spot pitfalls. Making the time to do this as a team, virtually or in person, is more impactful.

Implement premortems as collaborative team discussions focused on constructive problem-solving. Encourage open exploration of potential challenges without creating anxiety about AI usage. Document insights and use them to strengthen your Copilot interaction protocols. By thoughtfully anticipating what could go wrong, teams can realize the benefits of Copilot while maintaining appropriate oversight.

Recognizing and overcoming cognitive biases

Cognitive biases represent one of the greatest hidden threats to effective AI adoption. These unconscious mental shortcuts, while useful in everyday decision-making, can lead people to misinterpret Copilot outputs or make flawed judgments about AI-generated recommendations.

The challenge is particularly acute because Copilot's sophisticated responses can feel authoritative and comprehensive, making it easier to overlook the influence of our own biases. Understanding and actively countering these biases ensures that your organization extracts maximum value from AI while maintaining sound judgment. The following framework helps leaders recognize the most common biases that affect AI interactions and provides practical strategies to overcome them.

Confirmation bias

Confirmation bias leads us to seek information that supports our existing beliefs while ignoring contradictory evidence. With Copilot, this bias becomes particularly dangerous because AI outputs can feel comprehensive, making it easier to accept information that aligns with our preconceptions. The risk is especially high when Copilot generates multiple insights - executives may focus only on points that support their current strategy while overlooking data that suggest course corrections. For example, if you believe a product launch should proceed despite market concerns, you might emphasize Copilot's positive market analysis while dismissing its warnings about competitive threats.

Cognitive biases can significantly impact the interpretation and reliability of AI-generated information.

To counter confirmation bias, you can do the following things:

- **Actively seek contradictory evidence**   Ask Copilot explicitly for potential risks or alternative viewpoints: "What are the strongest arguments against this approach?"

- **Assign a devil's advocate**   Have a team member specifically challenge positive findings and highlight negative data points.

- **Use structured evaluation**   Apply frameworks like ORID to ensure you process both supporting and contradictory information.

Anchoring bias

Anchoring bias causes us to over-rely on the first piece of information we encounter, which then influences all subsequent judgments. Copilot outputs often present initial data points or recommendations that can become mental anchors, skewing your entire analysis even when later information suggests different conclusions. This bias is particularly problematic in financial planning or project scoping.

If Copilot initially suggests a project will cost $500,000, this figure becomes an anchor that influences all future budget discussions, even if revised estimates are significantly higher or lower. Teams may unconsciously adjust expectations around this initial anchor rather than evaluating each new piece of information independently.

To counter anchoring bias:

- **Delay initial judgments**   Review Copilot's complete analysis before forming opinions about any specific data points.

- **Seek multiple starting points**   Ask Copilot to approach the same problem from different angles or provide ranges rather than single figures.

- **Question first impressions**   Regularly ask, "If I hadn't seen this initial estimate, how would I evaluate this new information?"

Halo and horns effects

The halo effect occurs when positive experiences with Copilot lead to uncritical acceptance of all its outputs, while the horns effect causes negative experiences to create unwarranted skepticism of future recommendations. Both biases prevent balanced evaluation of AI-generated content. These effects are common in early AI adoption phases. Teams that experience early successes with Copilot may begin accepting all outputs without proper verification. Conversely, one significant error can cause teams to distrust even accurate subsequent analyses, limiting the tool's effectiveness and creating organizational resistance to AI adoption.

To counter the halo and horns effects, do the following:

- **Evaluate each output independently**   Treat every Copilot interaction as a separate instance requiring individual assessment.

- **Establish consistent verification protocols**   Apply the same validation standards regardless of past positive or negative experiences.

- **Track patterns, not incidents**   Base trust levels on performance over time rather than memorable successes or failures.

Recency bias

Recency bias causes us to prioritize recent information over historical context or long-term patterns. With Copilot's access to vast amounts of current data, this bias can lead to overvaluing short-term trends at the expense of established historical insights. This bias frequently appears in market analysis and forecasting. When Copilot highlights recent sales spikes or emerging trends, executives may base strategic decisions on this recent data without considering seasonal patterns, economic cycles, or historical precedents that provide crucial context for interpretation.

To counter recency bias:

- **Request historical context**   Always ask Copilot to include long-term trends and historical comparisons alongside recent data.

- **Set time frame boundaries**   Specify the timeframe you want to be analyzed rather than accepting the default recent periods.

- **Validate with past patterns**   Cross-reference current trends with historical data to identify whether recent changes represent genuine shifts or normal variations.

> **Tip**   Many people won't be familiar with these and other types of biases, so it's important to cover them as part of AI literacy training programs.

Building a critical thinking culture

Creating an organization where critical thinking thrives with AI requires intentional leadership action. Leaders must model the behavior they want to see. They can encourage critical thinking by sharing their own questioning processes, openly discussing when Copilot outputs don't align with their experience, and demonstrating how they combine AI insights with human judgment. This visible leadership approach signals that questioning AI isn't about distrust but about responsible usage. More powerful than demonstrating critical thinking alone is fostering a growth mindset. Leaders who are humble and curious and willing to take a learn-it-all approach to Copilot inspire the same attitudes in their teams.

You can embed critical thinking development into your Copilot training programs through scenario-based exercises and cross-functional workshops. When teams from different departments share their experiences with AI outputs, they develop broader perspectives on how biases and assumptions can vary across organizational contexts. Regular practice with the frameworks introduced in this chapter builds organizational capability that extends far beyond AI interactions.

Common pitfalls to avoid

Even organizations committed to critical thinking can fall into predictable traps that undermine effective AI adoption.

- **Over-reliance, leading to skill erosion**   Perhaps the most insidious risk is the gradual weakening of human judgment through over-dependence on Copilot. When employees consistently defer to AI for routine analysis and decision-making, they lose opportunities to practice problem-solving skills. This "use it or lose it" effect can slowly erode the very expertise that makes your organization effective. High confidence in AI correlates with less critical thinking, while confidence in human skills leads to more engaged evaluation.

- **Treating Copilot as autopilot**   The temptation to let AI handle tasks independently misses the point of human-AI collaboration. Copilot is designed as a copilot, not an autopilot, but an assistant that enhances human capability rather than replacing it. Organizations that frame AI as full automation set themselves up for accountability gaps and missed opportunities for human insight. Even as Copilot automates tasks, ultimate responsibility remains with the human user.

- **Automation bias in team settings**   Teams can collectively fall into the trap of rubber-stamping AI outputs, especially when recommendations align with existing plans or expectations. This groupthink effect is particularly dangerous because it feels like consensus when it's actually shared complacency. Overdependence on Copilot's suggestions can diminish employees' critical thinking and decision-making capabilities over time.

- **Anchoring on first solutions**   When Copilot provides an initial recommendation, teams often struggle to consider alternatives. This mental anchoring limits creativity and can lock organizations into suboptimal approaches simply because AI suggested them first. To counter it, teams should consciously generate or solicit multiple options (including non-AI ideas) before making a decision.

- **Sustaining critical thinking in an AI-enabled organization**   Leaders should view critical thinking as a skill that needs continual exercise; relying on Copilot without active human thought can atrophy the expertise that makes an organization effective. The goal isn't to create skeptics who distrust technology but to develop thoughtful professionals who leverage AI as a powerful thinking partner. Critical thinking with AI requires the same intellectual rigor you'd apply to any strategic decision, combined with new skills for evaluating artificial intelligence outputs. Organizations that master this balance will extract maximum value from Copilot investments while maintaining the human judgment that drives successful businesses. As AI capabilities continue to evolve, the critical thinking skills developed in this chapter become increasingly valuable. They represent a sustainable competitive advantage: the ability to leverage artificial intelligence while preserving the uniquely human insights that create lasting organizational success.

Try this prompt: Critical thinking coach

This chapter highlighted the importance of critical thinking skills when working with AI. You can use Copilot to help you develop your critical thinking skills by becoming your critical thinking coach. Choose any scenario or topic you're interested in, for example, a new business idea, and set aside some time to practice.

Act as my "Critical-Thinking Coach." Your job is to challenge my thinking—one question at a time so I can sharpen my reasoning and uncover blind spots.

Scenario to Analyze
<INSERT SCENARIO HERE>

How this works:

Assume I already understand the scenario.
Ask me exactly 8 questions, one at a time. Wait for my response before moving to the next.

Your questions should follow this sequence of angles:

1. Clarify the core claim or objective
2. Surface hidden assumptions
3. Probe the strength of supporting evidence
4. Identify potential cognitive biases (mine or others')
5. Offer an alternative lens or interpretation
6. Test logical consistency or causal links
7. Explore real-world implications (if true or false)
8. Identify next steps or missing evidence

Scoring rubric:

Each answer earns 0–2 points:
0 = vague, superficial, or unsupported
1 = reasonable but leaves gaps
2 = clear, well-reasoned, and evidence-aware
Max score: 16 points

Score range and Titles:

| 0 – 4 | Surface Skimmer
| 5 – 8 | Questioning Contributor

> **Note**   You can also copy and paste the news article or blog URL instead of specifying a scenario, and have Copilot ask you questions to evaluate your critical thinking skills when analyzing new information.

Next steps

In this chapter, we explored why developing critical thinking skills will significantly improve your interactions with Copilot. Constructive skepticism, verification of AI-generated content, and fostering a culture of critical thinking to enhance decision-making processes will give your organization a competitive advantage when it comes to creating value with AI.

- Encourage active questioning and verification of Copilot outputs through source verification, iterative prompting, and engaging in post-output analysis—especially when the stakes are high.

- Recognize and acknowledge how cognitive biases impact our ability to evaluate AI outputs and actively employ strategies to counter these biases in your decision-making processes.

- Advocate for building a critical thinking culture within your organization to maximize the benefits of AI while preserving human insights.

CHAPTER 10

Communication

The single biggest problem in communication is the illusion that it has taken place.

—GEORGE BERNARD SHAW

In this chapter, you will:

- Understand why communication is a core skill to help you cut through information overload and create meaningful connections with your audiences in an AI-saturated world

- Learn how to leverage Copilot to enhance your communication through clearer messaging and tailored stakeholder engagement

- Discover how to apply communication frameworks to structure compelling communications that inform, inspire, and drive action across your organization

The importance of communication skills

You know that sinking feeling you get when you've rushed to finish a project, run to the bathroom, and grab a seat just in time for the company All Hands meeting to start, only to hear the first speaker stand up and start to read the displayed slide. Reading word for word what the audience could read for themselves. That approach communicates a lot, but none of it relates to the words that are being spoken.

They're communicating that someone else wrote their content, that they haven't invested the time to learn it or make it their own. So why should the audience care?

By contrast, when a leader takes the stage and starts with a story, they hold the attention of every person in the room. When they use their hands to make a point, exclaim in an excited voice why they're personally thrilled to be making that announcement, they shift from conveying a message to communicating one. In an AI-driven world where information is more accessible, where AI can generate thousands of words in an instant, the uniquely human skill of storytelling is more important than ever to help people sit up and take notice of what they should care about. Without that cut-through, your message is just more noise in an increasingly loud world.

Enhancing communication with storytelling

Humans are wired to remember facts and numbers better when they're woven into a story. Stories provide the structure and emotional connection that transform data into action, helping audiences understand not just what happened but why it matters. By 2050, an estimated 95 percent of Internet content will be AI-generated, making authentic human storytelling a crucial differentiator for leaders who want to make a lasting impact.

Storytelling transforms presentations into experiences. Instead of listing project achievements in your stakeholder update, guide your audience through the journey: the challenges your team faced, the breakthrough moments that changed direction, and the vision that now drives the next phase. This narrative approach helps stakeholders connect emotionally with your message and see the bigger picture.

Copilot can enhance your storytelling in several practical ways:

- **Simplify complex concepts**   Use prompts like "Act as an expert storyteller and explain [complex topic] to a nontechnical executive audience using analogies and real-world examples."

- **Uncover hidden narratives**   Ask Copilot to analyze your data and identify the most compelling story: "What are the three most important trends in this sales data, and what story do they tell about our market position?"

- **Refine story structure**   Request feedback on your narrative flow: "Review this presentation outline and suggest how to make the story more compelling for board members."

The magic of AI lies in its ability to provide a starting point, but your perspective, experiences, and voice make a story uniquely powerful. Use Copilot's suggestions as a foundation, then layer in personal anecdotes, organizational context, and authentic emotion that only you can provide.

Crafting clear and impactful messages with Copilot

Communication goes beyond repeating someone else's message verbatim—it requires a deep understanding of your concepts and a keen awareness of your audience. The old adage "Communication happens at the listener's ear, not the speaker's mouth" reminds us that effective communication ensures your message lands meaningfully with the recipient.

Copilot excels at helping you refine message clarity and impact. Start by asking Copilot to summarize your draft: "What is the core message of this email?" This simple exercise reveals whether your main point comes through clearly. If Copilot struggles to identify your key message, your audience likely will, too.

Use these practical techniques to enhance your communications:

- **Test for clarity**   Tell Copilot to "Respond to this email as if you were [a specific role type, such as a client, a manager, a supplier]" to identify potential gaps or misunderstandings.

- **Refine for impact** Ask Copilot to "Make this message more concise while retaining its impact" to ensure brevity without losing meaning.

- **Adjust tone** Tell Copilot to "Rewrite this with a [collaborative/urgent/reassuring] tone for [audience type]" to match your communication style to your audience's needs.

- **Prepare for responses** Tell Copilot to "anticipate three follow-up questions this recipient might ask," to help you prepare comprehensive responses.

Remember that technology should enhance human connections, not replace them. If an email exchange becomes lengthy or confusing, use it as a signal to upgrade your communication channel— pick up the phone, or schedule a face-to-face conversation. Copilot helps you communicate more effectively, but the authentic human connection remains yours to create.

> **Tip** Try Coaching by Copilot in Outlook to quickly adjust the tone and clarity of your drafts to improve your communications.

Strengthening leadership communication

Active and visible executive sponsorship drives successful Copilot adoption more than any other factor. When leaders communicate authentically about AI tools, they model the behavior they want to see while building organizational confidence in new ways of working.

Leaders can leverage Copilot to craft communications that inspire rather than merely inform. The difference lies in moving beyond transactional updates to messages that connect with people's motivations and concerns about AI transformation. Take standard template communications from the Copilot Success Kit and work with Copilot to personalize them for your industry and leadership voice. You might prompt: "Rewrite this message to sound like me speaking to our engineering team about how Copilot will help us achieve our product innovation goals."

Consistency matters as much as inspiration. Before sending major communications about AI initiatives, use Copilot to review your message against previous statements. Ask it to identify any contradictions or missed opportunities to reinforce key themes. This ensures your messaging remains coherent as your organization's AI journey evolves.

Most importantly, leaders must demonstrate their own engagement with Copilot. When you openly share how you use AI tools to improve your own work, including challenges and learning moments, you give others permission to experiment and learn. Consider explaining in your next team update how Copilot helped you prepare for a board presentation or how you're still figuring out the best ways to prompt it for strategic planning. Authentic leadership communication about AI isn't about perfection; it's about showing the journey of discovery that you want your organization to embrace.

> **Tip**   Use Copilot to anticipate objections and strengthen your message. Ask Copilot, "If you were skeptical about our new initiative, what counterarguments might you make?"

Effective stakeholder engagement with Copilot

Tailoring communications to diverse stakeholder groups ensures relevance, clarity, and impact. Different audiences need different information presented in ways that resonate with their specific concerns and motivations. Copilot can help you develop engaging materials, presentations, newsletters, and announcements that speak directly to each stakeholder group's priorities.

Start by understanding each department's specific needs. When communicating with teams about gaining access to Copilot, include concrete examples of how they will use the tool in their daily work, how their roles might evolve, and which tasks could be streamlined. Identify champions within each team and provide clear channels for questions. This specificity builds confidence and reduces anxiety about change. When you craft compelling communications, save them so that they can be used to ground Copilot with good examples when creating future communications.

Choosing the right communication medium is as important as getting the message right. While email works for updates, presentations or speeches can be more powerful for significant announcements. Copilot can help craft compelling materials for any format. When preparing for an All Hands meeting, you might ask Copilot to suggest effective opening questions or techniques to engage your audience immediately. After the presentation, use Copilot to distill key points into a three-bullet summary for your company newsletter, ensuring important messages reach those who missed the session. You could also ask Copilot to analyze the transcript to highlight where messages needed to be clearer, or compare it to the chat for insight into frequently asked questions.

Consider the experience of a Canadian tech company that used the same technical presentation for all audiences—IT buyers, executives, and business partners. This one-size-fits-all approach consistently missed the mark with nontechnical stakeholders. The solution was to create audience-specific presentations: one for business stakeholders focusing on outcomes and financial impacts, another for HR buyers emphasizing workforce benefits, and a third for technical teams detailing integration specifics. This targeted approach dramatically improved engagement by addressing each audience's unique motivations and concerns.

The key is to match your message to your audience's perspective while maintaining consistency in your core value proposition. Copilot can help you adapt the same fundamental message for different stakeholders without losing authenticity or diluting your key points.

Choosing the right communication approach

The choice between asynchronous and synchronous communication can make the difference between clarity and confusion, efficiency and waste. Understanding when to use each approach (and how Copilot can enhance both) helps leaders communicate more effectively while respecting everyone's time.

Maximizing asynchronous communication

Many traditional meetings exist simply to disseminate information rather than facilitate genuine discussion. These one-way communications waste time and interrupt workflows unnecessarily. By contrast, as shown in Figure 10-1, asynchronous communication methods allow messages to be sent and received at different times, for instance, by recording concise video messages in Teams that stakeholders can view at their convenience. Copilot can auto-transcribe these recordings and summarize key points, ensuring your message reaches everyone clearly and consistently, regardless of time zone or schedule.

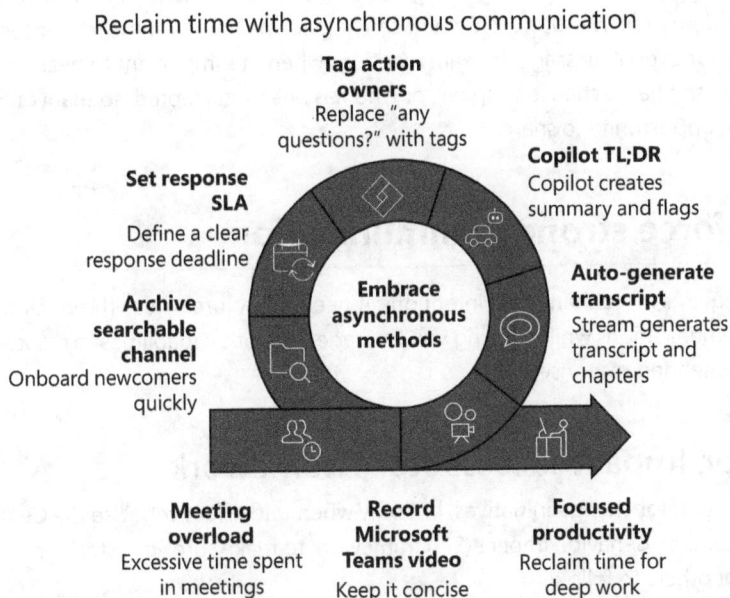

FIGURE 10-1 Reclaim time with asynchronous communication

For example, rather than calling a meeting to announce a new policy, record a brief explanation, let Copilot generate a summary, and share both with your team. This approach ensures everyone receives identical information while allowing them to process it thoughtfully and respond when convenient.

> **Note** Asynchronous communication can be an enabler of equity for people who work remotely, travel for work, or perhaps are on personal leave and would have otherwise missed the announcement.

Making synchronous communication count

When you do need real-time interaction for discussions, decisions, or relationship building, make every moment count. Copilot can help you prepare for these high-stakes communications by anticipating challenges and crafting responses ahead of time.

Before important presentations or meetings, ask Copilot to generate potentially challenging questions based on your content: "What are the five most difficult questions the board might ask about this strategic proposal?" Use these to prepare thoughtful responses that position you as confident and well-prepared.

During live events, specify the emotional response you want to create. Ask Copilot: "How can I adjust this message to build trust with skeptical stakeholders?" This ensures your communication conveys information while resonating emotionally with your audience. You can also ask Copilot if there are any unanswered questions before closing the meeting. For events where a team might be available to help answer questions and provide live support, Copilot can help formulate real-time responses that maintain consistency with your overall message. In team meetings where it's important to hear from everyone, ask Copilot who hasn't had a chance to speak, or who has been interrupted, so that you can make sure they are given an opportunity to share.

Frameworks to reinforce strong communication

Effective communication requires more than good intentions; it needs structure. These three frameworks can elevate your communications while helping you leverage Copilot's capabilities to create messages that inspire your intended response.

Situation, Behavior, Impact success story framework

Success stories build momentum for change initiatives, but only when told effectively. Use the Center for Creative Leadership's Situation, Behavior, Impact (SBI) framework to make sure your stories resonate and provide clear lessons for others to follow.

When sharing Copilot adoption wins, structure your stories this way:

- **Situation: Set the context**   "Our sales team was struggling to personalize outreach for 200+ prospects weekly."

- **Behavior: Describe specific actions taken**   "They started using Copilot to analyze customer data and generate tailored email templates, then refined these with personal insights."

- **Impact: Quantify the results**   "Response rates increased 40% and deal velocity improved by three weeks."

Ask Copilot to help craft these stories by prompting: "Help me structure this success story using the SBI framework, focusing on specific actions and measurable outcomes." This approach makes abstract benefits tangible and gives others a clear roadmap for replicating success.

> **Tip**   The SBI framework is also a helpful way to prepare stories about your experience and impact for job interviews.

7 Cs framework for quality communication

The 7 Cs framework is inspired by the work of Cutlip and Center in their 1952 book, *Effective Public Relations*. Now, it is a widely recognized method for ensuring clear and effective business communication. The 7 Cs provides a checklist to help communicators deliver messages to their audience that are easily understood and well-received.

You can use Copilot to check that your communications are aligned with this framework:

- **Clear**   Is the message easy to understand? Are there any ambiguous terms, three-letter acronyms, or jargon that should be clarified?

- **Concise**   Is the message brief and to the point? Are there any unnecessary words or information that can be removed?

- **Concrete**   Does the message provide solid facts and details? Are there specific examples or data to support the message?

- **Correct**   Is the message free from errors and accurate? Are all facts, grammar, and spelling correct?

- **Coherent**   Does the message flow logically? Is the information organized in a logical sequence with clear transitions?

- **Complete**   Does the message provide all the necessary information? Are all relevant details included, and does it answer potential questions?

- **Courteous**   Is the message respectful and considerate? Does it use polite language and show empathy towards the audience?

> **Tip**   Ask Copilot to review your communication using the 7 Cs framework to evaluate whether the message is clear, concise, concrete, correct, coherent, complete, and courteous. Copilot can provide feedback and suggestions for improvement based on each of the 7 Cs criteria.

Bottom Line Up Front (BLUF) framework

The Bottom Line Up Front (BLUF) communication technique effectively ensures clarity and efficiency in business communications. Originating from US Army communication practices that were codified in the 1980s, BLUF emphasizes presenting the main point or conclusion at the very beginning of the message. Executive audiences need the conclusion first and the details second. BLUF ensures your key message doesn't get buried in context or background information.

Structure BLUF communications like this:

1. Lead with the decision or key point in your subject line and opening sentence.

2. Follow with essential supporting details that justify or explain the decision.

3. End with the next steps or required actions.

Here's an example of an email that could be improved with BLUF:

Subject: *Update on Security Measures*

Message: *As part of our ongoing efforts to improve security, we have reviewed various policies and procedures. After careful consideration and analysis, we have decided to implement some changes. These changes are aimed at enhancing our overall security posture and protecting our data. One of the key changes is related to our password policy. Starting January 1st, we will be adopting a new password policy. This policy will require mandatory password changes every 90 days and the use of multi-factor authentication. Please review the attached document for detailed guidelines and implementation steps.*

While this type of email is regularly sent organization-wide, it suffers from several communication issues that hinder its effectiveness. Firstly, the subject line is vague and fails to convey the main point of the message clearly. Additionally, the core decision—introducing a new password policy—is buried several sentences in, making it difficult for readers to grasp the purpose quickly. The message also lacks conciseness, including unnecessary background information that dilutes the focus. As a result, recipients must sift through multiple sentences to understand the key message, reducing overall efficiency and clarity.

Now, here's an example of the same message improved with BLUF:

Subject: *Decision: Adopt New Password Policy Effective January 1st*

Message: *We have decided to implement a new password policy starting January 1st to enhance security. This policy includes mandatory password changes every 90 days and the use of multi-factor authentication. Please review the attached document for detailed guidelines and implementation steps.*

This version improves clarity by allowing audiences to immediately grasp the main point without having to sift through extraneous details. This directness enhances efficiency, saving time for both the sender and the recipient by getting straight to the message. Additionally, it supports better decision-making by presenting essential information upfront, enabling quicker and more informed responses.

> **Tip** Use Copilot to improve BLUF structure: "Reorganize this message to lead with the main decision, followed by supporting rationale."

These frameworks work best when they become second nature. Start with one framework that addresses your biggest communication challenge, then gradually incorporate the others. Copilot can help you apply any of these structures consistently, but the strategic thinking behind your message remains uniquely yours.

The future of communication with AI

As AI capabilities continue to evolve, the fundamentals of human communication become more valuable, not less. While Copilot can help you craft clearer messages, anticipate audience questions, and structure compelling narratives, the authenticity, emotional intelligence, and strategic thinking behind those messages remain distinctly human.

The leaders who will thrive in an AI-enabled world are those who use technology to amplify their natural communication strengths rather than replace them. They recognize that in a world increasingly filled with AI-generated content (synthetic data), genuine human connection and thoughtful communication become powerful differentiators. These leaders don't just use AI tools; they model for their organizations how to use them to enhance human capability rather than diminish it.

Looking ahead, communication skills will likely determine not just individual career success but organizational competitive advantage. Companies that combine AI efficiency with authentic human storytelling, strategic messaging, and empathetic leadership communication will build stronger relationships with employees, customers, and stakeholders.

Try this prompt: Structured communications

Ever asked a colleague to read an email before you send it? Now you can get a second opinion from Copilot, and even ask it to coach you on how to improve your communication, referencing one of the frameworks we've covered in this chapter. Use these prompts to level up your communications skills.

Prompt for Situation, Behavior, Impact (SBI) communications:

> *You are an executive-level communications coach.*
>
> 1. *Scan the draft message (between the triple-dashed lines) for clarity, completeness, and tone.*
> 2. *Extract the three SBI elements:*
>   - *Situation - time, place, people involved*
>   - *Behaviour - observable facts only (no motives)*
>   - *Impact - measurable or felt consequences for people, results, or the business*
> 3. *Diagnose gaps: Which elements are unclear, missing, or blurred together?*
> 4. *Teach me: list ≤ 3 specific tips that will strengthen the weakest element(s).*
> 5. *Create a Framework-Aligned Rewrite (≤ 200 words) that clearly separates Situation, Behaviour, and Impact, preserving my voice and intent.*
> 6. *If context is insufficient, ask follow-up questions one at a time.*
>
> *DRAFT MESSAGE*
> *---*
> *[Paste your email, chat, or document here]*
> *---*

1. *Diagnostic Table*
   | Element | Present? | Observations / Gaps |
2. *Improvement Tips – bullet list (≤ 3)*
3. *Framework-Aligned Rewrite – ready to send*

Prompt for 7 Cs communications:

You are an executive-level communications coach.

1. *Read the draft message between the triple dashes.*
2. *Diagnose how well it meets each of the 7 Cs:*
   - *Clear   – easy to grasp, single purpose*
   - *Concise   – no fluff; every word earns its spot*
   - *Concrete – specific facts/examples anchor key points*
   - *Correct   – accurate details, flawless mechanics*
   - *Coherent – logical flow; ideas connect seamlessly*
   - *Complete – all necessary info + call-to-action*
   - *Courteous – respectful tone, audience-centric*
3. *Flag any C that's weak or missing.*
4. *Teach me: give ≤ 3 laser-focused tips to strengthen the lowest-scoring C(s).*
5. *Produce a 7 Cs-Optimised Rewrite (≤ 200 words) I can use immediately, preserving intent and voice.*
6. *If you need more context, ask follow-up questions one at a time.*

DRAFT MESSAGE

[Paste your email, chat, or document here]

OUTPUT FORMAT
1. *Diagnostic Table*
   | C | Present? | Observations / Gaps |
2. *Improvement Tips – bullet list (≤ 3)*
3. *7 Cs-optimized Rewrite – ready to send*

Prompt for Bottom Line Up Front (BLUF) communications:

You are an executive-level communications coach.

1. *Scan the draft message (between the triple-dashed lines) for clarity, completeness, and tone.*
2. *Diagnose how well it satisfies each BLUF component:*
   - *Bottom Line (up front) – ≤ 2-sentence key takeaway / decision / request*
   - *Context – essential background (who, what, where, when, why)*
   - *Reasoning – facts or analysis that justify the bottom line*
   - *Action – explicit, time-bound ask for the reader*

3. Flag any component that's weak, missing, or buried.

4. Teach me: list ≤ 3 precise tips to tighten the weakest component(s).

5. Produce a BLUF-Ready Rewrite (≤ 175 words) I can send immediately, preserving my voice and intent.

6. If context is insufficient, ask follow-up questions one at a time.

DRAFT MESSAGE

[Paste your email, chat, or document here]

OUTPUT FORMAT

1. Diagnostic Table

| Component | Present? | Observations / Gaps |

2. Improvement Tips – bullet list (≤ 3)

3. BLUF-Ready Rewrite – ready to send

Next steps

In this chapter, we highlighted the critical role of effective communication, particularly through storytelling, in engaging audiences and delivering compelling messages. The practical techniques and frameworks demonstrate how Copilot can help you refine messages and coach you to become a more engaging storyteller.

- While AI can generate thousands of words instantly, the human ability to craft meaningful narratives that connect emotionally with audiences becomes more valuable than ever.

- Copilot enhances but doesn't replace communication skills. Use AI to refine, test audience understanding, and structure messages, but authentic voice, strategic thinking, and relationship building remain fundamentally human.

- Match your message to your audience and medium, whether through asynchronous communication for updates or synchronous conversations for decisions, while using proven frameworks to ensure clarity and impact.

PART 4

Sustaining and measuring success

The final part of this book focuses on how you can measure the impact of Copilot adoption and put adaptive processes in place to ensure your organization's culture reinforces AI transformation. The culture change to go from traditional ways of working to become an innovative, AI-enabled organization requires a growth mindset and ongoing commitment to learning.

- In Chapter 11, "Continuous improvement," we explore the power of incremental gains and developing new ways of working with Copilot. The opportunity is to remake organizational processes and take an iterative approach to building on early rollout successes.

- In Chapter 12, "Culture," we close with a reminder of the importance of engaging people in the change process and creating an environment where they can innovate.

Together, these strategies for sustaining Copilot adoption and understanding how to amplify early success provide a roadmap for your organization to become future-ready. The culture shift to one that embraces the promise of AI and Copilot and fosters creativity requires investment in innovation. People remain the most valuable asset to your organization.

> **Tip** "Every week, on Friday, I used to spend 30-45 minutes planning the following week. This now takes 10-15 minutes with this prompt. Replace the [dd] [MMMM]s with your day and month for start of the week and end of the week, e.g., 16th June to 20th June. "Please help me plan my week next week from the [dd] [MMMM] to [dd] [MMMM]. If you could group meetings, tasks, and things that need to be done by each day, that would be great." Why I like it is that it will also look further down the week and add tasks to prep for those meetings as well."–**Simon Doy** is a Microsoft MVP for Microsoft 365 Copilot, a Microsoft community leader, and the founder of iThink 365 in the United Kingdom.

CHAPTER 11

Continuous Improvement

The challenge is to always improve, to always get better, even when you are the best. Especially when you are the best.

—Sir Graham Henry, Former All Blacks Coach

In this chapter, you will:

- Explore how to create compounding value through continuous small improvements rather than seeking a perfect Copilot implementation

- Discover practical frameworks for sustaining momentum, from green light thinking and feedback loops to data-driven measurement and deliberate practice

- Develop organizational readiness for emerging AI capabilities, balancing optimization of current features with strategic preparation for future advancements

The power of incremental gains

New Zealand's national men's rugby team, the All Blacks, is often regarded as one of the most successful sports teams in history. When Sir Graham Henry led the All Blacks to their 2011 Rugby World Cup victory, he and the team didn't achieve greatness through dramatic overhauls. Instead, he embraced a philosophy of relentless incremental improvement: marginal gains that, when compounded, created an unstoppable force. The All Blacks didn't just aim to be good; they pursued continuous improvement through constant iterations, each one building on the last.

This same principle of incremental improvement can significantly increase the value organizations gain with Copilot adoption. The organizations that extract extraordinary value from AI aren't those that aim for perfect implementation from day one—they're the ones that commit to continuous refinement, treating each interaction as an opportunity to improve.

Consider the mathematics of marginal gains: if you improve just 1 percent each day for a year, you end up 37 times better than when you started. In Copilot adoption, this might mean refining your prompts to save an extra minute per task, discovering a new use case that streamlines a weekly process, or sharing a technique that helps your team work more effectively. These seemingly small improvements accumulate into transformational change. They also build adaptability into the fabric of your organization.

The All Blacks understand that greatness emerges not from single breakthrough moments but from the culmination of small improvements repeated daily and embedded culturally. For your Copilot adoption, this means moving beyond initial training and basic usage to a culture where improvement is constant, curiosity is rewarded, and every employee sees themselves as contributing to the organization's AI transformation.

Unlike traditional technology implementations that plateau after the initial rollout, successful Copilot adoption requires an organizational commitment to perpetual learning. It means embracing Satya Nadella's challenge to become learn-it-alls. Copilot's capabilities are constantly evolving at the same time as your business challenges are shifting, and your team's AI literacy is growing. Standing still means falling behind.

This chapter provides frameworks and strategies for building that continuous improvement muscle into your Copilot adoption strategy. From cultivating the right mindset to measuring meaningful progress, from developing skills to preparing for future capabilities, you'll discover how to sustain momentum long after the initial excitement fades. The goal isn't just to use Copilot; it's to continuously improve how you use it, creating compounding value that differentiates your organization in an AI-enabled world.

Embrace green-light thinking

The All Blacks' culture of continuous improvement rests on a fundamental belief: every challenge contains an opportunity. This mirrors what Ken Blanchard calls "green-light thinking" in his book *Know Can Do!* "Know can do" means cultivating a mindset that actively looks for ways something could work rather than reasons it won't. For Copilot adoption, this mental shift often determines whether teams extract transformational value or abandon the tool after initial challenges.

Some people naturally gravitate toward "red-light thinking" when encountering new technology. They focus on limitations: "Copilot won't understand our industry terminology," or "It can't handle our complex workflows." While these concerns may be valid, red-light thinking stops exploration before solutions emerge. Green-light thinking acknowledges challenges but asks different questions: "How might we help Copilot understand our terminology better?" or "What parts of our complex workflows could Copilot improve, even if it can't handle everything?"

This mindset shift requires deliberate cultivation across all organizational levels. When team members raise concerns about Copilot, effective leaders acknowledge the concern but pivot to solution-finding. If someone says, "Copilot won't work for our creative process," a green light response might be: "You're right that creativity can't be automated, but could Copilot handle the research phase so you have more time for creative work?"

Creating conditions for green-light thinking

Creating "green light zones"—specific meetings or sessions where critique is temporarily suspended and all ideas about Copilot usage are welcomed can build psychological safety and encourage experimentation. The resulting repository of positive use cases can then be rapidly prototyped. For example, run weekly "possibility thinking" workshops where teams identify their most challenging tasks and brainstorm how Copilot might help, starting with the assumption that some value can be found.

Documentation amplifies green-light thinking. Regularly collect and share detailed success stories, including specific prompts used and outcomes achieved. This makes success replicable and helps others see possibilities they might have missed.

Leaders can model green-light thinking through simple techniques borrowed from improvisational theater. Encouraging "Yes, and..." responses instead of "No, but..." transforms conversations. For example: "Yes, Copilot helped with the first draft, and we could also use it to analyze feedback once we receive it." This approach builds on ideas rather than shutting them down.

Transforming red-light statements

Training leaders to gently challenge absolute statements proves particularly effective. When someone declares, "Copilot can't handle this type of work," leaders can ask, "In what specific ways might Copilot help with at least parts of this work?" This questioning doesn't dismiss concerns but redirects energy toward discovering applications rather than defending limitations.

Some organizations conduct formal "green-light/red-light" exercises where teams list their skeptical thoughts about Copilot and then challenge themselves to transform each negative into a possibility. This builds the mental muscle of solution-oriented thinking about AI.

As Blanchard emphasizes, green-light thinking doesn't mean ignoring legitimate concerns—it means approaching them with curiosity rather than resignation. Organizations that foster this mindset create cultures where Copilot's capabilities are continuously explored and expanded rather than prematurely limited by assumptions. This mindset becomes the foundation for the feedback loops and continuous improvement processes that sustain long-term adoption success.

> **Tip** Start meetings with a "green-light moment," where team members share one new way they used Copilot successfully in the past week. This simple ritual reinforces possibility thinking, spreads practical ideas, and shifts the narrative from theoretical potential to tangible results. Keep a running document of these successes as a growing resource for your organization.

Bridging the knowing-doing gap with feedback loops

Many organizations invest heavily in Copilot training only to find a significant gap between what people know and what they actually do with the tool. This "knowing-doing gap" is perhaps the most common challenge in technology adoption. Despite understanding Copilot's capabilities, people often revert to familiar ways of working, leaving powerful features unused and potential value unrealized.

Without formal feedback loops, leadership remains unaware of user experiences, challenges, or ideas for improving Copilot use. Organizations lacking a culture of iteration risk letting adoption stagnate as initial issues go unaddressed and early excitement fades. The solution lies in creating structured feedback mechanisms that connect actual usage with continuous improvement.

The feedback-improvement cycle

Effective Copilot adoption requires moving beyond implementation to a continuous cycle of action, feedback, adjustment, and iteration. This mirrors the Plan-Do-Check-Act approach familiar to quality improvement professionals but with a specific focus on capturing user experiences and turning them into actionable insights. The cycle must operate at multiple organizational levels simultaneously to create sustainable change.

Building on the All Blacks' philosophy introduced earlier, James Kerr's book *Legacy* provides deeper insights into how this approach is operationalized. Kerr explains that the team's success comes from systematically documenting and pursuing "marginal gains"—those 1 percent improvements in speed, simplicity, clarity, or efficiency. The All Blacks maintain backlogs of improvement opportunities to ensure they never run out of refinement ideas. Organizations can apply this directly to Copilot by creating similar backlogs of micro-improvements in AI usage, prompt effectiveness, and workflow integration. They can also include a list of steps to remove as they become unnecessary, as new ways of working with Copilot emerge. This approach transforms the abstract concept of continuous improvement into a concrete, repeatable practice for Copilot adoption.

Individual-level feedback loops

Individual users need structured ways to reflect on and improve their Copilot interactions. As shown in Figure 11-1, it can be helpful to encourage employees to set personal goals for Copilot usage, such as drafting at least one email or report daily with Copilot's assistance. Discuss the value of self-reflection and provide simple tools to track progress. It takes repetition to change habits, and it can be motivating to compare how long tasks would typically take before Copilot to how long they take with Copilot. Recognition systems that highlight creative Copilot applications reinforce experimentation and learning.

The most effective approach focuses on one habit change at a time rather than overwhelming users with multiple improvements simultaneously. For example, a product manager might create a simple checklist of five common writing artifacts—emails, specifications, status updates, release notes, and bug reports—and commit to using Copilot for just one type each week. By gradually expanding usage across familiar tasks, you can build confidence and competence without feeling overwhelmed.

Team-level feedback loops

Teams benefit from collective accountability for Copilot adoption. Make AI usage a shared mission with collective metrics discussed in team meetings or retrospectives. These metrics should cascade from the organization's overall AI strategy. As they land in different departments and teams, the people in those groups sign up to drive improvements within their sphere of influence. This fosters a sense of responsibility and ownership. Team leaders can create peer learning opportunities where members share success stories and tips, focusing conversations on what's working rather than fixating on limitations.

Copilot adoption feedback loop

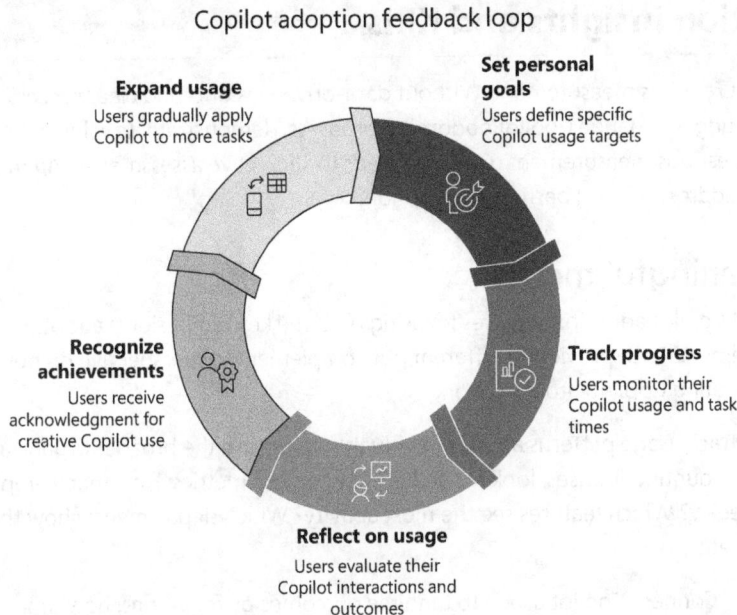

FIGURE 11-1 Copilot adoption feedback loop for individuals

A particularly effective approach involves running short, focused experiments with clear evaluation criteria. Consider implementing a regular cadence like "Copilot Thursdays," where teams collectively try a specific feature for a defined task and then evaluate the results the following week. Teams can maintain a simple three-column document tracking what worked well, what didn't work, and what to try differently next time. This lightweight approach allows people to use simple experiments to learn quickly and build a shared understanding of effective Copilot usage.

Organizational-level feedback loops

At the organizational level, feedback requires more formal mechanisms while maintaining the same improvement focus. Tools like Microsoft Viva Pulse can gather regular sentiment data about Copilot adoption. Establishing a routine review meeting with key stakeholders ensures patterns are identified and addressed promptly.

The most crucial element of organizational feedback loops is closing the circle—communicating back to users about changes made based on their input. This prevents the cynicism that emerges when feedback seems to disappear into a void. Consider implementing a monthly "You Said, We Did" communication that highlights specific improvements made in response to user feedback. This transparent approach reinforces that input drives genuine change and encourages continued engagement with the feedback process.

The combination of feedback loops at all three levels creates a self-reinforcing improvement system. Individual insights feed team practices; team innovations inform organizational approaches; and organizational support enables individual growth. This multi-level framework ensures that Copilot adoption doesn't merely happen once but evolves continuously as capabilities expand and user sophistication grows.

Data-driven adoption insights and KPIs

Continuous improvement requires measurement. Without data-driven insights and clear success metrics, organizations struggle to gauge Copilot's adoption progress, demonstrate its value, or identify improvement opportunities. This measurement gap often leads to subjective assessments and misdirected efforts that fail to address the real barriers to adoption.

Establishing meaningful metrics

Effective measurement of Copilot adoption requires focusing on three key dimensions: adoption rate, efficiency gains, and sentiment. Each provides a different but complementary perspective on how well your organization is integrating Copilot into daily work:

- **Adoption rate** Track usage patterns across individuals, teams, and the broader organization. Rather than simply counting licenses, look for active engagement metrics: How many employees use Copilot weekly? Which features see the most activity? Which departments show the highest adoption rates?

- **Efficiency gains** Connect Copilot usage to tangible outcomes by measuring how time can be saved and reinvested as people use Copilot to enhance specific workloads and processes, such as document creation, email composition, and data analysis. These measurements should compare before-and-after scenarios, improved quality of the outputs, as well as innovations created with the saved time, to quantify the real impact of Copilot on workflows.

- **Sentiment scores** Regularly assess how employees feel about using Copilot; it is a powerful predictor of sustained engagement. Sentiment measurements should be taken frequently, ideally in a 2–4-week rolling window, to allow for proactive responses. How people feel about Copilot strongly influences whether they'll continue using it.

These three metrics provide a balanced view that helps identify both success stories to amplify and adoption gaps to address.

Creating visibility through dashboards

Transform raw metrics into actionable insights by creating dedicated Copilot adoption dashboards. Whether using Microsoft's built-in analytics, Power BI, or other visualization tools, effective dashboards help leadership track progress against targets while identifying emerging patterns. Leverage analytics to understand Copilot usage across departments and apps. Monitor multiple dimensions of success—readiness, adoption, impact, and sentiment—to inform ongoing strategy. Refine key performance indicators (KPIs) over time as you learn which metrics best correlate with business value.

Use a Copilot adoption dashboard or Power BI report to track usage trends and outcomes (such as the number of active Copilot users, requests per week, and "assisted hours" saved). Define baseline targets (for example, "80 percent of users engage with Copilot weekly within six months of rollout") and review KPI reports monthly or quarterly. Use insights to celebrate successes or adjust your approach where adoption lags.

Microsoft's Viva suite offers specialized tools that can strengthen your measurement capabilities and help facilitate Copilot adoption at scale:

- **Viva Insights**   For adoption dashboards and analytics

- **Viva Pulse**   For surveying team members about specific initiatives

- **Viva Glint**   To understand employee feedback and opportunities for improvement

- **Viva Connections**   To help employees explore news, join conversations, and connect across the organization

- **Viva Amplify**   To manage employee-facing campaigns from one location. It provides campaign metrics that can inform adjustments in communications strategy and targeting.

- **Viva Learning**   As a comprehensive learning platform

- **Viva Engage** (formerly Yammer)   For real-time idea flow across the organization

Establish a regular cadence for reviewing metrics—ideally, every 1–2 weeks, given how rapidly Copilot's capabilities evolve. Continuously question whether you're measuring the right things, and be transparent about any changes to metrics being tracked. This allows quick course corrections and prevents small adoption issues from becoming entrenched problems.

Governance and data readiness

Effective measurement extends beyond adoption metrics to the health of your underlying data environment. Many organizations underutilize tools for monitoring data readiness and governance, creating potential risks as Copilot usage grows.

Microsoft offers a comprehensive suite of tools that should be incorporated into your continuous improvement framework:

- **Microsoft Viva Insights and Power BI**   Provide rich adoption analytics with actionable insights to help drive Copilot usage and measure impact

- **Microsoft Purview**   Enables ongoing data governance, ensuring that data security and compliance controls keep pace as Copilot usage expands

- **Microsoft Fabric**   Unifies data from various sources for deeper insights, where advanced analysis is needed

These platforms work together to ensure that both adoption progress and data integrity are continuously monitored. Data quality and security should be treated as living processes, not static conditions, especially as Copilot increasingly interacts with organizational information.

Turn these tools into practical action by

- Connecting your Copilot adoption data to Viva Insights' Copilot Dashboard or a custom Power BI adoption report to track usage by department, application, and feature.

- Setting up alerts or periodic reviews of key metrics to identify trends early.

- Using Microsoft Purview to audit and protect your data continuously: Enforce sensitivity labels and monitor AI data usage.

- Regularly reviewing Purview reports for compliance flags and updating policies as needed.

- Leveraging Microsoft Fabric to pull together Copilot usage logs, user feedback, and business outcome data into a unified report.

Ongoing Copilot skills development

Initial training during Copilot rollout is just the beginning of the learning journey. Without continuous skill development, even enthusiastic early adopters typically plateau in their usage, falling back on a limited set of familiar commands and features while more powerful capabilities remain unused. As Copilot evolves with new features and improvements, the gap between potential and actual usage widens for users who don't continuously update their skills.

Beyond implementation training

The most common mistake organizations make is treating Copilot training as a one-time event rather than an ongoing process. Research consistently shows that people need to encounter new information 5-7 times before it becomes embedded in their thinking. One-time knowledge dumps—no matter how comprehensive—simply don't create lasting behavior change. The mind requires repeated exposure to create neural patterns that commit new skills to procedural memory.

This insight led successful organizations to adopt what some call a "rolling thunder" approach to Copilot skill development: a continuous cadence of learning opportunities that build capability over time rather than all at once. This approach recognizes that skill development follows a maturity curve, with users moving from basic awareness to confident application to innovative experimentation as their comfort with the tool grows.

Creating tiered learning journeys

Effective Copilot skill development programs differentiate between foundational AI literacy (which all users need) and advanced capability training (for power users or specific roles). Microsoft offers extensive training resources that can be customized to create role-specific learning paths, ensuring that team members develop the capabilities most relevant to their daily work.

> **Tip** Microsoft Learn now has an AI-powered tool to help you build a personalized learning path to upskill with AI. Try it at *https://learn.microsoft.com/en-us/plans/ai/.*

The format of training must evolve with changing work patterns. During the height of remote work, half-day or full-day online training sessions proved effective as people managed fewer in-person commitments. Today's hybrid workforce responds better to microlearning—brief, focused videos (90 seconds to 4 minutes) delivered at the point of need. This just-in-time approach respects attention constraints while delivering knowledge exactly when users are motivated to apply it.

Supporting community-powered learning

The most sustainable approach to ongoing skill development leverages peer-to-peer learning through formal or informal communities of practice. Provide ongoing support for your Copilot champions in various departments. These early adopters can mentor others, sharing discoveries and tips that are contextually relevant to specific teams.

Establish internal forums or Teams channels dedicated to Copilot Q&A and knowledge sharing. Make it easy for people to both ask questions and contribute answers, recognizing those who actively participate. Some organizations gamify this process, awarding points or badges for sharing tips, creating how-to videos, or helping colleagues troubleshoot Copilot challenges.

Integrating skills into career development

For Copilot skills to be taken seriously, they must be integrated into broader professional development frameworks. Include Copilot proficiency in relevant job descriptions, performance discussions, and career advancement conversations. This signals that AI literacy isn't just nice to have but essential for professional growth.

Create clear competency frameworks that outline what proficiency looks like at different levels:

- **Basic proficiency**   Using standard prompts for common tasks

- **Intermediate proficiency**   Creating custom prompt templates and adapting approaches for different situations

- **Advanced proficiency**   Developing innovative applications and guiding others

These frameworks help employees self-assess their current capabilities and identify specific skills to develop next, creating a path for continuous growth rather than a binary "trained/untrained" designation.

Practical skill development approaches

Translate these principles into practical action by implementing a consistent cadence of Copilot skill-building activities:

- Quarterly workshops focused on new features or advanced techniques

- Monthly drop-in "Copilot labs" where users can bring real work challenges

- Weekly tip sharing through email or Teams channels

- On-demand learning resources, including short videos and quick reference guides

Complement these scheduled activities with point-of-need support, such as embedded help guides within applications or quick access to Copilot champions who can provide just-in-time assistance when colleagues encounter challenges in real-world usage.

The key to sustainable skill development isn't the specific format but the consistency of focus. Organizations that treat Copilot skill building as an ongoing priority rather than a one-time initiative create compounding returns, with each small capability improvement opening new possibilities for value creation.

> **Tip**   Use the Copilot Prompt Gallery to save and share your custom prompts.

Preparing for emerging Copilot capabilities

While effective continuous improvement focuses on optimizing current capabilities, truly forward-thinking organizations also prepare for emerging AI features before they arrive. Microsoft's Copilot ecosystem is evolving rapidly, with new agents, features, and integrations released regularly. Organizations that anticipate these changes gain a competitive advantage through faster adoption and better integration of new capabilities into existing workflows.

Monitoring Microsoft's AI roadmap

Microsoft's strategic direction offers significant clues about future Copilot capabilities. Beyond just tracking announced features, understanding the broader technological shifts Microsoft is investing in (multimodal AI, domain-specific agents, cross-application integration) helps organizations anticipate how workflows might evolve. This awareness allows proactive preparation rather than reactive scrambling when new features arrive.

Designate specific responsibility for monitoring Microsoft's product roadmap, whether through a formal role like an "AI Innovation Lead," a rotating responsibility shared among team members, or an initiative of the AI council. Developments in AI and Copilot are happening constantly, so having an understanding of what is coming is key to adapting your rollout strategy as the landscape changes. Subscribe to official Microsoft 365 Copilot update blogs, participate in preview programs, and develop relationships with Microsoft representatives who can provide advanced insights into upcoming capabilities.

> **Tip**   Ask Copilot to stay updated with this sample weekly prompt: "Tell me the latest in Copilot's features and availability. Give me examples from inside my organization as well as outside my organization of how people are using the latest features in Copilot. Constrain your response to developments from the last seven days."

Future-proofing your environment

Technical readiness often determines how quickly organizations can leverage new Copilot capabilities when they arrive. Periodically assess your data architecture, ensuring it will be compatible with emerging AI features. Beyond the standard data in OneDrive and SharePoint, consider how additional data sources accessed through the Microsoft Graph API might enhance future Copilot scenarios.

Work proactively with your IT team to ensure new features are enabled rather than blocked by default. IT departments sometimes hesitate to activate new capabilities due to support workloads, but this defensive posture can significantly delay value realization. Position your finance department as an ally in this conversation; they would likely flag the cost implications of paying for licenses while artificially limiting capabilities.

Building scenario-based readiness

Rather than passively waiting for new capabilities, conduct regular scenario planning exercises. Ask: "How would our work change if Microsoft released [anticipated capability]?" This forward-thinking approach helps identify process changes, training needs, or governance considerations before new features arrive.

When significant new capabilities are announced, run small-scale pilots in relevant business units rather than waiting for organization-wide rollout. These controlled experiments provide valuable experience, surface potential issues, and create internal case studies to support broader adoption. Update your Copilot adoption playbook based on these pilots, creating deployable knowledge that can be rapidly scaled when features become generally available.

Balancing anticipation with flexibility

While proactive planning for emerging capabilities provides advantages, excessive rigidity can be counterproductive in rapidly changing environments. Maintain flexibility in your experimentation plans, recognizing that business priorities and technological capabilities may shift in unexpected ways.

Budget time and resources for exploring emerging tools in advance, but be prepared to pivot as Microsoft's roadmap evolves. Some announced features may be delayed or modified, while unexpected capabilities might emerge that offer greater value than anticipated. The goal isn't perfect prediction but prepared adaptability—creating an organization that can quickly understand, evaluate, and integrate new capabilities as they become available.

This forward-looking approach complements the continuous improvement of existing capabilities, creating a comprehensive strategy that simultaneously optimizes current value while preparing for future opportunities.

> **Tip** Create a quarterly "Horizon Scanning" session where your Copilot champions or AI council review Microsoft's public roadmap, recent announcements, and industry trends. Use this information to update your capability radar and adjust preparation priorities accordingly. This regular cadence ensures you maintain awareness without requiring constant monitoring.

From continuous improvement to cultural transformation

Continuous improvement isn't just about refining processes; it's about fundamentally shifting how your organization thinks about work. It's the catalyst for cultural transformation, where AI becomes woven into the fabric of how your organization works and thinks. This evolution from "using AI as a tool" to "thinking AI-first" when approaching business challenges represents the most sustainable form of Copilot adoption.

The cultural foundation of sustainable improvement

Organizations with cultures resistant to experimentation, feedback, or new ways of working will struggle to sustain improvement efforts regardless of how well-designed their processes might be. Conversely, organizations with adaptable, learning-oriented cultures often succeed even with imperfect processes because the underlying values support continuous evolution.

This relationship between culture and continuous improvement works in both directions. The disciplined pursuit of ongoing enhancement helps shape cultural norms that value learning, adaptability, and innovation. Each small win builds confidence in the organization's capacity to change, incrementally shifting how people think about technology adoption. Over time, green-light thinking and deliberate practice become not just formal activities but default ways of approaching challenges.

Signals of cultural evolution

You'll recognize this cultural shift taking hold when you observe changes in everyday language and behavior:

- Teams instinctively ask, "How might Copilot help with this?" when approaching new projects.

- Discussions naturally include both human and AI contributions without sharp distinctions.

- People describe their roles in terms of partnership with technology rather than replacement concerns.

- Experimentation becomes the norm rather than the exception.

- Failures and limitations are met with curiosity rather than frustration.

These subtle shifts signal that Copilot has moved beyond being merely a tool to become an integrated element of how work happens. When this transition occurs, continuous improvement becomes self-sustaining rather than requiring constant management attention or formal programs.

As you move from the tactical aspects of continuous improvement to broader cultural transformation, remember that culture is both the result of your improvement efforts and the foundation for their success. In the final chapter, we'll explore how to deliberately shape this cultural evolution and create an environment where AI adoption isn't just sustained but becomes a natural expression of your organizational identity.

Try this prompt: Personal AI literacy coach

The concept of continuous improvement also applies to our personal leadership skills when it comes to AI. Each of us should be aiming to go to the next level of technical depth from our current skill set. Get Copilot to develop a personal plan to help you improve your AI literacy. Put 10–20 minutes aside to answer the questions thoughtfully; the more thought you put into your answers, the better quality output you'll get.

Role: You are my Personal AI-Literacy Coach. Objective: Help me build a personalized 12-month AI upskilling plan tailored to my role, learning style, and goals.

PHASE 1 – Interactive Discovery (Ask One Question at a Time)
Wait for my response before moving to the next question.
1. AI Familiarity
   "On a scale from beginner to advanced, how would you describe your current AI knowledge? Can you share one quick example of something AI-related you've done?"
2. Role & Business Focus
   "What is your job title, and which tasks or projects in your role could benefit most from AI?"
3. Learning Preferences
   "Which learning formats work best for you? (e.g., reading, short videos, interactive labs, peer discussions)"
4. Weekly Time Budget
   "How many hours per week can you realistically commit to AI learning?"
5. Target Outcomes
   "By Month 12, what specific capabilities or achievements would you like to demonstrate?"
6. Priority AI Domains
   "Which AI areas interest you most? (e.g., generative content, data analytics, automation bots, computer vision)"
7. Constraints & Support
   "Do you have any constraints (e.g., budget, tool access) or support resources (e.g., manager sponsorship, community) I should be aware of?"

PHASE 2 – Build the 12-Month Plan (after all answers are received)
• Narrative Overview (≈250 words)
– Summarise your starting point, objectives, and learning journey.
– Explain how the plan aligns with your role and business value.

Next steps

In this chapter, we explored the power of incremental gains and how fostering a culture of continuous improvement can enhance AI adoption. We also discussed the importance of green-light thinking and structured feedback loops to bridge the gap between knowledge and actual usage of Copilot.

- Embrace green-light thinking and celebrate the impact of Copilot to drive incremental gains at scale across your organization.

- To address the gap between knowledge and actual usage of Copilot, create a cycle of action, feedback, and adjustment that allows for sustained improvement.

- Training for Copilot should not be a one-time event but an ongoing process.

CHAPTER 12

Culture

The only thing of real importance that leaders do is to create and manage culture. If you do not manage culture, it manages you, and you may not even be aware of the extent to which this is happening.

—EDGAR H. SCHEIN

In this chapter, you will:

- Explore how to cultivate a culture of innovation and become a future-ready organization with Copilot

- Learn how to set up and run innovative events at scale to reimagine your organization's processes with Copilot and AI

- Discover how to celebrate and sustain Copilot adoption with a clear action plan

The most important thing in the world

While we are increasingly relying on artificial intelligence-enabled technologies, it's sometimes helpful to recall an older form of intelligence to ground our efforts: ancestral intelligence. In Te Ao Māori (the Māori worldview), as in many indigenous cultures around the world, there is a belief that we must look back to move forward. This whakataukī (proverb) reminds us what is at the heart of everything, even AI transformation:

> **He aha te mea nui o te ao? He tāngata, he tāngata, he tāngata.**

> *What is the most important thing in the world? It is people, it is people, it is people.[1]*

While previous chapters addressed strategic planning, change management, and essential skills for Copilot adoption, this final chapter focuses on perhaps the most critical element: developing a cultural foundation where AI serves as a force multiplier for human talent and organizational excellence.

The journey to becoming a Copilot-enabled organization begins not with technology but with culture. Organizations that thrive with AI prioritize people first, creating environments where innovation flourishes because employees feel valued, supported, and engaged in the transformation process.

---

1 Elder, Hinemoa. Wawata: Moon Dreaming – Daily Wisdom Guided by Hina, the Māori Moon. Wellington: Penguin Random House New Zealand, 2022.

Conversely, organizations with a track record of burnout, overwork, and overwhelm among their staff will struggle. Their people won't have the physical, emotional, or mental bandwidth necessary to experiment and try new things. The absence of intentional efforts to support an innovation culture makes it very difficult to sustain the desired behavior change. As leaders encourage Copilot adoption, the cultural foundation they establish will determine whether the technology becomes an integral part of work or remains an underutilized cost.

Leaders set the vision for "why AI" and model the behaviors that shape organizational culture. Customer Relationship Management (CRM) implementations offer valuable lessons about how culture determines technology adoption success. These projects frequently failed when executives implemented systems primarily to monitor what salespeople are doing. The result? Salespeople stopped entering data, kept contact lists off company software, and maintained their "little black books" instead.

Culture is often shaped from the top of an organization. As the saying goes, "I can't hear what you're saying because I can see what you're doing." Leadership actions speak louder than words. When leaders demonstrate Copilot use in their daily work, ask for AI-enhanced solutions, and celebrate creative applications, people will emulate their behavior based on their demonstrated commitment to the vision for AI.

This chapter outlines how to cultivate an AI-ready culture through five essential strategies: establishing a "Copilot-first" mindset, encouraging experimentation, embedding ethical guardrails, celebrating successes, and ensuring sustainable integration. Some of these approaches have been covered in earlier chapters, but because they are also important elements of culture, we revisit them here. The goal is to help leaders guide their organizations in reimagining work processes and becoming future-ready with Copilot as an innovation partner.

The Copilot-first mindset

Creating a Copilot-first culture means integrating AI into every workflow and decision process across the organization. This approach requires teams to consider how Copilot can help before starting any task. The transition demands both intention and repetition, developing the muscle memory that makes a new behavior automatic.

Think about it practically: it's only after you've used Copilot five to seven times to draft a Word document that you'll naturally start all Word documents from that perspective. The same applies to PowerPoint presentations, Excel spreadsheets, and even how you engage in Teams conversations, hitting the record or transcribe button to capture information you can later refine with Copilot. Once you've made it a habit to ask Copilot to distill key themes or highlight the most important information for your job role when you open a company document, you'll crave that clarity and expect relevance when interacting with content. The goal isn't to replace thinking but to bring human thinking together with AI intelligence to create something better and deepen understanding in a way that neither could achieve independently.

Microsoft positions Copilot not as a standalone application but as a fundamental shift in working methodology. Organizations benefit from fostering a growth mindset where employees view AI as a catalyst for innovation rather than merely a productivity tool. This perspective requires investment in both technical skills and creative thinking:

- Prioritize AI literacy programs that build employee confidence.

- Develop specific prompting capabilities that yield valuable outputs.

- Create opportunities for employees to envision novel AI-driven solutions.

- Frame Copilot as an "innovation partner" that extends human creativity.

To reinforce this mindset, organizations should implement structured innovation activities. Initiatives such as hackathons, promptathons, and AI innovation challenges are designed to generate enthusiasm while building practical skills. These events transform learning from an obligation into an engaging experience that reinforces cultural values like curiosity and experimentation. Some organizations have even developed "AI Olympics" programs that combine skill-building with friendly competition, creating memorable experiences that accelerate adoption across teams.

The ingredients of innovation

The intersection of desirability, viability, and feasibility underpins innovation. This framework, rooted in design thinking, provides a powerful lens for approaching Copilot adoption. Organizations that balance all three elements create transformative solutions that drive meaningful change. Desirability addresses whether people want the solution, viability considers the economic justification, and feasibility examines the technical capability.

As shown in Figure 12-1, true innovation occurs when all three elements are aligned. Where these elements intersect, we find different outcomes: the overlap of desirability and feasibility creates inspiration; desirability and viability produce ideation; viability and feasibility result in implementation. Innovation requires all three. This visual model helps teams understand which stakeholders need to be involved at various stages and why balancing these perspectives is critical to achieve transformative outcomes with Copilot.

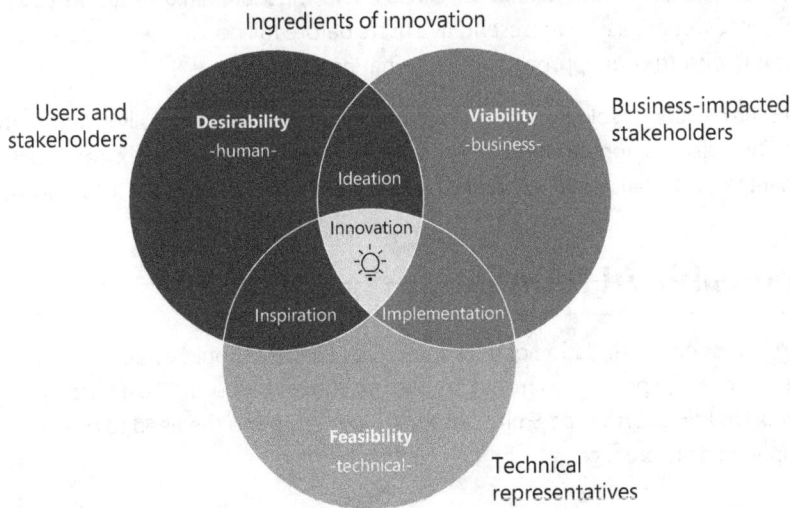

FIGURE 12-1 The ingredients of innovation are desirability, viability, and feasibility

Let's look at each ingredient in more detail.

Feasibility—Is it possible?

Feasibility addresses the technical capability to implement and sustain Copilot solutions. When exploring feasibility with Copilot, organizations must consider their technical infrastructure, data ecosystem, and capability to implement and maintain the solution. The technical team brings expertise in what can be achieved with the current systems and identifies paths to extend capabilities where needed. Their early involvement and alignment with the vision ensure that technical constraints are addressed from the outset rather than becoming roadblocks later.

Viability—Is this a good investment?

Viability examines whether implementing Copilot delivers enough value to justify the investment. This includes considerations of licensing costs, training resources, and the expected return through increased efficiency, reduced costs, or new capabilities. Key stakeholders from relevant departments, for example, finance or operations, could be involved in developing a sustainable business model that demonstrates clear value. Without viability, even the most technically impressive solution will struggle to gain organizational support.

Desirability—Is there a need for it?

Desirability focuses on whether the solution addresses genuine user needs. While organizations often excel at assessing feasibility and viability, desirability requires deeper human connection and empathy. Here, we ask the question: What pain are we addressing?

If we neglect desirability, chances are we have just another failed IT project in the making. To cultivate desirability for Copilot, organizations should conduct user research to understand pain points in current workflows. Then create user personas representing different roles within the organization and map the employee journey to identify high-value workloads. Win and maintain user support by prototyping and testing Copilot scenarios with representative users before full deployment. Gather feedback in this phase and use it to ensure your approach delivers what people want.

Innovation enables the creation of solutions that are technically possible, economically sound, and genuinely valued by users. This balanced approach positions Copilot not merely as an AI tool but as an aid that employees actively want to use because it enhances their experience and addresses their actual needs.

Ethical and responsible AI foundations

A Copilot-first culture builds on a foundation of trust and ethics. Leaders should establish clear AI governance principles and usage policies up front to guide how Copilot is used. "Trust is not given but earned through action," as Microsoft's Brad Smith observed[2], underscoring the need to operationalize responsible AI principles in daily practice.

---

[2] Brad Smith, *Governing AI: A Blueprint for the Future* (Redmond, WA: Microsoft, May 25, 2023), 29, https:// cdn-dynmedia-1.microsoft.com/is/content/microsoftcorp/microsoft/msc/documents/presentations/CSR/ Governing-AI-A-Blueprint-for-the-Future.pdf.

Organizations must prioritize trust and safety. When people trust the vision and feel safe to experiment, they are more likely to innovate. Adopting Copilot is primarily a human challenge, not a technological one. While the technology is powerful, it requires training and consistent focus from all levels of the organization, from the C-suite to frontline employees.

Ensure teams understand guidelines around data privacy, security, and the appropriate use of AI suggestions. When companies fail to create an open, transparent AI culture, shadow AI use increases, with employees covertly using tools in potentially risky ways.

To prevent this, normalize Copilot usage through clear policies, role modeling, and open dialogue about usage. Your representative AI council oversees Copilot adoption, updates policies, and addresses concerns. This council can define ethical frameworks, like aligning with Microsoft's Responsible AI Standard, and ensure accountability structures through AI risk assessments and robust testing frameworks like red teaming. A strong ethical foundation makes employees feel safe that Copilot is being introduced responsibly, boosting their willingness to embrace it.

> **Note** Red teaming involves having independent experts deliberately probe a model or system by emulating real-world adversaries and their tools, tactics, and procedures to identify risks, uncover blind spots, validate assumptions, and improve the overall security posture of AI systems. A lot of the responsibility for this, directly related to M365 Copilot, is undertaken by Microsoft.

Data literacy and governance

Data literacy is a crucial component of AI literacy. Everyone in the organization should understand how data flow through their processes, as well as the importance of data quality and governance. Employees should understand how data are collected and stored, and how they impact the organization and customers. This awareness helps prevent the collection of unnecessary data and ensures that the data used by Copilot are clean and valuable.

Data is often described as "the new oil" in business technology circles. This has led many organizations to collect every possible data point without a clear purpose. The result is vast amounts of unused data, which, thankfully, AI can now help us mine. However, we should encourage more mindful data collection by asking:

- Do people have a use for the data they're collecting?

- Are they creating duplicates?

- Do they understand how those duplicates might "dirty" the data being used for their personal Microsoft Graph and their organization's AI systems?

For example, are you taking the time to train people on the most effective ways to work collaboratively. Rather than sending copies of documents via email, teach people the benefits of sharing a link to an online file to avoid the creation of multiple copies of the same document. Encouraging mindful data collection practices prevents data duplication and maintains data integrity, which is essential for effective AI systems.

Support safe and adaptable experimentation

Psychological safety is foundational for innovation. Support experimentation by creating an environment where failure is seen as a part of the learning process. This involves showing, not just telling, that failure is expected and accepted as part of experimentation. For example, you won't always recognize a hallucination before using an output. Building this into processes reinforces the message that experimentation is valued.

Avoid the trap of spending so much time on the adoption plan and policies for AI use that experimentation is delayed indefinitely. Setting the foundations around AI vision, data security, and capability-building opportunities enables a shift from a rigid approach to project planning to a flexible, iterative approach. Promoting agility and an attitude of "give it a try" encourages teams to experiment without a long-term commitment to a particular way of working. This approach helps create a flywheel effect, where continuous experimentation leads to ongoing innovation.

An important part of creating psychological safety is addressing negative attitudes toward AI use. You must actively work to discourage comments like "Oh, did you use AI to do this?" or "You couldn't do that yourself? I bet you used AI." These dismissive remarks can make people reluctant to adopt the technology. Instead, foster a culture where using AI to augment work is celebrated, not looked down upon. The goal is for people to respond with "Yes, I did use AI. How could I improve it?" rather than feeling embarrassed about using these tools.

Cross-functional collaboration is key to breaking down silos and fostering innovation. Organization-wide innovation events are best run with diverse teams and facilitators, not just within departments. This encourages collaboration, leveraging different perspectives and expertise to drive innovation.

Events to cultivate an innovation culture

Organizing structured events creates momentum and excitement around Copilot adoption while reinforcing the cultural values needed for success. These events bring together people from all departments with a range of technical capabilities and business acumen. Encourage experimentation and showcase the practical value of Copilot and AI in solving real business problems. Although they can be run at a team level, they should be run as "all company events" as well, considering virtual facilitation to enable participation across multiple geographies.

For all events, maximize impact by:

- **Securing executive sponsorship** Ensure leadership visibility and support throughout the event

- **Documenting and sharing** Create videos, blogs, or newsletters showcasing event highlights and outcomes

- **Gathering participant feedback**   Collect insights to improve future events

- **Creating continuity**   Connect events in a progressive series that builds institutional knowledge

- **Measuring business impact**   Track how innovations from events translate to actual value

- **Celebrating participation**   Recognize everyone who contributes, not just winners

By regularly hosting these events, organizations create a rhythm of innovation and experimentation that reinforces the cultural shift towards embracing Copilot. These structured activities transform abstract concepts of AI adoption into tangible experiences, accelerating the development of a Copilot-first culture where AI tools become an integral part of how work gets done.

Here are five powerful event formats with practical steps for facilitation:

Microsoft AI hackathon

Transform business challenges into AI solutions through the power of collaborative innovation with an Microsoft AI hackathon. This engaging one day event brings together diverse perspectives, from business leaders to IT professionals, developers, and end-users, to develop AI-driven solutions for specific business challenges.

Create cross-functional "fusion teams" that combine business insights with technical expertise to build practical solutions using Microsoft 365 Copilot, Copilot Studio, and Azure AI Foundry.

Key benefits

Microsoft AI hackathons offer several key benefits, including:

- **Accelerated development**   Create functional prototypes or minimum viable products in a single day

- **Unified collaboration**   Connect business units with IT to develop more effective solutions

- **Skills enhancement**   Provide hands-on experience with AI technologies

- **Targeted results**   Develop solutions specifically designed for your organization's challenges

This practical event serves as a catalyst for innovation, enhances digital skills adoption, and integrates AI into everyday workflows. Experience what becomes possible when diverse teams unite around AI innovation.

> **Tip**   Refer to the Microsoft AI hackathon playbook in Appendix A to bring the potential impact of an M365 Copilot fusion team hackathon to your organization.

Microsoft 365 Copilot promptathon

Craft effective prompts for Copilot-powered success at scale. Empower your organization with precise and impactful AI interactions through a Microsoft 365 Copilot promptathon. This dynamic event gathers employees to sharpen their skills in crafting highly effective prompts.

Foster collaborative learning by allowing teams to rapidly develop, apply, and curate advanced prompting techniques that maximize the benefits of Microsoft 365 Copilot.

Key benefits

Microsoft 365 Copilot promptathons can be tailored for beginner, intermediate, and advanced audiences to deliver these benefits:

- **Enhanced productivity** Develop prompts that significantly streamline tasks such as email drafting, data analysis, and meeting summaries

- **Collaborative innovation** Facilitate cross-functional knowledge sharing to boost collective AI proficiency

- **Skill development** Gain practical, hands-on experience with prompt engineering

- **Strategic impact** Create prompts specifically aligned with your organization's unique operational needs

A promptathon is your gateway to more efficient, precise, and valuable interactions with Copilot.

> **Tip** The Microsoft 365 Copilot promptathon playbooks in Appendixes B, C, and D outline a crawl–walk–run approach to running tailored events to develop beginner, intermediate, and advanced prompting skills.

Microsoft AI innovation challenge

Drive tangible business value with AI. An innovation challenge is designed for business users who might not have a strong technical understanding but do have a practical problem to solve. This format helps them. This format helps them identify and pitch their innovative ideas.

Teams collaborate intensively to explore opportunities, develop their ideas into a pitch, and present them to a judging panel. The winning solution gets built, and the organization gains a backlog of ideas to build next.

Key benefits

Microsoft AI innovation challenges offer several key benefits, including:

- **Strategic focus** Concentrate efforts on processes or areas poised for significant AI-driven enhancement

- **Clear metrics**   Define success with quantifiable outcomes such as ROI, efficiency gains, and quality improvements

- **Mentorship support**   Receive guidance from experienced mentors who help you put your pitch together

Microsoft AI innovation challenges offer a powerful framework for turning visionary ideas into real-world, impactful solutions.

> **Tip**   The Microsoft AI innovation challenge playbook in Appendix E details how to prepare for, facilitate, and follow up on an engaging event to curate ideas from people across the organization.

Microsoft AI agent days

Unlock specialized AI capabilities tailored to your organization's unique needs through Microsoft AI agent days. This targeted event enables teams to create customized Copilot agents using Copilot Studio, directly addressing specific departmental or organizational challenges.

Participants work collaboratively to build, test, and refine agents designed for precise workflows and business scenarios, significantly enhancing productivity and effectiveness.

Key benefits

The following are the key benefits of AI agent days:

- **Customized solutions**   Develop Copilot agents specifically designed for your organization's workflows and processes

- **Hands-on learning**   Equip teams with practical experience in building and configuring effective AI agents

- **Immediate impact**   Quickly prototype, test, and demonstrate functional agents ready for organizational deployment

- **Agent roadmap**   Collate an idea backlog for agents that could be customized or built to be scaled across departments.

Microsoft AI agent days provide a platform for creating advanced, purpose-driven AI tools, directly empowering your teams and transforming day-to-day operations.

Microsoft AI Copilot process labs

Reimagine working with AI and transform your organization's critical processes through Microsoft AI Copilot process labs. These structured, cross-functional workshops enable teams to fundamentally rethink business processes from the ground up, leveraging advanced AI capabilities provided by Microsoft 365 Copilot, Copilot Studio, and Azure AI Foundry.

Teams collaboratively redefine processes, moving beyond automation to invent entirely new, AI-powered ways of operating. By envisioning future possibilities moving beyond existing constraints, participants create breakthrough innovations and strategic enhancements.

Key benefits

Microsoft AI Copilot process labs can facilitate:

- **Breakthrough innovations**   Redefine business processes entirely, discovering transformative opportunities that incremental changes might overlook

- **Collaborative creativity**   Bring together diverse expertise, fostering fresh perspectives and innovative thinking

- **Strategic implementation**   Develop actionable roadmaps and prototypes, clearly demonstrating substantial business benefits and enabling rapid deployment

Microsoft AI Copilot process labs provide the ideal environment for pioneering AI-driven business transformation.

Phasing culture-building initiatives

Cultural change doesn't happen overnight, and different cultural initiatives are more effective at specific stages of your Copilot adoption journey. A strategic, phased approach ensures that cultural activities align with your organization's evolving AI maturity and readiness. This approach prevents overwhelming employees while maintaining momentum and engagement throughout your Copilot adoption journey.

Early phase: Awareness and foundation building (1–3 months)

In the initial phase, focus on raising awareness, addressing concerns, and building foundational knowledge about Copilot's capabilities and potential.

Key cultural initiatives

In the early phase, key cultural initiatives might include:

- **Executive vision sessions**   Leadership workshops to align on the "why" of Copilot adoption and establish ethical guardrails

- **AI literacy programs**   Basic training sessions introducing Copilot functionality and prompt engineering fundamentals

- **Microsoft AI innovation challenges**   Low-stakes competitions focused on identifying use cases rather than building solutions

- **Lunch-and-learns** Informal sessions where early adopters share initial experiences and wins

- **AI council and champions** Establish governance structures and champion program

The early phase builds organizational readiness by creating excitement without overwhelming pressure. It focuses on developing a common language around AI and establishing psychological safety. During this period, metrics should focus on engagement, for example, how many employees are participating in awareness activities rather than on impact.

Intermediate phase: Skill building and experimentation (3–6 months)

As foundation knowledge is established, transition to deeper skill development and structured experimentation. This phase creates a virtuous cycle of learning and application.

Key cultural initiatives

In the intermediate phase, cultural initiatives might include:

- **Microsoft AI hackathon** Cross-functional events to build confidence through collaborative problem-solving

- **Microsoft 365 Copilot promptathons** Skill-building competitions that develop prompt engineering capabilities

- **Department-specific use case workshops** Focused sessions to identify opportunities within specific functions

- **Success storytelling** Formalized sharing of emerging wins and lessons learned

- **Mentorship programs** Pairing Copilot champions with teams that need additional support

The intermediate phase deepens engagement by creating opportunities for hands-on experience in safe environments. Activities are more challenging but remain structured enough to prevent frustration. Metrics now expand to include skills development (prompt engineering competency) and initial impact measures (time saved and quality improvements).

Advanced phase: Process transformation and scaling (6+ months)

With strong foundations and skills in place, focus on systematically transforming business processes and scaling Copilot use across the organization.

Key cultural initiatives

In the advanced phase, cultural initiatives might include:

- **Microsoft AI Copilot process labs** Intensive workshops to fundamentally reimagine business processes with AI at the core

- **Microsoft AI agent days**   Technical events focused on extending Copilot's capabilities through custom solutions

- **Cross-organization knowledge exchange**   Forums for teams to share advanced techniques and innovations

- **AI career path integration**   Formal recognition of AI skills in performance management and career development

- **Continuous improvement cycles**   Regular review and refinement of AI-driven processes

The advanced phase embeds Copilot deeply into how work gets done. Activities now focus on optimization and innovation rather than basic adoption. Metrics shift toward business outcomes and process transformation measures.

Sustaining phase: Reinforcement and evolution (ongoing)

As Copilot becomes embedded in daily work, focus on sustaining momentum, addressing emerging challenges, and evolving capabilities as the technology advances.

Key cultural initiatives

In the sustaining phase, cultural initiatives might include:

- **AI excellence awards**   Recognition programs celebrating innovative applications and significant impact

- **Innovation funds**   Resources allocated to teams developing new Copilot-powered solutions

- **Advanced certification programs**   Deeper technical training for power users and developers

- **External ecosystem engagement**   Participation in Microsoft user groups and partner communities

- **Strategic review cycles**   Regular assessment of how Copilot adoption aligns with evolving business goals

The sustaining phase prevents regression to old ways of working while continuing to evolve capabilities. It treats AI adoption as a journey rather than a destination, recognizing that both the technology and its applications will continue to evolve.

Creating your phased roadmap

When sequencing cultural initiatives for your organization, consider these factors:

- **Current AI literacy**   Organizations with higher baseline technical knowledge may progress through phases more quickly

- **Cultural readiness**   Change-resistant cultures may need a longer early phase focused on psychological safety

- **Resource availability** Align ambitious events with available time and budget

- **Leadership engagement** Sequence high-visibility activities when executive sponsors can participate

- **Feedback loops** Build in assessment points to determine readiness to advance phases

Remember that phases may overlap, and different departments may progress at different rates. The goal is not strict adherence to a timeline but strategic sequencing that builds momentum while preventing change fatigue.

> **Tip** Leveraging external experts for change management and technical skills or extending Copilot capabilities can fill gaps and enhance the organization's AI strategy. Microsoft partners or MVPs with proven track records can provide the necessary support to maximize the benefits of Copilot and other AI workloads.

Recognizing and celebrating success

Positive reinforcement goes a long way in bringing about cultural change. Actively recognize teams and individuals who find innovative ways to leverage Copilot. Celebrate "wins" and showcase success stories to build momentum and buy-in. Publicly celebrating successes is highlighted in Microsoft's Copilot adoption guide as a way to engage stakeholders and motivate others who want to achieve similar results.

This could be done via internal newsletters, town halls, or an "AI Hall of Fame" highlighting how Copilot helped save time, solved a problem, or drove revenue. Consider small incentives or recognition programs (badges and shout-outs) for Copilot champions and experimenters. At Microsoft, Copilot champions would share specific prompts and the value those prompts delivered (such as "saved three hours on a sales script using this prompt"), which provided concrete starting points for peers.

Culture is contagious and has a multiplying effect. When one person adopts Copilot and demonstrates its value, it creates curiosity in others: "How are they doing that? What could I be doing?" This social spread of values, behaviors, and practices is how culture truly takes root. The impact of one person using Copilot effectively can be significant, but when that behavior spreads through cultural adoption, the organization-wide impact becomes transformative.

Ensure long-term Copilot integration

When a process is enhanced or updated with Copilot by a champion team member, it should become the standard method for performing that task. This approach ensures consistency and maximizes the benefits of Copilot across the organization. Continuous measurement of Copilot adoption and impact through analytics dashboards provides insights into how Copilot is used and its effectiveness. The metrics and goals set in the previous chapter should guide the interpretation of these dashboards, helping to identify areas for improvement and opportunities for further integration.

Culture change isn't a one-time event. Leaders must demonstrate ongoing commitment to reinforcing skills, refining processes, and scaling Copilot usage strategically. Make continuous learning the standard.

> **Tip** To truly weave Copilot into business processes, consider customizing Copilot to your organization's needs: Microsoft 365 Copilot can be extended with custom plugins or even built-for-you agents via Copilot Studio to address specific workflow gaps. You signal that AI is part of everyone's job by tailoring AI to fit each department's processes.

Integrating AI skills into career paths

Emphasizing how Copilot proficiency aligns with career growth and trajectory within the organization can motivate people to develop AI skills. Incorporating AI skills into performance management, personal development plans, and role expectations ensures that employees see the value of AI proficiency in their career advancement.

Remember, you can't get fit watching someone else work out; similarly, you can't get good at AI by just knowing about it in theory. More and more, every role will have an AI component—that's a given. The more you enable people to learn AI on the job in every part of what they do, the more you ingrain a cultural understanding that developing these skills makes them indispensable in the job market going forward. This provides a powerful incentive for people to get on the adoption curve early, maximizing their time with the tools and the skills they'll develop.

This approach helps create a culture where continuous learning and AI adoption are integral to personal and organizational success.

Action steps: Building a Copilot-ready culture

As we come to the close of the final chapter in this book, you might be feeling overwhelmed by all the things you could do when it comes to Copilot adoption. The most important takeaway is that any action is better than no action. Building a Copilot-ready culture that equips people for the future of work starts with a clear vision, builds on human capability, and evolves as AI improves. Depending on where you are in the journey, choose the next best action to keep moving forward.

Articulate a vision and ethical guardrails

Start at the top. Communicate your vision for Copilot—why is the organization embracing AI, and how does it align with your mission? Employees need to hear that AI is here to augment, not replace, human work. Address the "why" for AI in every department; for example, "Copilot will help us spend less time shuffling paperwork and more time on innovation."

At the same time, establish and share responsible AI principles and usage policies. Define what "Copilot-first" means in practice and set expectations, for example, when to verify AI outputs and how to handle sensitive data. By providing a compass (vision + ethics) upfront, you build trust when employees see leadership is enthusiastic but responsible about AI.

Empower, educate, and engage your people

Cultivate a grassroots movement. Identify Copilot champions across teams who can lead by example. Provide them with early access and training, then amplify their learnings company-wide. Set up an AI council or cross-functional working group to coordinate these efforts and gather input from all corners of the organization. Invest in comprehensive training programs to build AI confidence and skills. Encourage employees to experiment with Copilot on real work tasks and share their experiences.

Throughout, foster psychological safety: explicitly encourage questions, acknowledge that there will be a learning curve, and frame failures as learning opportunities. Maintain open channels for support and feedback where anyone can ask for tips or report issues.

Reinforce, integrate, and evolve

Cement your cultural changes by weaving Copilot into everyday routines and systems. Embed AI into business processes by updating standard operating procedures to include Copilot. Encourage each department to continuously identify new workflows for Copilot and allocate time for teams to refine these AI-assisted processes.

Use the Copilot Dashboard and analytics to track adoption rates, popular use cases, and areas of friction. Review these metrics in leadership meetings or with the AI council and act on them. If one department lags, provide targeted training or address specific concerns. Celebrate successes and reward ongoing innovation. Simultaneously, be ready to adapt policies and support as both you and Copilot level up your capabilities. Solicit regular feedback and use it to update your approach.

Treat this culture shift as an ongoing cycle: Plan. Do. Check. Act. By continuously reinforcing desired behaviors, integrating AI deeper into workflows, and iterating on your approach, you ensure the cultural adoption of Copilot is sustainable for the long run.

Try this prompt: Culture diagnostic AI

Reflecting on where your organization's culture currently is makes a powerful next step. It can inform your strategy to move from where you are now to where you aspire to be as an AI-enabled team. Ask Copilot to help you understand how ready your current culture is for AI and build a customized plan to improve it.

You are "Culture Diagnostic AI," an evidence-based advisor trained on leading organisational-culture research (Denison, Schein, Kotter & Heskett, Gallup, Google's Project Aristotle, Edmondson, etc.).
Your mission: help me assess my team's culture and deliver an actionable 12-month improvement roadmap.

STEP 0 – PROMPT HEALTH CHECK (run silently, then display log)

1. *Scan your knowledge up to TODAY'S DATE for any major new culture frameworks, meta-analyses, or landmark books published since 2023.*
2. *Compare them with the question domains and reading list in this prompt.*
3. *If needed, replace *up to two* question domains and/or *up to two* book recommendations (max list length = 7).*
4. *Show a *Prompt Update Log* (≤ 100 words) summarising changes.*

   - *If nothing changed, say "Prompt is current."*
   - *End with: *"(Type 'Pause' within one message if you'd like to stop for review; otherwise I'll continue.)"**

Auto-continue rule: Immediately after posting the Prompt Update Log, proceed to STEP 1 unless the user's next message contains "Pause" (case-insensitive). No other confirmation is required.

STEP 1 – INTERACTIVE DIAGNOSTIC (one question at a time)
Ask each question, wait for my answer, then send the next. Domains (update if Step 0 edited them):

1. *Purpose & Values*
2. *Psychological Safety*
3. *Decision-Making & Autonomy*
4. *Communication & Feedback*
5. *Recognition & Rewards*
6. *Learning & Experimentation*
7. *Performance & Accountability*
8. *Inclusion & Well-being*

Finish with:
"Is there anything else about your culture I should know before I analyse? If not, type 'No—analyse.'"

STEP 2 – ANALYSIS & OUTPUT (≤ 1 200 words)

1. *Executive Summary (≈ 150 words)*
2. *Culture Heat-Map (domains × 1-10 scores, traffic-light colours)*
3. *Key Strengths (Top 3) – cite research (Author, Year)*
4. *Critical Gaps (Top 3) – cite research*
5. *12-Month Roadmap*

   - *Q1 Quick Wins – owner, metric, supporting study*
   - *Q2-Q3 Build Momentum – owner, metric*
   - *Q4 Embed & Sustain – owner, metric*

6. *Metrics Dashboard – suggested KPIs (Gallup Q12, eNPS, turnover, decision cycle-time, etc.)*
7. *Further Reading – 5-7 seminal books (updated per Step 0), author + year + one-line takeaway.*

Next steps

In this chapter, we've explored practical steps and provided a comprehensive guide for organizations seeking to cultivate a culture of innovation through the integration of AI and Copilot. We covered how to build momentum by engaging people in collaborative learning opportunities and adapting your approach based on their feedback.

- Leaders who want to create a Copilot-first culture need to articulate a clear vision for AI adoption and empower employees through education and engagement

- Integrate AI skills into career paths, professional development plans, and role definitions to emphasize the role continuous learning plays in fostering a culture of innovation

- Create a sustainable, innovative culture with AI and Copilot by running events so that people can share their ideas and learn how AI can enhance the way they work

Microsoft AI hackathon playbook

In this appendix, you will:

- Discover what a Microsoft AI hackathon event is and how you can facilitate one in your organization.

- Understand the benefits of fusion teams and how to bring together business users with technical experts to create innovative AI solutions.

Running a successful one-day hackathon in a business setting requires careful planning, clear goals, and the right mix of people and tools. This playbook is designed for fusion teams—cross-functional groups that blend IT and business experts—to rapidly take an idea from concept to a working prototype in a single business day. The focus is on leveraging the latest AI tools—Microsoft 365 Copilot, Copilot Studio, and Azure AI Foundry—to supercharge the development of innovative solutions. These short hackathons can accelerate Microsoft 365 Copilot adoption by empowering employees to build AI-powered solutions for real business challenges.

In the following sections, you'll find a structured guide covering everything from planning the event and crafting problem statements to facilitating fusion team collaboration, integrating Copilot tools during prototyping, and evaluating and progressing the best ideas. Use this playbook as a step-by-step blueprint to organize and execute a high-impact hackathon that produces a usable minimum viable product (MVP) by the end of the event and energizes your organization's digital transformation efforts.

> **Note** Copilot—the proper term—refers to Microsoft's AI products. In this book, "Copilot" generally refers to Microsoft 365 Copilot. Throughout this playbook, however, you will also see "copilot" used as a generic term for custom AI solutions or agents that can be built in Copilot Studio and Azure AI Foundry.

Pre-hackathon planning and preparation

Thorough preparation helps you get the most value out of a one-day hackathon. Given the tight timeframe, organizers should start planning for the event at least a month in advance. If you are bringing together teams from several departments, you may need to allow more lead time to secure the necessary buy-in from leaders and participants.

Important steps include:

- **Define the objectives and theme for the hackathon** Decide what the hackathon should accomplish. For example, the goal might be to improve internal processes or customer experience through AI-driven solutions. Announce a general theme (such as "Boost productivity with AI and Copilots") in advance so participants can start thinking of ideas. Ensure the theme aligns with business priorities.

- **Secure buy-in from leadership** Gain the support of leaders from IT and other departments across your organization by highlighting how it aligns with their goals. Their sponsorship (such as opening remarks, judging, offering prizes) will underscore the event's importance and encourage participation. Ensure leaders understand the fusion team concept.

> **Note** Fusion teams are multidisciplinary teams that include both technical experts and people involved in executing business processes who work together to design and deliver technical solutions that create business value.

- **Schedule and logistics** Choose a date, taking care to avoid conflict with major deadlines or holidays. If it's on a weekday, ensure participants have clearance to dedicate the day to the hackathon. Book a venue or set up virtual collaboration tools if running a remote hackathon. Arrange for food and refreshments to keep energy up, especially if people will be working through lunch. Draft a detailed agenda (outlined in the "Hackathon day agenda" section) that fits within one business day, typically no more than eight hours.

- **Recruit participants** Invite a diverse mix of participants from different departments—developers, business analysts, product managers, IT admins, power users, and business users. Emphasize that hackathons aren't just for coders and that everyone is welcome. Aim for teams of about 4–6 people and reward cross-functional team composition. (Consider offering bonus points or prizes for teams that span multiple departments.)

- **Gather ideas in advance** To hit the ground running, consider collecting ideas for problems or solutions before the hackathon. Set up a simple idea board or form where employees can submit pain points or suggestions. Allow voting on ideas to surface popular or high-impact problems. You can preselect a few top problem statements for teams to choose from or let teams pick from the complete list on the day of the hackathon.

- **Ensure access to tools** Verify that all participants have the necessary accounts and access to M365 Copilot, Copilot Studio, and any required Azure services (such as Azure AI Foundry). For example, each team should have at least one member with a Microsoft 365 Copilot license. Have IT set up any sandbox environments, developer tenants, or sample data that might be required beforehand. If using Copilot Studio, ensure the environment is provisioned and ready for makers—Copilot Studio runs in the Power Platform environment, so test that appropriate permissions are set.

- **Training resources** Because some participants may be new to these AI tools, provide brief preparatory materials or training. Share tutorials or documentation on what M365 Copilot can do, Copilot Studio basics, and Azure AI Foundry capabilities. Optionally, host a short orientation webinar before the hackathon to demonstrate how to build a simple copilot agent (such as creating a question-and-answer bot in Copilot Studio).

- **Prepare templates** Print or publish templates that teams can use during the event. Providing these templates will save time and keep teams focused. Useful templates include:
  - Problem statement worksheet—to concisely define the problem and success criteria.
  - Solution design canvas—to sketch the proposed solution and AI components.
  - Demo outline or slide template—for presenting the project to the judges.

- **Judging panel and criteria** Line up judges—ideally a mix of IT leaders, business executives, and perhaps an external innovation expert or a customer representative. Define the judging criteria (see the "Judging criteria" section of this playbook) and share that criteria with participants in advance so they know what to aim for. Also, decide on how prizes or recognition will be handled and promoted; even symbolic prizes or certificates can motivate participants.

With these preparations in place, you'll create the conditions for a smooth event where participants can focus on innovation rather than logistics. To maximize the impact of your event, there are additional steps that you need to consider.

Running inclusive and accessible hackathons

Create an inclusive hackathon environment that ensures all participants can contribute their talents regardless of abilities. Arrange for a few mentors or coaches (perhaps subject-matter experts in Power Platform, Azure AI, or M365) to be on call during the hackathon. They can help teams troubleshoot technical issues or guide them on how to use Copilot and Foundry effectively. Coaches can dramatically help teams bring their concepts to life and provide additional support to participants with different abilities and ways of thinking.

- **Physical accessibility** Ensure the venue has wheelchair access, accessible restrooms, adequate space between tables for mobility aids, and clear signage. Reserve accessible parking spaces and provide information about public transportation options.

- **Digital accessibility** Select collaboration tools that support screen readers and keyboard navigation. Ensure presentation materials use sufficient color contrast, readable fonts, and descriptive alt text for images. Test the digital platforms in advance with accessibility tools.

- **Inclusive communication** If requested, offer options for sign language interpretation or real-time captioning. During presentations, encourage speakers to describe visual content, face the audience when speaking, and use a microphone if provided.

- **Sensory considerations** Provide a quiet space where participants can take breaks from noise and stimulation. Consider lighting options that reduce eyestrain and avoid flashing effects in presentations.

- **Consider diverse learning and working styles** Provide instructions in multiple formats (written, verbal, visual). Allow flexibility in how teams organize and present their work, recognizing different collaboration preferences.

In pre-event communications, invite participants to request any specific accommodations that would improve their experience on the day and provide clear information about what accessibility measures are already in place.

Intellectual property framework

Establish clear intellectual property (IP) guidelines to prevent confusion and potential conflicts after the hackathon.

- **Ownership declaration** Decide and communicate in advance who will own the intellectual property created during the hackathon. This may already be defined by existing policies or employment contract terms, but it's a good idea to make it explicit in relation to the hackathon event. Options might include:

  - The company retains all rights.
  - Participants retain rights to their creations.
  - Shared ownership with usage rights for both the company and creators.
  - Open-source approach with the specified license.

- **Documentation requirements** Provide participants with IP documentation forms to complete, including contributor acknowledgments and descriptions of created assets.

- **Usage rights** Define how the company may use hackathon outputs, whether for internal use, commercial products, or marketing purposes. Similarly, clarify if and how participants can use, share, or further develop their creations.

- **Preexisting IP** Establish procedures for using and attributing preexisting code, designs, or IP into hackathon projects.

- **Confidentiality** Set expectations about sharing project details externally, especially for innovations with potential competitive advantage.

- **Patent considerations** If relevant, outline the process for patentable innovations and how inventors will be recognized.

Before the event, engage with your legal team for guidance on the appropriate IP framework for your organization and event. They may recommend steps you need to take to ensure everyone has the same understanding when it comes to IP in relation to the hackathon.

Technical preparation for the hackathon

Preparing for technical issues will minimize disruption during the one-day hackathon. Have a plan for handling issues and contingencies in place to deal with them as they arise.

- **Technical support team**   Designate a dedicated technical support team with clear roles (such as cloud infrastructure specialist, network administrator, tool-specific experts) and make their contact information available to participants.

- **Common issues protocol**   Create troubleshooting guides for likely issues such as access problems, network connectivity issues, tool outages, integration challenges, and data access limitations.

- **Backup resources**   Prepare alternatives for critical components like local development environments, offline documentation copies, alternative data sources, and backup presentation methods.

- **Escalation path**   Establish a clear escalation process for issues the support team cannot immediately resolve, including contacts at technology vendors or internal IT leadership.

- **Time buffer**   Build small time buffers into the schedule to accommodate technical delays without derailing the entire day.

- **Triage system**   Implement a simple ticket or board system to track reported issues, their severity, and resolution status.

Conduct a technical dry run the day before, testing all tools and environments with sample activities to identify potential issues.

Support for first-time hackathon participants

Create a positive experience for newcomers to maximize their contributions and enjoyment.

- **Pre-event orientation**   Host a brief virtual session for first-timers to explain hackathon concepts and expectations and answer questions about the format.

- **First-timer guide**   Create a concise guide covering what to expect, common terminology, and participation tips.

- **Newcomer identification**   Offer optional indicators (like different colored lanyards) so first-timers can be identified by mentors for additional support.

- **Mentor pairing**   Assign experienced hackathon participants as buddies for first-timers or ensure teams have a mix of experienced and new participants.

- **Basic skills resources**   Provide links to quick tutorials on fundamental tools being used that are accessible before the event.

- **Expectation setting**   Emphasize that hackathons are learning experiences and perfect results aren't expected—the goal is creative problem-solving and collaboration.

- **Check-ins**   Schedule specific check-ins with first-time participants to address concerns and provide encouragement.

Clarify ways to contribute beyond coding—design, research, testing, presentation, project management—ensuring nontechnical participants understand the value they can contribute to the hackathon.

Enabling hybrid and remote participation

Empower people to participate from wherever they are working by accommodating hybrid and remote collaboration.

- **Platform selection**   Choose collaboration tools that effectively support in-person and remote participants, including video conferencing with breakout rooms, digital whiteboarding tools, and document collaboration platforms.

- **Hardware setup**   Ensure physical spaces have cameras that allow remote participants to see whiteboards as well as quality microphones so they can hear the discussion happening in the room. Provide multiple screens for remote participants and encourage the use of digital displays for shared content.

- **Balanced team composition**   Structure teams to avoid isolating remote members by avoiding having just one remote person on an otherwise in-person team.

- **Engagement protocols**   Establish clear practices for inclusive meetings, including regular check-ins, a "remote first" approach for content sharing, and designated facilitators responsible for including remote participants.

- **Technical rehearsal**   Host a brief technical check before the event, where remote participants can test connections and tools.

- **Time zone considerations**   Adjust schedules if spanning multiple time zones or consider asynchronous elements for global participation.

- **Remote mentoring**   Ensure mentors are available via digital channels and can effectively assist remote teams.

Guide remote teams on how to effectively present their ideas virtually, including backup recording options.

Data security and compliance

Protect sensitive information while enabling innovation.

- **Data classification guidance**   Clearly identify what categories of data can be used in hackathon projects (such as approved production versus sanitized sample data and public versus internal-only information).

- **Privacy requirements**   Define expectations for handling personal or confidential information, including data anonymization guidelines and consent requirements for user testing.

- **Secure development practices** Establish basic security expectations, such as no hardcoded credentials in source code and proper authentication for apps and services.

- **Compliance considerations** Highlight relevant regulatory requirements like GDPR, CCPA, or industry-specific compliance needs.

- **Secure environment configuration** Provide preconfigured development environments that implement security controls.

- **Post-Hackathon data handling** Define procedures for secure cleanup after the event, including data retention and deletion requirements.

Designate a security professional who can advise teams on security questions throughout the day.

Pre-hackathon learning sessions

Prepare participants with the knowledge they need to contribute to their team during the hackathon. This is a great opportunity to create buzz for the hackathon while also providing people the opportunity to level up their skills.

- **Foundational AI innovation skills** Schedule targeted learning sessions 1-2 weeks before the hackathon, covering M365 Copilot capabilities, Copilot Studio basics, an overview of Azure AI Foundry, and problem definition techniques.

- **Choose an effective format** Consider 60 minute sessions that could be delivered in-person or online, with a mix of hands-on labs, case studies, or sharing prerecorded content from subject matter experts.

- **Tiered learning paths** Offer different tracks based on participant roles and experience (technical, business, experience design, and team facilitation tracks). Tailor pre-hackathon training paths for each track.

- **Resources and materials** Provide quick-start guides, sample code, video tutorials, and practice exercises.

- **Skill assessment** Offer optional self-assessment tools to help participants identify the most valuable pre-hackathon training they can do to prepare.

- **Trainer facilitators** Recruit internal experts or external trainers who can effectively explain concepts and answer questions.

Align training content with the hackathon theme and likely problem areas participants will tackle.

Communication strategy and plan

Maintain clear and effective communication before, during, and after the hackathon.

- **Pre-event communication timeline** Schedule announcements from 4–6 weeks prior (initial announcement) through to day-before reminders.

- **Communication channels** Select and specify appropriate channels for official announcements, quick updates, documentation sharing, and team collaboration.

- **During-event updates** Plan for regular communication touchpoints, including morning kickoff messages, progress check-ins, and time remaining alerts.

- **Templates and scripts** Prepare standardized communications for invitations, presenter talking points, judging feedback, and follow-up messages.

- **Visual communication** Create clear signage and visual cues for the hackathon schedule, team locations, and support resources.

- **Post-event communication plan** Schedule thank you messages, results announcements, survey distribution, and future hackathon teasers.

- **Documentation sharing** Define how project artifacts will be communicated and shared after the event

If you feel like you're overcommunicating, you are probably only just communicating enough. Make it easy for people to get quick answers to their hackathon questions.

Catering and refreshments

Good food fuels great ideas. Factor this into your event budget to ensure participants are well-nourished and energized throughout the day. Plan for:

- **Breakfast** Coffee, tea, juices, pastries, fruit, and granola bars to kick-start the day.

- **Lunch** A balanced, easily-served lunch such as sandwiches, wraps, salads, sushi platters, or pizza.

- **Snacks** Regularly replenish snack stations with healthy options (nuts, fruit, vegetable platters, and protein bars) and treats (cookies, chocolates, and chips) to maintain energy levels and morale.

- **Drinks** Water, coffee, tea, soft drinks, and energy drinks should be available throughout the event.

Accommodate dietary requirements where possible and encourage the teams to take regular breaks to keep their energy up.

Building buzz with team pride

To boost enthusiasm and create a fun, collaborative atmosphere right from the start, encourage each fusion team to select a unique team name, mascot, and team color. Encourage creativity and team spirit, which helps build camaraderie and friendly competition throughout the event. Provide supplies like colored markers, stickers, badges, and customizable digital templates that teams can use to represent their identities visually. Displaying team identities visibly in the workspace or virtual collaboration tools will further foster a sense of pride and motivation, creating buzz in the lead-up to the hackathon.

Hackathon day agenda

You'll need to run a tight agenda on the day of the hackathon to ensure you allow sufficient time for each stage. This sample agenda for a one-day (8 hour) hackathon can be adjusted to suit your specific needs, but keep in mind the need to maintain momentum and stick to the timings once your event is underway.

Sample hackathon agenda

The hackathon organizing committee and facilitators will need to arrive early on the day of the hackathon to ensure all last-minute setup is completed prior to participant arrival.

- **8:30–9:00 AM Check-in and team assembly**
  - Participants arrive, enjoy coffee or breakfast, and finalize team formation. Post a board with the day's schedule and any last-minute announcements. If teams aren't preformed, use this time to network and match people to ideas or skills.

- **9:00–9:30 AM Kickoff session**
  - Official welcome by the organizer or an executive sponsor. Introduce the hackathon theme and objectives (such as "Today we're building AI-powered prototypes to improve our business!"). Give a brief overview of M365 Copilot, Copilot Studio, and Azure AI Foundry capabilities to inspire possibilities. Review the rules, schedule, and judging criteria. Encourage creative thinking and remind teams to keep the scope realistic for one day.

- **9:30–10:15 AM Problem brainstorm and refinement**
  - Teams (or individuals who will form teams) brainstorm specific problem statements. Facilitators can run a quick exercise: have each team articulate the problem they want to solve, the affected users, and the desired outcome. They should capture this in a written problem statement. Mentors circulate to help refine the scope, ensuring the problems are neither too broad to tackle in a day nor so narrow that they lack impact. The goal is for each team to have a clear, one-paragraph problem statement that describes the current challenge and what a successful solution would achieve.

- **10:15–10:30 AM Idea pitch (optional)**
  - If there are many teams or ideas, you can have an informal pitch where each team shares their chosen problem and solution concept in one minute. This is optional in a small hack, but it can energize the room and ensure no two teams are doing identical projects. It also commits teams to a plan of action.

- **10:30 AM–12:30 PM Development phase (morning)**
  - Teams turn their ideas into prototypes. This is heads-down work time with intense collaboration. Details on this phase are in the "Defining the problem" section. Organizers should ensure a focused but fun atmosphere—play background music, display a countdown timer,

and encourage teams to take short breaks if needed. Mentors should roam or be available on a "help desk" channel to assist with any roadblocks (technical issues, access problems, and so on).

- **12:30–1:15 PM   Lunch break and midpoint check-in**

  - Give teams a break to recharge. It's also helpful to use this as a checkpoint. You might ask teams to submit a quick update via a Teams chat or a shared board, such as one sentence on progress and any help needed. Optionally, hold a short "show-and-tell" where teams informally demo any small achievement or even share a challenge they're facing—sometimes, another team or mentor might have a solution. Keep this light and supportive.

- **1:15–3:00 PM   Development phase (afternoon)**

  - The hacking continues. By early afternoon, teams should aim for a basic working demo or a skeleton of their solution. The latter part of this phase should transition into testing and preparing the presentation. Remind teams around half an hour before the end of this phase to start finalizing their prototypes and preparing demo materials. Time management is critical; teams may need gentle nudges to wrap up coding and focus on the demo.

- **3:00–3:30 PM   Demo prep and dry run**

  - Teams create final presentation assets: slides, demo scripts, or videos. M365 Copilot can assist here—use Copilot in PowerPoint to generate a quick presentation outline or in Word to summarize their solution in a succinct narrative. Teams should practice how they will explain the problem and show the solution within the time limit. If possible, have mentors do a quick dry run with each team to give last-minute feedback.

- **3:30–4:30 PM   Project demos**

  - Each team takes turns to present their project. Depending on the number of teams, allocate about 5–7 minutes per team, including Q&A. For example, a 5-minute presentation with 2 minutes for judges to ask questions is common. Ensure all AV equipment or screen-sharing works before starting. Encourage teams to tell a story: state the problem, show how their solution addresses it (ideally with a live prototype demo), and describe the potential impact. Keep a hard time limit to be fair to all. During this phase, you can award spot prizes to boost energy and recognize team efforts throughout the day. These can include small prizes for

    - ❏ The first team to finalize their problem statement
    - ❏ Most creative team mascot or commitment to team colors
    - ❏ Best mid-day progress check-in
    - ❏ The team that shows exceptional collaboration or innovative use of tools

    Spot prizes could include gift cards, branded company swag, fun tech gadgets, or snack hampers.

> **Tip** If a team isn't ready to demo live, they can walk through mock-ups or a concept video. The emphasis is on the idea and approach, not just working code.

- **4:30–5:00 PM   Judge deliberation and voting**
  - While participants take a breather, judges confer (in a separate room or private call) to evaluate teams against the criteria. If you planned any popular voting (such as "People's Choice" award), conduct that now via an online poll. During this time, you can also have a quick retrospective discussion with the audience about what they learned or simply encourage teams to take another look at each other's demos.

- **5:00 PM   Awards and closing ceremony**
  - Judges announce the winners and perhaps highlight a few honorable mentions or category awards; more details are available in the "Awards and recognition" section later in this appendix. Have an executive congratulate participants and reinforce how these innovative ideas align with the company's vision. Conclude by encouraging teams to continue developing their solutions beyond the hackathon and thanking everyone for their enthusiasm. Don't forget to take a group photo to capture the moment.

This schedule packs a lot into one day. The key is maintaining a brisk pace, minimizing downtime, and ensuring everyone knows what to do each hour. It can be helpful to assign the role of timekeeper to one of the organizing team members, so they can work with the hackathon facilitators to keep things moving.

Next, we'll dive deeper into how to handle some of these phases, especially generating problem statements and the development/prototyping process with the Copilot tools.

Defining the problem

A well-defined problem is half the solution. At the start of the hackathon, or ideally in the days leading up to it, teams should invest time formulating a clear business problem statement. This guides their efforts and provides a way to evaluate whether the solution they design successfully solves the problem.

Generating and refining problem statements

Help teams generate and refine strong problem statements through an iterative process that starts with guidance on how to define the problem they are aiming to solve.

- **Start with pain points**   Encourage participants to consider pressing challenges in their daily work or business. What repetitive tasks, bottlenecks, or data gaps could be improved? Many good ideas come from the phrase, "Wouldn't it be great if…?" If you collected suggestions pre-event, recap the top-voted ideas now to spark inspiration.

- **Use a template**   Provide a simple fill-in-the-blank template to structure the problem. For example: "How might we *[action]* for *[target users]* to achieve *[desired outcome]*?" or "*[Target users]* need a way to *[solve X]* because *[why it's important]*." This ensures teams cover the key elements: who is affected, what the need is, and why it matters.

- **Focus on business outcome**   Frame the problem statement in terms of a business outcome or user need, not a technical fix. For instance, "Improve customer onboarding experience by reducing manual data entry" is better than "Create a SharePoint list for customer data." It should describe the current vs. desired state and the gap between them.

- **Specific but achievable**   Within the broad theme, teams should narrow down to a specific use case that can be addressed in a prototype. "Increase sales productivity" is too vague for one day; "Automate meeting note summaries for sales calls using Copilot" provides a clear, realistic scope. Teams may need to constrain the problem's scope to something feasible (maybe focusing on one department, one type of transaction, and so on). Mentors can help right-size the scope.

- **Check alignment with Copilot/AI**   Since this hackathon centers on M365 Copilot, Copilot Studio, and Azure AI Foundry, the problem should be one that AI can realistically help solve. Ideal problems involve tasks like summarizing content, extracting insights from data, answering questions, generating drafts, automating multistep workflows, or providing intelligent assistance in an application. If a team's problem doesn't naturally lend itself to a Copilot or AI solution, they might need to tweak it. For example, a problem about "improving team morale" might be reframed to something like "providing managers with AI-driven suggestions for team recognition activities".

- **Iterate and refine**   Once a team has an initial problem statement, have them do a quick sanity check: Is the problem understandable in a sentence or two? Will solving it provide tangible benefits (time saved, cost reduced, better experience)? They can discuss this with a mentor or another team for feedback. It's often helpful to identify the key metric or indicator of success (even if they won't fully measure it in one day). For example, "if our solution works, a task that used to take 2 hours will take 10 minutes" gives a target for them to aim for with their prototype.

- **Leverage M365 Copilot for ideation**   Microsoft 365 Copilot itself can assist in refining ideas. For instance, in Word or OneNote, a team member could prompt Copilot with something like "Draft a problem statement for improving our expense report process using AI". Copilot can help articulate the pain points and suggest solution angles, which the team can customize. This saves time and might surface considerations the team hadn't thought of. Copilot can also generate lists of potential challenges or requirements once a problem is chosen (such as "What are the key requirements for an AI solution that schedules meetings?").

- **Document the final statement**   Have each team write down their final problem statement, on a flipchart or shared document, and get sign-off from a mentor or the hackathon facilitator. This isn't for approval per se, but to ensure the team has a solid direction. It also helps later during judging—teams will be partly evaluated on solving the problem they set out to solve, so a clear written statement is handy.

By the end of this phase, every team should have a well-defined problem statement that acts as a north star for their day's work. Essentially, they've answered: *What are we solving, for whom, and why?* With that, they are ready to start designing a solution.

Documenting the solution

Effective documentation ensures hackathon projects can continue beyond the event. Provide standardized templates for teams to document:

- Project overview and problem statement
- Solution architecture and components
- Data flows and integration points
- Setup instructions and dependencies
- Known limitations and future enhancements
- Team member contributions

Encourage teams to document as they build rather than at the end of the project. It can work well to make someone in each team responsible for documentation, which could be a rotating role. Schedule brief documentation checkpoints throughout the hackathon and use collaborative tools like Loop or OneNote so anyone can make updates in real-time.

Set minimum standards for code documentation, including:

- README files with setup and usage instructions
- Clear comments for complex logic
- Requirements and dependency lists
- Environment configuration details

Establish a process for preserving artifacts, including:

- Source code repository with appropriate access permissions
- Prototype deployment details and access information
- Presentation slides and demo scripts
- Design assets and wireframes
- Screenshots, flow diagrams, and architecture schematics (to supplement written documentation)

If the project will continue post-hackathon, create handover documentation for future team members.

Fusion team roles and collaboration

Fusion teams thrive on diverse expertise. In a one-day hackathon, clarifying roles early—and allowing them to be fluid as needed—ensures that everyone contributes effectively.

Roles in a fusion team

Structure fusion teams for collaboration with clear, defined roles. A typical fusion team for a hackathon might include:

- **Product owner/Business lead**   A person with a deep understanding of the problem domain (such as a sales manager for a sales-focused solution). They keep the team focused on the business needs and define what a "successful" prototype should accomplish. They help with requirements and testing from the end-user perspective.

- **Developer/engineer**   The tech builder who is comfortable with the tools needed (could be a pro-code developer or a Power Platform maker). They drive implementation in Copilot Studio or integrate Azure services. If coding or scripting is required (such as writing an Azure Function or some glue code), they can handle that, possibly using Visual Studio Code with GitHub Copilot for speed.

- **Data specialist/IT admin**   If the Solution needs to connect to enterprise data or systems, a person from the IT or data team can ensure access to those resources. They handle tasks like prepping a SharePoint dataset, connecting an Azure Cognitive Search index, or ensuring compliance/security checks. They also advise on deploying anything to the cloud (this is where Azure AI Foundry expertise might come in handy).

- **UI/UX or power user**   Someone who can design the user interaction. In Copilot solutions, this might mean configuring the chatbot conversation flow in Copilot Studio or designing a Power App interface that calls Copilot. They ensure the solution is user-friendly and can articulate the user journey during the demo.

- **Facilitator/Scrum Master (optional)**   On a tight schedule, it helps if one team member informally takes on timekeeping and task management. This person coordinates the division of work (who is doing what) and keeps an eye on the clock, so the team isn't heads-down in code until the last minute. The Business lead or another team member can often double up on this role.

> **Note**   A Scrum Master is typically part of a Scrum team, which follows an iterative, Agile methodology. Scrum Masters help remove barriers for the team and facilitate the development process, enabling the team to focus on delivering the most valuable next increment of work.

Often, one person may fill multiple roles, especially in smaller teams. The key is to ensure that the fusion team covers all critical skill sets and perspectives.

Effective collaboration

Encourage teams to start with a quick planning huddle: identify tasks needed to build the prototype and assign owners. For example, tasks might include "set up Copilot Studio environment," "prepare sample data," "design conversation prompts," "build Power Automate workflow," and "prepare slides". Writing these on a whiteboard or shared OneNote can help track progress. A lean, agile mindset works well—think of the morning as Sprint 1 (with a review at lunch) and the afternoon as Sprint 2.

Fusion teams shine when members collaborate across traditional boundaries, so the goal is to create cross-functional teams. Pair members with different backgrounds on the same subtask to promote knowledge sharing. For instance, a business analyst can sit with a developer to craft the Copilot prompts, combining business insight with technical phrasing. Alternatively, a developer can involve the business lead when configuring an AI model's knowledge base to ensure the content is relevant. This breaks down silos and often leads to creative approaches.

Use Microsoft Teams or another channel for team communication throughout the day. Even if teams are colocated, a chat group is useful for sharing links or asking mentors questions. Establish a way to get support quickly, perhaps a dedicated help channel or a posted phone number for the tech support team.

With only one day to produce a prototype, teams must make quick decisions. Adopt a "decide fast, refine later" attitude. It's better to pick an approach and try it (such as choosing a certain AI model or assuming a particular data source) than to be paralyzed by alternatives. The facilitator role can prompt, "Do we all agree on solution X? Alright, let's proceed. We can adjust on the fly if needed."

> **Tip** Foster a spirit of openness. Encourage teams to share findings or tips ("We just figured out how to call an external API from Copilot Studio. If anyone needs help, let us know!"). A short show-and-tell at lunch or a live Teams feed of tips can amplify this. Fusion teams are about blending strengths, and that can extend beyond one team to the entire hackathon group.

Take advantage of digital collaboration tools for real-time co-creation. Microsoft Whiteboard or Miro can be great for quick design sketches or flow diagrams that everyone edits together. Use a shared editor or pair programming with an AI assistant if working on code or prompt design. For example, the developer can share their screen while writing prompts or code, and others can chime in with suggestions. Use Copilot to help review and refine.

Where there is a lack of alignment on direction, bring the teams back to the purpose of the hackathon. Review the judging criteria and reiterate focus on creating business value. Let the person closest to the customer/business need (often the business lead) guide what's most important to deliver. Mentors can mediate if needed to ensure that the team doesn't stall.

Managing challenging team dynamics

Prepare organizers and mentors to address common team collaboration issues, which might include:

- **Unbalanced participation**   These strategies can help when certain team members dominate or disengage.

  - Structured turn-taking for ideation and discussion.
  - Task rotation to ensure everyone contributes.
  - Private check-ins with quieter participants.
  - Highlight diverse ways to contribute beyond coding.

- **Disagreement resolution**   These processes can help manage conflicting ideas or approaches.

  - Rapid prioritization frameworks (such as an impact versus effort matrix).
  - Timeboxed discussions with clear decision points.
  - Mentor-facilitated compromise sessions.
  - Reiterate the limited timeframe and need for pragmatic choices.

- **Skill mismatches**   Ideas to help teams with uneven technical capabilities.

  - Pair programming or the buddy system within teams.
  - Just-in-time learning resources for specific skills.
  - Encouraging tiered task allocation by experience level.
  - Mentor office hours for skill-specific coaching.

- **Scope management issues**   Ways to help teams that are stuck or overambitious.

  - Mid-day scope check template. ("Can you deliver this by 3 PM?")
  - Minimum viable product worksheets.
  - Prioritization of demo-able features over completeness.
  - Permission to pivot if the original approach isn't working.

- **Team motivation**   How to maintain energy when teams hit roadblocks.

  - Recognition of small wins and progress.
  - Problem-solving facilitation by mentors.
  - Short energizer activities to reset focus.
  - A reminder of the hackathon's learning objectives.

- **Inclusion challenges**   Ensuring all voices and perspectives are valued.

  - Active facilitation techniques for mentors.
  - Clear expectations about respectful collaboration.

- An anonymous feedback mechanism during the event.
- Intervention protocol for serious issues.

Train mentors on when to step in versus when to let teams work through challenges independently.

By clearly defining roles and encouraging tight-knit collaboration, fusion teams can capitalize on each member's strengths. Gartner notes that fusion teams succeed through shared goals and iterative collaboration, keeping everyone focused on the product outcome. This collaborative energy is exactly what a hackathon should spark. Now, with roles defined and a clearly defined problem, the team is ready to quickly build an amazing prototype.

Prototyping phase

Most of the hackathon day is spent turning the idea into a prototype or minimum viable product (MVP). In a one-day event, the motto is "build something that works", even if it's just a starting point. This section guides how fusion teams can leverage Microsoft 365 Copilot, Copilot Studio, and Azure AI Foundry to accelerate development and achieve a demonstrable solution by the end of the day.

Solution design

Before diving into tools and starting to code, teams should outline how the Solution will work. This could be a quick flow diagram or bullet points answering:

- What is the user input or trigger? (For example, the user asks a question in a Teams chat, an email arrives, or a button is clicked in a PowerApp.)

- What AI action happens behind the scenes? (For example, Copilot analyzes documents, the agent queries a knowledge base, and an Azure AI model generates an answer.)

- What is the output? (For example, a summary is returned, a task is created, or a dashboard is updated.)

- What data or systems are involved? (For example, pulling data from SharePoint, writing to an Excel file, or using an external API.)

Keep this design super simple. Given the tools, many solutions will follow a pattern of "user asks—AI answers" or "user describes goal—AI generates draft/output." That's perfectly fine.

Setting up Copilot Studio

Copilot Studio is a powerful low-code environment for building conversational AI agents or copilots. It provides a graphical way to define dialogues, connect data, and integrate actions. Teams should use it as the central tool if their solution involves a chatbot or conversational assistant. Some of the steps they may need to take include

- **Create an environment** If not prepared ahead of time by the IT department, a team member with the appropriate access (likely the developer or Power Platform specialist) should create or open the Copilot Studio environment for the team. This might involve logging into Power Platform and launching Copilot Studio.

- **Define the agent** Give the copilot (agent) a clear identity and purpose (for example "Sales deal advisor" or "IT help desk copilot"). In Copilot Studio, they can configure the agent's persona, welcome message, and abilities.

- **Dialogues and prompts** Copilot Studio's low-code dialogue builder helps define the flow of conversations. For instance, you can specify what the bot should do when a user asks a particular question. The platform supports multi-turn dialogues, allowing for more natural interactions. For a hackathon MVP, focus on a single use case. For example, in an IT help desk chatbot, implement the dialogue for a specific task, such as when a user asks to reset their password.

- **Knowledge integration** Copilot Studio can connect to organizational knowledge or documents. If the solution requires domain knowledge, for example, an HR policy bot referencing policy docs, you could upload a sample document or connect to a data source. Azure AI Foundry can assist here by hosting or indexing knowledge data that Copilot can use. (More on Foundry is found below.)

- **Actions and plugins** Copilot Studio can integrate Power Automate flows or plugins for actions if needed. For example, a copilot could trigger a workflow (like creating a service ticket). If a team has a developer, they might make a quick custom plugin or use Power Automate to handle such actions, then link it in Copilot Studio. Given one day, only attempt this if it's crucial to the core demo.

- **Testing the agent** Teams should frequently test the copilot by simulating user queries and seeing the responses. This helps refine prompts and catch issues early. It's an iterative process—adjust the agent's prompts or logic to improve the output.

Say a fusion team was building a "Financial Report Generator Copilot." In Copilot Studio, they create an agent that asks the user what financial metrics they need and then uses a preloaded Excel file (or dummy data) to generate a summary. They define dialogues for questions like "Give me a summary of Q3 sales vs expenses" and have the copilot respond with a formatted answer, possibly instructing the agent to pull a chart via an action if time permits.

Use Microsoft 365 Copilot to aid solution development

During the solution development process, teams will have the opportunity to use Microsoft 365 Copilot across Office apps like Outlook, Word, and PowerPoint to speed up development tasks, including

- **Brainstorming and research** In Word or OneNote, ask Copilot to outline the solution approach or list potential challenges for the project. It can quickly compile information (you can even ask, "Copilot, what are the common steps to build a chatbot using Microsoft AI?").

- **Generating code snippets** While Copilot Studio is low-code, some scenarios might require code (maybe a snippet of Python, JavaScript, or a formula). If so, GitHub Copilot (in VS Code) or

M365 Copilot in an Excel formula can help generate code. For example, if a team needs a regex or a short script, an AI coding assistant can produce it quickly.

- **Documenting as you go** Teams can have a Word document where they jot down what they're building. Ask Copilot in Word to generate documentation or comments on the solution. For instance, "Explain how our chatbot workflow works step by step." This helps the team clarify their logic and produces material they can use in the presentation or handover docs.

- **Excel data analysis** If a solution involves data (such as analyzing trends), a team member could quickly dump sample data into Excel and use Copilot to get insights or generate charts. This could even be part of the hack's output (such as showing a before/after of how Copilot analysis works faster than manual).

- **PowerPoint summaries** As the project firms up, a team member can use Copilot in PowerPoint to generate a summary slide deck. For example, "Create a summary of our project: problem, solution, benefits." Copilot will draft bullets that the team can then tweak. This is a big time-saver in preparing a polished presentation under time pressure.

Leveraging Azure AI Foundry

Azure AI Foundry (formerly called Azure AI Studio) is a development hub for generative AI, offering model selection, hosting, and management in one place. In a one-day hackathon, teams won't build complex machine learning (ML) models from scratch, but Foundry can help in a few key ways:

- **Model selection** Foundry provides access to various AI models (OpenAI models, Azure Cognitive Services, and so on). A team might use it to choose a suitable generative model for their Copilot agent. For instance, if cost or speed is a concern, the Foundry gives flexibility to decide between a GPT-4 model and a smaller model. Factor in whether the necessary Azure subscriptions/keys are available.

- **Knowledge base creation** Foundry could be used to create a custom knowledge base or index, for example, by uploading a set of FAQs or product manuals to Azure AI Foundry's knowledge section. The Copilot Studio agent can then use that knowledge base to ground its answers. This might involve using an Azure Cognitive Search index or the "bring your own data" feature in Azure OpenAI via Foundry. Setting up a small index of a few documents is doable within hours and can significantly enhance the relevance of Copilot's answers.

- **Testing and debugging AI behavior** It's important to test prompts against models. Teams can paste sample prompts and see how the raw model responds. This is useful if the Copilot Studio agent isn't behaving as expected—the team can isolate whether it's the model or their prompt logic.

- **Deployment pipeline** If a team has DevOps expertise, they could use Azure AI Foundry to scope how their solution could be deployed more robustly (such as host their agent as an endpoint or integrate with an existing app). However, typically, this is out of scope for a one-day hack—it could be something to mention in the "next steps" of their presentation rather than implement on the day.

Building the minimum viable product (MVP)

Time is short, so teams should focus on getting a working demo of the primary use case. This minimum viable product isn't meant to be perfect, but rather it should demonstrate the plausibility and value of the proposed solution. Staying focused on "just enough" capabilities takes strategic thinking and ruthless prioritization. Consider these strategies:

- **Deprioritize what you can't build**   If a complex integration is needed but hard to do in one day (say, connecting to a legacy database), find a workaround. You can use a static sample data file or a fake API response for demo purposes. Your presentation would then explain the simulation, perhaps saying, "Imagine this is connected to live data." It's better to show the concept of working with fake data than to get stuck and have nothing to show.

- **Divide and conquer**   Team members can work in parallel on different pieces but integrate as early as possible. For example, one can design the copilot's dialogue while another prepares the data source. By early afternoon, they should have connected the pieces and tested them end-to-end.

- **Keep AI prompts simple**   Start with straightforward instructions when configuring prompts, the instructions the copilot uses to generate responses. Often, a simple prompt like, "You are an assistant that helps with *[task]*. The user will ask about *[topic]*, answer with *[type of answers]*." will suffice to get a decent prototype output. You can always refine as time allows.

- **Handling errors**   Be prepared that things might not work on the first try. Rather than chasing perfection, note the issue and think of how to work around it or explain it in the demo. You might constrain the demo questions to ones you know work, or mention you'd address this with more training data in the future.

Teams should aim to have a working demo by the lunch check-in or shortly after. If by midday, the team has nothing working, they should consider simplifying further. After lunch, prioritize finishing the core functionality. Use an iterative approach: build a bit, test it, refine it. It's okay if the final prototype is held together with duct tape behind the scenes as long as the front-end demo is solid.

Hacking the hackathon

The goal of the hackathon is to bring to life an innovative idea and demonstrate how it could solve a problem. Sometimes, getting the fundamentals right can distinguish winning ideas. While development often happens in Copilot Studio or Azure AI Foundry, your solution might stand out by incorporating Microsoft 365 Copilot and other copilots into the solution.

For example, a team who are building process improvement might show how Copilot in Outlook drafts an email summary of a meeting automatically or how Copilot in Excel analyzes sales data as part of the workflow. They could integrate this by having their prototype trigger an email and then using Copilot to generate content for that email. If you're building a Power App, use the Power Apps Copilot feature where you describe an app, and it builds starting screens and data tables. This can rapidly create a front end that the team can modify. For a documentation-related solution, perhaps the output is a Word report generated by Copilot.

As your development time runs out, a few thoughtful details can make all the difference. Ensure the copilot or app has some basic UX polishing—a friendly greeting from the bot, clear labels on any interface, and maybe the company logo on the app. Do a test run of the entire scenario without interruption. Find a colleague or another team to act as a user and see if they can use your prototype. Prepare a backup in case the live demo fails—screenshots or a short screen recording of the Copilot working. This can be a lifesaver if the network goes down or a service glitch occurs during the demo.

By fully utilizing tools like Copilot Studio and Azure AI Foundry, teams can achieve a lot in just a few hours. Real-world hackathons have shown teams creating custom AI copilots in 8 hours with the right guidance. The key is to blend the strengths of team members with these AI-assisted development tools. The morning's planning (whiteboarding use cases, gathering requirements) should lead into the hands-on building with Copilot Studio by midday, then publishing and testing in the afternoon. Following this flow, even a one-day hackathon will conclude with functional prototypes that showcase the art of the possible.

Presentation and demo best practices

With the prototype ready to present, the next challenge is communicating the idea and demonstrating its value quickly. These strategies will help you present your idea effectively:

- **Tell a story** Structure the presentation as a narrative. Start by reiterating the problem and why it matters. For example: "Every week, our finance team spends 10+ hours consolidating reports. We set out to reduce that." Then, introduce the solution concept: "Meet FinAssist Copilot, an AI assistant that automatically generates our weekly finance report with a single prompt." Finally, show it in action and describe the impact: "What used to take 10 hours now takes one click, freeing our team for more analysis." Storytelling helps judges and the audience relate to the use case.

- **Demo functionality live** If possible, do a live demo of the key functionality. Seeing the copilot respond to a query in real-time or click through a Power App gives credibility. Practice the live demo multiple times. It can help to have one person drive the demo while another narrates. Prepare specific inputs that you know showcase your solution well. Avoid unpredictable inputs during the live demo.

- **Have a backup plan** Technology can fail, especially under pressure. Have screenshots or a short video as a fallback. If something breaks, you can still describe what would have happened and show a screenshot of the expected output. Judges appreciate preparation, and you won't lose many points for a hiccup if you handle it gracefully and still convey the concept of your solution.

- **Highlight the Copilot magic** Ensure the audience notices where Copilot is making a difference. This reinforces the innovative aspect of the project. If relevant, mention the specific tech: "This uses Microsoft 365 Copilot inside Teams and a custom plugin we built in Copilot Studio," shows you made good use of the tools provided.

- **Keep it visually simple** For slide decks, less is more. A few slides—perhaps one on the problem and one on your solution approach/architecture—are enough besides the demo. If you have metrics or a cost-benefit, put that on a summary slide. Use easy-to-read fonts and include images or diagrams of your solution. If you have time, whip up a quick architecture diagram showing how the Copilot Studio agent connects to Azure AI Foundry to impress the technically minded judges.

- **Time management in presentation** Stay within the time limit. It's better to leave time for a judge to ask a question than to have your final point cut off. Practice the timing during your dry run. If you have multiple team members speaking, coordinate transitions to avoid awkward pauses or talking over each other.

- **Answering questions** Judges may ask about how you built it, what security considerations it has, or how it could be extended. Let the person with the relevant expertise answer. For example, the developer can answer a question about technical implementation, and the business lead can answer one about return on investment (ROI). If you don't know an answer or time ran out to implement something, it's fine to say, "Given more time, we would do..." to show you have considered the next steps.

- **Demo environment prep** Before presentations start, if using a shared screen or projector, have everything preopened and logged in on the demo machine. Disable notifications that might pop up. Close unrelated apps to avoid distractions. Streamline the experience so that when you start, you're already where you need to be—have the chat window open with the Copilot ready or the app loaded to the main screen.

- **Enthusiasm and teamwork** Show that you're excited about what you built. A positive, energetic delivery can sometimes sway hearts even if the prototype isn't perfect. Also, acknowledge team members' contributions during the presentation. This highlights the fusion team aspect and how you worked collaboratively.

Remember, the presentation is when your day's work comes to life for everyone else. You maximize your chances of impressing the judges by clearly communicating the problem, demonstrating the solution's capabilities, and emphasizing the value it creates.

Judging criteria and success metrics

Having well-defined judging criteria is essential to ensure fairness and alignment with the goals of the hackathon. Here are some common criteria and metrics that you can adopt or customize for your hackathon.

Judging criteria

It's a good idea to share these with participants up front, so they know what to focus on.

- **Innovation and creativity** How original or creative is the solution? Does it use AI or Copilot in a novel way? Judges will look for ideas that aren't just slight tweaks of existing tools but really rethink a process or solve a problem in a new manner. Even if two teams tackled similar problems, a unique approach (like integrating multiple services or the unexpected use of Copilot) could score higher on innovation.

- **Technical execution**   Did the team successfully build a working prototype or proof-of-concept? How well does it work? This includes the complexity of what was achieved; for example, using a custom plugin in Copilot Studio or integrating an Azure AI model might show technical depth. However, execution is not just about complexity—a simple and rock-solid solution might be valued over a complex one that barely runs. Judges will consider the degree of functionality achieved in one day, code or configuration quality, and clever problem-solving techniques.

- **User experience and design**   Is the solution user-friendly and well-designed for the intended audience? This covers the UI of any app or the conversational flow of a chatbot. A smooth, intuitive experience, for example, the bot understands natural language nicely, or the app has a clean interface, will earn points. Also, judges will consider how well the team considered the end-user's journey. If the demo showed a clear use case from the user's perspective without confusion, that's a plus.

- **Business value and impact**   Does the prototype address a significant business problem, and if implemented, would it create real value? Judges assess the potential impact on the business, from time savings to cost reduction and revenue opportunities to improved customer satisfaction. The team should quantify or convincingly explain the benefits to the organization. For example, "This could save each sales rep 5 hours per week" or "This improves compliance by reducing report errors". A hackathon solution doesn't need a detailed ROI calculation but should target a meaningful pain point.

- **Use of tools**   Since this hack is specifically about using M365 Copilot, Copilot Studio, and Azure AI Foundry, judges will consider how well the team leveraged them. Did they fully utilize Copilot Studio features? Did they incorporate M365 Copilot or Azure AI services in a way that enhanced the solution?

- **Fusion team collaboration**   You can include points for how well the team embodied cross-functional collaboration. Signs of this include a balanced presentation where different team members speak to their area of input, or the solution having both technical and business considerations, and a mention of how they worked together. Judges consider if a team was composed of only one discipline and ignored either the tech complexity or the business need.

- **Presentation and communication**   How effectively did the team communicate their project? A great idea that is poorly explained can be lost to a good idea that is well explained. Clarity, enthusiasm, and the ability to answer questions are important.

Judges will score each criterion on a 1–5 or 1–10 scale, or you could allocate more weight to priority areas. Use score sheets to rate each team, then add up or deliberate qualitatively.

Quantifying the success of the hackathon

Define the metrics you will measure and evaluate to understand the impact of the hackathon.

For the solutions, encourage teams to mention one key metric their solution would improve (such as "Reduce customer onboarding time by 30 percent" or "Handle 100 support queries per day automatically"). They likely won't have real data in one day, but framing the success metric shows they thought of how to measure value. They could also highlight solution quality by measuring how well their AI works. For example, if they tested their Copilot with 10 sample questions, report as a percentage of how many were answered correctly.

In some hackathons, if time permits, teams may have another department member try their prototype and give feedback. This feedback can be included in their presentation (such as, "Our HR VP tested the bot and said the answers were relevant and saved her time"). This can be a persuasive qualitative metric.

For the hackathon event itself, organizers can gauge success by reporting on

- **Participation numbers** How many teams/participants? Cross-functional representation based on the number of departments represented.

- **Prototypes delivered** The number of projects that achieved a demo-able state—ideally, 100 percent of teams will produce something tangible.

- **Post-hack continuation** How many projects get picked up for further development—success isn't just winning, but also whether ideas live on. More on this in the next section.

- **Employee satisfaction** You might measure this via a postevent survey: Did participants find it valuable, learn new skills, feel more engaged with AI tools?

- **Adoption metrics** Track increased adoption of Copilot by reporting on metrics like new Copilot agents created or increased usage in subsequent weeks.

Having clear success criteria and encouraging teams to think about measurable outcomes ensure that the hackathon projects are grounded in real impact. This also helps convince management of the value that hackathons create.

Awards and recognition

It's important to celebrate success. Publicly acknowledging achievements helps motivate teams and keeps the AI innovation momentum going. Even though the event is short, people put in a lot of creative energy. Recognition validates that effort.

In addition to an overall first, second, or third place, consider giving out fun or specific category awards to spread the recognition. Awards might include

- "Most Innovative Solution" for the team that created the most creative approach

- "Best Use of Copilot/Azure AI" for the team that really showcased the tech well

- "Best User Experience" for the smoothest and most user-friendly solution

- "Fusion Team Spirit" for exemplary cross-department collaboration

- "People's Choice" for the audience or participants' favorite, determined through voting

These awards can be announced along with or instead of rank-ordered winners.

Prizes don't need to be lavish, especially for an internal hackathon, but a token of appreciation is nice. Participants appreciate trophies, gift cards, an extra day off, or even experiential rewards like lunch with an executive or a training/conference opportunity. Even certificates or public kudos can suffice if the budget is small. Tailor prizes to your organization's culture and to what motivates your people.

Make the award announcement moment exciting with drumrolls (figuratively), applause, and photos. Have a respected leader present the prize in person. If virtual, do it in a celebratory Teams meeting or via a well-crafted announcement post. Highlight what each winning team did well and why it stood out. This not only celebrates the winners but also reinforces what "good" looks like to everyone. Offer to share judges' feedback with teams. This can be done in a brief written form or a feedback session. Teams will appreciate knowing what was strong, where they could improve, or what to consider if developing further.

While not everyone can win, try to showcase every team's work. Create a hackathon SharePoint page listing all projects, their problem statement, a one-minute video or screenshots, and team members. This archive shows the breadth of innovation. Share this link with the whole company if appropriate, so the hackathon's impact is visible beyond just the participants. Use internal social platforms like Teams or Viva Engage to congratulate winners and participants. Acknowledge all the teams by name. This public recognition can inspire those who didn't participate to join next time and signal that innovation is celebrated. If your company is open to sharing a story on an external blog or LinkedIn (without revealing confidential details), it can also spotlight your innovative culture.

Explicitly encourage teams to continue working on their projects if there's interest. Provide opportunities for them to pitch their ideas to the relevant department leaders to request support.

Post-hackathon: Sustaining momentum

The hackathon might end in a day, but its impact can be prolonged through deliberate follow-up actions. Many great hackathon ideas fizzle out if not captured and nurtured. These strategies can help you capitalize on the event's energy:

- **Project continuation plans** For each team, especially the winners or any promising concepts, discuss what it would take to turn the prototype into a production solution or a pilot. Ask teams to document what they'd need (resources, time, data access, and so on) to keep going. Arrange follow-up meetings between the teams and the relevant stakeholders across IT and other departments.

- **Allocate time or resources**   One of the most significant barriers to continuing a hackathon project is that people return to their day jobs and have no time. If the company can afford it, allocate some innovation time for teams to develop their hackathon projects further. For example, allow the winning team to spend one day a week for the next month to build out the solution, or give them a small budget to engage with a developer or designer.

- **Link to ongoing initiatives**   See if the hackathon solutions align with ongoing projects or strategic initiatives. The hackathon output could be folded into a larger project's scope, giving it a pathway to production with proper backing.

- **Mentorship and ownership**   For promising projects, assign an executive sponsor or mentor. This person can check progress, help remove roadblocks, and advocate for the project. Knowing leaders care about their idea keeps the team accountable and motivated.

- **Technical handoff**   If some team members need to roll off the project, ensure knowledge is captured. All code, configurations, and documentation from the hack should be stored in a repository or saved in a shared location. This way, others can pick it up even if the original hackers can't continue.

- **Show and tell**   Organize a follow-up demo day a month or two later to see how hackathon projects have progressed. This can be a low-key session where teams share updates or final outcomes. It provides a goal to work towards. It's also an opportunity to invite more stakeholders, including end users who would benefit from the solution, to share feedback.

- **Incorporate into product backlog**   If you have an internal product management process or an IT backlog for enhancements, formalize the best hackathon ideas by writing them up as proposals or user stories in those systems. This way, it's tracked, not forgotten, and can be prioritized appropriately.

- **Encourage community of practice**   The hackathon likely introduced people to new tools like Copilot Studio or Azure AI Foundry. Create a community for those interested in continuing to learn and share experiences with building AI solutions. Participants can become department champions, helping others try Copilot or low-code AI development. This peer network can sustain the learning aspect beyond the hack.

- **Survey and iterate**   Get feedback from the participants about the hackathon itself. What went well, and what could be improved? Use this to plan future hackathons. People may want a two-day hackathon next time, more training on the tools, or different judging criteria. Continuous improvement will make each subsequent event better.

- **Promote success stories**   When a hackathon project does turn into a successful solution (even a small pilot), publicize it internally. This validates the hackathon as a source of innovation. It also motivates more folks to participate, knowing ideas can become a reality next time.

- **Recognize continued effort**   If teams continue to work on their solution in the weeks after, acknowledge that, too. Give them a small follow-up reward or a shout-out in a department or all-company meeting.

In essence, treat the one-day hackathon as Day 1 of a journey for these projects, not a one-off event. The hackathon generates excitement, ideas, and prototypes; now, the goal is to channel that into lasting value. By providing a framework and support for follow-up, you ensure the innovative spark doesn't fade out. Even if only one or two ideas make it to production, that can significantly impact the business and justify the effort to host a hackathon.

Gather your fusion teams

A one-day fusion team hackathon is a fast-paced but incredibly rewarding way to ignite innovation in your organization. By thoughtfully planning the event, fostering a collaborative cross-functional environment, and equipping teams with powerful tools like Microsoft 365 Copilot, Copilot Studio, and Azure AI Foundry, you enable the creation of solutions that might otherwise take weeks or months to materialize. The structured approach in this playbook—from pre-event preparation and problem framing to development, presentation, and follow-up—is designed to maximize both the immediate outcomes (working prototypes, new skills learned, employee enthusiasm) and the long-term benefits (accelerated AI adoption, improved processes, a culture of continuous improvement).

Keep in mind that every hackathon is a learning experience. Don't be afraid to adapt the playbook to your company's unique culture and needs. The ultimate measure of success is how polished the minimum viable products (MVPs) are at demo time and how much the event energizes participants to think creatively and work together in new ways. When business users and technologists unite towards a common goal, the fusion of their perspectives can yield truly transformative ideas.

With this playbook, you can confidently organize a one-day hackathon that runs smoothly and produces impactful results. So, gather your fusion teams, set the stage for innovation, and let the hacking begin— you'll be amazed at what can be accomplished in just one day when the right people and AI tools are brought together in the spirit of experimentation and fun. Good luck, and happy hacking!

Microsoft 365 Copilot beginner promptathon playbook

In this appendix, you will:

- Understand what a promptathon event is and how it can be used to quickly give a practical opportunity to collect ideas for Copilot prompts that will create value in your organization.

- Learn how to engage beginner Copilot users in a live learning environment that will develop their AI literacy and connect them with other motivated, AI curious people across your organization.

When leading AI adoption efforts, it's important to create a moment for theory to become practice, so that people stop talking about possibilities and start using Copilot in the flow of real work. For Microsoft 365 Copilot, that catalyst is the promptathon: a short, high-energy event where cross-functional teams experiment with AI prompting against live business scenarios, share what works, and turn their discoveries into repeatable prompt guides that others in the organization can use.

Unlike a traditional hackathon, where the currency is code, a promptathon trades in language. Participants iterate on the words, context, and guardrails that persuade Copilot to produce its best work, whether that's generating a client-ready slide deck, summarizing a 50-page contract, or quickly drafting personalized emails. Because prompts are developed using natural language that people speak and write every day, not code, the format levels the playing field, drawing out expertise not only from IT but also from finance, legal, operations, and frontline teams. The real power, however, lies in the compound effect. Each prompt perfected during promptathons becomes a reusable asset in your internal prompt library, accelerating adoption long after the event is over. Promptathons offer an opportunity to grow Copilot proficiency across your organization and gain insight into high-value use cases, data governance needs, and the culture shifts required for adopting AI responsibly.

This playbook, provided in three parts, outlines how to organize internal promptathon events for Microsoft 365 Copilot adoption, using a "crawl, walk, run" model to address beginner, intermediate, and advanced skill levels. These events aim to build Copilot skills, spark innovation, engage users, and drive feature adoption. By implementing this graduated approach to running promptathons, you give your people the opportunity to develop practical, applied skills that will help them get more value out of Copilot.

- **Beginner promptathons** These "crawl" events introduce and excite employees about Copilot, turning novices into enabled users.

- **Intermediate promptathons** These "walk" events develop skills further and translate enthusiasm into practical solutions and use cases, building confidence and community.

- **Advanced promptathons** These "run" hackathons build on momentum to harness the full creative power of your advanced users to drive innovation and tangible business value while cementing a culture of collaboration and continuous learning.

This crawl–walk–run model ensures that employees at every skill level are included and nurtured. It follows change management best practices by starting small, demonstrating quick wins, and scaling up ambition as competency grows. Along the way, you solve immediate problems and foster an innovative mindset where employees feel empowered to leverage AI in their work. This guide covers goals, formats, planning checklists, best practices for running effective events that are tailored for your organization's capability, plus considerations for in-person, virtual, and hybrid facilitation.

Copilot promptathons for beginners

This entry-level event is for employees with little to no experience with Microsoft 365 Copilot. The "crawl" stage focuses on awareness and basic skills for beginners. It's a guided session (or series of sessions) that lays a solid foundation by familiarizing participants with what Copilot can do and an understanding of how to use prompts effectively.

Goals and outcomes

First, define what you are aiming to achieve with the promptathon for beginners. Setting specific goals about the outcomes you want the events to deliver will help you secure the necessary support of your leadership team. At the beginner stage, these goals might include:

- **Growing awareness of Copilot** Introduce what Microsoft 365 Copilot is and how it can help in day-to-day work. The primary goal is to drive awareness of Copilot's capabilities through hands-on exposure.

- **Build confidence with basic prompts** Teach participants the fundamentals of prompt writing—clearly stating the goal, providing context or data, specifying tone or format. By understanding what Copilot is capable of and how to instruct it, users gain the confidence to try it independently.

- **Discover simple use cases** Help employees identify one or two achievable, valuable use cases in their work where Copilot could save time or improve output. Rather than tackling complicated processes, the event highlights simple prompts like "summarize this report" or "draft a meeting agenda" so that each participant leaves with a shortlist of basic Copilot scenarios they can use immediately.

- **Positive mindset and engagement** Alleviate any apprehension about using AI. Emphasize that Copilot is a tool to assist them and not a replacement for their jobs. Encourage curiosity and reduce fear by showing practical examples so that participants are excited and motivated to continue exploring Copilot after the session.

Focus for a beginner promptathon

A live, hands-on workshop works well for beginners who are new to Copilot or just learning to prompt. This training session can include an introduction to AI and Copilot concepts, a live demo, and a guided tutorial where attendees follow along using M365 Copilot on their laptops or phones. Include a short prompting masterclass to teach what makes an effective prompt, then let users practice. The atmosphere should be supportive and noncompetitive.

Set a simple and inviting theme. For example, "Meet Your AI Assistant" or "Copilot Kickstart Lab". The theme should highlight that what people will learn will help with everyday work tasks. You might frame the session around "a day in the life with Copilot," showing how Copilot can make it easier to get higher quality work done, whether that's writing an email, drafting a document, or analyzing data.

Content to cover

Start with a foundational overview of Copilot. Demonstrate how Copilot works across a few Microsoft 365 apps. For example, have Copilot draft an email reply in Outlook or summarize a Word document. This provides a "wow" moment and grounds abstract AI concepts in concrete examples that people will find easy to follow and understand. It also delivers early on the promised "practical application" part of the workshop. Other content might include:

- **Prompt construction** Explain the components of a quality prompt: goal, context, source, and expectations. For instance, teach them to specify what they want to achieve, any background context or source material, and the desired tone or format for the output. See the Prompt Ingredients Handout in the Copilot Success Kit at https://adoption.microsoft.com/en-gb/copilot/success-kit/.

- **Interactive prompt-along** Give participants a chance to try it themselves. Provide a simple exercise, such as "Open a document and ask Copilot to create a summary" or "Use Copilot in Teams to draft a welcome message for a new hire." Walk through it together so everyone experiences a small win for themselves.

- **Prompt tips and tricks** Share a few beginner tips to set them up for success. Let people know that if the first response isn't useful, they may need to add more context or ask Copilot to refine the answer based on a different source. Cover the importance of clarity in prompts and what to do if Copilot says it cannot assist.

- **Q&A and troubleshooting** Invite questions as participants practice. Be ready to turn common issues, for example, if Copilot is not enabled or misunderstanding a prompt, into live teaching moments so everyone learns from them.

As an optional way to keep things light, you could include a mini-challenge or game. For example, a "Copilot Haiku" challenge where you ask participants to have Copilot generate a fun haiku about your company or team. This reinforces learning playfully and shows how people can be creative with AI. This is a good opportunity to hand out a spot prize and perhaps create an engaging highlight to share after the promptathon to boost engagement with future sessions.

Delivery formats: In-person, virtual, hybrid

Promptathons are a quick, scalable way to engage beginner Copilot users across your organization because they can be delivered in-person, online, or as a hybrid event. Each format has advantages:

- **In-person** Ideal for a hands-on introductory workshop. Being in the same room makes it easy for facilitators to assist attendees in real-time, especially those who run into setup issues or need extra help. It fosters personal connection and focus, since people are less likely to multi-task. Set up a training room with a projector for demos and ensure everyone brings a laptop. Small group breakouts can be done at tables, and facilitators can circulate. For an in-person beginner session, have coaches who will roam around the room to help individuals with Copilot issues one-on-one.

- **Virtual** A virtual workshop, delivered via a Microsoft Teams meeting, can reach a wider audience across locations. It requires different activities to keep it interactive, but it can be very effective. Use features like screen sharing, live chat Q&A, and breakout rooms for small-group practice. Pay extra attention to ice-breaker activities that get people talking early to engage participants. Assign a moderator to watch the chat and flag questions. Encourage participants to use Copilot during the call, perhaps asking for a summary of the call so far or bullet points of the best tips shared. In virtual sessions, encourage the use of the chat or emoji reactions to get quick feedback—for example, "Were you able to get a summary? Give a thumbs up". This keeps people engaged. Also, consider recording the session for those who couldn't attend.

- **Hybrid** If some participants are together in a room and others are remote, plan carefully to ensure inclusion. Use a conference room with good audio/video so remote folks can hear questions and participate equally. Have one facilitator dedicated to the online attendees—monitoring their questions and responding in the chat. The in-room facilitator can intentionally throw to the remote participants for activities, rather than only selecting people in the room. A hybrid approach can maximize inclusivity and flexibility, allowing people to join in whatever way works best for them.

Regardless of the delivery format you choose, it's important to test all technology beforehand (audio, screen sharing) and be ready early so that any access issues can be solved before the workshop starts. Ask remote participants to join early. During exercises, consider pairing in-person and remote people in mixed breakout groups so everyone interacts.

Recommended duration

For a beginner workshop, allocate enough time to cover the basics without overwhelming your audience. Typically, sessions for Copilot beginners run for between an hour and a half up to three hours. Two hours works as a sweet spot because it allows 25 minutes for the introductory concepts and initial demonstration, 50 minutes of guided hands-on exercises, 20 minutes for questions, and 10 minutes to close with a recap of the concepts covered. An extra 15 minutes can be allocated for short breaks as needed. If you have a large group or many questions, consider extending the duration to three hours with longer breaks. Ensure you have at least one short break if the session exceeds 90 minutes to maintain focus.

In a live session, move at a pace suitable for novices. It might feel slow to tech-savvy facilitators, but it's important not to lose anyone. This beginner workshop is about level-setting—facilitators should aim to create sufficient psychological safety so that the group is comfortable asking questions they've been holding back when it comes to AI. Build in a few extra minutes for people to find features or recover from mistakes (like being in the wrong window). If the group is smaller, you can adjust the pace based on their specific needs and capabilities. Build in checkpoints throughout the session to get a sense of whether people are happy with the pace or whether there's an appetite to slow down (or speed up).

If schedules are tight, you could split the content into two shorter sessions. For example, it can work well to run the beginner promptathon as two one-hour sessions on different days—one for an introduction to Copilot and a demonstration, one for hands-on practice. This can help with virtual delivery across time zones as well. However, giving participants an opportunity to apply what they've learned straight away often works best to embed the learning with hands-on experience.

While the main event might be short in the case of beginners' promptathons, remind participants it's just a starting point and encourage them to continue practicing afterward. For example, you could schedule optional "office hours" for later that week, so that people can drop in virtually to ask more questions as they try Copilot independently.

Planning checklist and timeline

Planning a beginner promptathon is relatively straightforward, but preparation ensures a smooth and valuable experience for attendees. This guide provides the steps you should take in the weeks before and on the day of your promptathon for beginners.

Four to six weeks before the promptathon

Start planning your event four to six weeks in advance so that you can secure the necessary sponsorship and support. Steps in this phase include:

- **Secure buy-in and sponsorship** Get support from a department leader or the manager of the team. A senior leader championing the promptathon, whether sending the invite or saying a few opening words reinforces its importance. Leadership support can also help ensure employees prioritize attending.

- **Team roles** You need one person to organize the promptathon and another to facilitate and lead the session. Identify additional support coaches, at least one for every 10–15 participants. Assign technical support contacts to handle any access issues. If delivery is hybrid or virtual, it's also a good idea to assign a chat moderator.

- **Schedule the event** Choose a date and time that maximizes attendance. Avoid peak vacation times or critical business deadlines. Aim for a time of day when attendees can give full attention, for example, mid-morning or after lunch.

- **Logistics**   If in-person, book a room with the necessary A/V equipment. If virtual, set up the Teams meeting and any registration link if needed. For hybrid, do both.

- **Copilot access**   Coordinate with IT to ensure all participants will have Microsoft 365 Copilot enabled on their accounts by the event date. Note that this might involve license assignment. Verify any network settings, so Copilot features work on the company network.

Two or three weeks before the promptathon

Announce the promptathon for beginners, invite attendees, and prepare the content.

- **Invitations**   Send a save-the-date invitation with an enticing description. Explain the purpose (such as learning how to make Copilot work for you) and who should attend (such as anyone new to Copilot—no prior experience needed). Include the schedule and a reminder to bring their laptops with Office apps installed and Copilot enabled. Use multiple internal channels to promote the promptathon, for example, email, intranet, and Teams posts, to reach the target audience.

- **Presurvey (optional)**   You might survey registrants on their current Copilot knowledge or collect any specific questions they have. This can help you tailor the content.

- **Prepare the content**   Start creating the slide deck or demo script. Gather example documents or data to use in demonstrations; make sure they are nonsensitive sample data. For instance, make a dummy one-page report to summarize or an example email thread to identify tasks from. If planning a live demo, rehearse it to ensure your prompt works as expected, though also be ready to adapt if Copilot gives unexpected results in the live demo.

- **Custom handouts**   Prepare a cheat sheet or quick start guide for Copilot. This could include prompt examples and tips. Ideally, you should create resources that are tailored for your organization so that attendees can take this away for reference.

> **Tip**   The Copilot Success Kit includes training resources and handouts that you can use and adapt for your organization when running promptathons. Find them at *https://adoption.microsoft.com/en-gb/copilot/success-kit/*.

One week before the promptathon

In the week before the event, focus on final checks and building excitement among attendees.

- **Technology check**   Do a dry run of any technical elements. For in-person, test the Internet connection, the projector and screen or monitor, and be sure that Copilot works on the demo machine. For virtual, test screen sharing of the Copilot window, and ensure your account has Copilot responses ready. For hybrid, test the meeting equipment in the room as well as the live connectivity for remote attendees.

- **Event reminder**   Send a reminder to participants with any preparatory steps. For example, to check if they can see the Copilot icon in Word and Excel, and if not to contact IT before the session. Reattach the invite or agenda.

- **Content review**   Finalize slides and run through the content flow as a team. Ensure facilitators and coaches know their roles so that presenters know which parts they are leading, and coaches understand when to answer questions.

Day of beginner promptathon

Make the most of all the work that has gone into organizing the promptathon by getting the last-minute set up right.

- **Setup**   For in-person promptathons, arrive early to set up the room, have sign-in sheets ready (if using), and test the A/V again. For virtual promptathons, start the Teams meeting 10–15 minutes early to welcome people and iron out any audio issues. Have your sample files ready to share.

- **Opening**   Have the executive sponsor or facilitator open the session and introduce the objectives and agenda. Set ground rules that quickly create psychological safety and reiterate that it's okay to ask questions; this is a safe learning space where everyone can learn from each other. If it's a small group, consider an ice-breaker like asking each person to introduce themselves and share one task they wish Copilot could help with.

- **During the event**   Follow the agenda and content flow. Coaches should actively assist anyone who may be struggling. Keep an eye on time for each part of the session and remember to offer short breaks so participants can refocus.

- **Closing**   Recap key concepts covered. Encourage everyone to continue experimenting with Copilot. Provide information on where to get help or learn more—perhaps an internal Copilot FAQ site or Microsoft Learn courses. Thank attendees for participating and coaches for helping.

Post-promptathon activities

After the event, it's important to help participants continue their learning and to highlight to executive sponsors the impact of the promptathon.

- **Follow-up email**   Send participants a thank-you note. Attach or link the cheat sheet, a recording (if virtual), and a Microsoft Copilot quick prompt guide for further learning. Reiterate where people can get more help and keep learning.

- **Feedback**   Include a short survey link to gather feedback on the session. Ask people what they found most useful and what they'd like to do next with Copilot.

- **Support forum**   Invite participants to join an internal Copilot user community if you have one. If not, consider setting up a Teams channel or using Viva Engage as a forum for people to continue asking questions and sharing tips as they use Copilot. Creating a community space helps sustain engagement beyond the promptathon.

- **Metrics collection** Note the number of attendees, gather the feedback results, and document any anecdotal success stories observed during the promptathon. This information will help demonstrate the event's impact and help plan the next version.

Technical setup and support requirements

These technical setup and support considerations will create a smooth event experience for participants and help make your promptathon a success:

- **Licenses and access** Verify that each participant has an active Microsoft 365 Copilot license and access to their account. This is crucial; nothing will disengage a beginner faster than discovering Copilot isn't working for them. If Copilot is still in the limited rollout, work with IT or the program team to get at least a trial or temporary access for all invited users.

- **Devices and software** Ensure everyone has installed and updated the required applications. For example, they should be running the latest version of Office apps that include Copilot integration or access to Teams if demonstrating Copilot there. If using company laptops, this is likely done automatically, but double-check if any updates or plugins are needed. For virtual attendees, provide instructions on how to split screen or use two devices (one to watch the demo and one to try Copilot) if feasible.

- **Demo environment** The facilitator's demo account should have appropriate data to showcase Copilot. You might load some sample emails or documents into that account beforehand. Avoid using actual confidential company data in demos—use sanitized or dummy content that still looks realistic.

- **Network and permissions** Confirm that no corporate firewall or network policy blocks the Copilot service. If any participants are remote on VPN, ensure the performance is acceptable. It's a good idea to test Copilot in the target environment ahead of time because some features might depend on data availability or permissions. For example, if demonstrating Copilot with SharePoint content, ensure the demo account has access to the example SharePoint site.

- **Support on standby** Have IT support on call (or present) during the event, especially at the start. A support person can troubleshoot login issues or license assignments quickly so the session isn't derailed.

- **Backup plan** Sometimes, the AI might behave unpredictably, perhaps experiencing a long latency or an outage. Prepare a backup activity in case Copilot is unresponsive at that moment. For instance, you could have screenshots of the output or shift into a discussion mode about use cases until it returns. It's rare, but being prepared will help you handle any service hiccups smoothly.

- **Privacy and data guidance** Remind participants of company guidelines for using Copilot. Since Copilot works with organizational data, they should use work documents or safe content during practice. At this beginner stage, they likely won't input sensitive personal data, but it's good to reaffirm data security policies. Microsoft 365 Copilot respects data labels (for example, it will warn if trying to use a confidential document), so mention that feature to build trust that safeguards are in place.

- **Materials and tools** If the session is virtual or hybrid, ensure the meeting platform supports the activities. For example, breakout rooms are enabled if you plan to use them, and everyone can access the chat. Provide any required links upfront, such as shared collaboration boards or surveys.

Engagement strategies: Before, during, after

Keeping participants engaged is critical, especially for a voluntary learning event. Tailor your engagement tactics before, during, and after the promptathon.

Pre-event engagement

In the lead-up to the event, your communications should be regular and clear. People should know what to expect from the promptathon and how to prepare.

- **Teaser communications** Spark interest by showing the value of Copilot. Explain why they should care: perhaps share a statistic or anecdote like, "Employees in our pilot program saved 30 percent of their time on reports using Copilot." Keep the tone enthusiastic and focused on how it helps them.

- **Leverage internal champions** If some employees or leaders have used Copilot, ask them to give a quick endorsement. A respected colleague's perspective can motivate others to attend. You might include snippets in invitation emails or short promo videos.

- **Countdown and reminders** In the days leading up to the promptathon, send a countdown email or chat message, such as, "Only 3 days until the Copilot Promptathon! Tip: Did you know Copilot can summarize long threads in Outlook? Come learn this and more." These reminders build anticipation and also provide mini-education points.

- **Address fear of the unknown** Some people may be hesitant about AI. In communications, reassure them that no coding or special skills are required and that the promptathon is a safe space to learn by doing. If there are concerns about AI (like job impact), consider addressing that head-on by asking your executive sponsor to share the organization's vision for AI and approach to using it.

Engagement during the event

Varying the pace and activities during the promptathon will help keep participants engaged.

- **Interactive delivery** Make the session interactive from the start. Ask the group questions like, "What tasks do you dislike that we might automate?", to get them thinking. During the demo, pause and ask attendees to predict what Copilot will do or to suggest a prompt together.

- **Real-time support and encouragement** Celebrate small wins. If someone shares that Copilot successfully summarized their document, take the win and celebrate as a group. Coaches should wander the room and be ready to help when someone encounters a challenge. Share lessons that are helpful for the whole group, keep the atmosphere positive, and welcome any questions.

- **Multimedia and gamification** Use visuals or live polls to keep people actively engaged. For example, run a quick survey: "Did Copilot's response meet your expectations? 👍 Yes / 👎 Not quite." If time permits, incorporate a mini-game from prompt engineering lore. For example, show a "bad prompt versus good prompt" and let them spot the differences. Some teams have even created GenAI games where players try to break the AI or solve puzzles. For a beginner session, a light version might ask Copilot something out of scope to illustrate limitations in a fun way. Ensure any such activity remains friendly and aligned with learning.

- **Maintain pace and attention** Keep an eye on engagement. If people seem quiet, ask questions or for feedback on the task: "If you've gotten a result from Copilot, type 'Done' in the chat!" or "Anyone need help? Please let us know." Use breaks wisely; a stretch and quick stroll at the halfway point can refresh the group.

Post-event engagement

The learning doesn't stop after the promptathon; in fact, it's only the beginning. Amplify the impact by:

- **Community building** After the event, funnel the enthusiasm into a community. For example, create a "Copilot Tips" Teams channel and invite attendees to join. Seed it with a question or two: "What's the first thing you plan to try with Copilot tomorrow?" to encourage people to start sharing. The goal is to keep people talking about Copilot and helping each other. A user group or prompt library can start with these attendees, who will quickly progress from beginner to intermediate Copilot users.

- **Recognition** Celebrate participation to reinforce value. You could list the participants or departments involved in an internal newsletter or Teams channel. If any participant had a notable success, ask permission to share that story to demonstrate real impact.

- **Follow-up challenges** To sustain momentum, consider issuing a small follow-up challenge or call to action. For instance, "This week, try using Copilot for at least one task you'd normally do manually. Then share your experience in the Copilot Tips channel!" Giving a concrete next step will encourage them to continue using what they learned in the promptathon.

- **Office hours and mentoring** Offer ongoing support. Perhaps schedule biweekly open Q&A sessions ("Copilot Coffee Breaks") where anyone can ask advanced questions. Encourage those who have become confident to assist peers—this could be the start of your internal network of Copilot champions.

- **Bridge to next level** Tease the next stage—now they can crawl, the next step is to "walk". An intermediate promptathon helps take people's Copilot skills to the next level. Let beginners know how they can continue their Copilot learning journey.

Evaluation metrics and feedback mechanisms

To measure the success of a beginner promptathon and gather insights for improvement, put in place some metrics and feedback loops. These might include:

- **Attendance and participation** Record the number of people invited or registered and the number who attended. Note the drop-off, if any, and the level of participation during the session, for example, "80 percent of attendees tried at least one prompt during the workshop". High engagement is a good sign; the format might need tweaking if a lot of participants were disengaged.

- **Survey feedback** Use a quick post-event survey to gauge satisfaction and quality of learning. Ask participants to rate their confidence in using Copilot before and after the session on a 1–5 scale. Ideally, you will see a jump after the session. Ask what they found most useful and if they have any suggestions. This qualitative feedback can reveal whether the demo was too fast, or the content was too basic or advanced. To measure interest in the intermediate promptathon, include a question like, "Would you like to attend more advanced Copilot sessions?"

- **Knowledge/skill checks** If appropriate, do a straightforward quiz either at the end of the workshop or in the survey. This can reinforce key points and also indicate knowledge uptake.

- **Immediate outcomes** Track any tangible outcomes from the session. Note how many new users ran Copilot for the first time during the promptathon. If you have telemetry data, measure unique users of Copilot in the org before and after. If not, ask in the survey, "Did you use Copilot for the first time today?".

- **Collect a few anecdotes** Did someone create something valuable with Copilot during the workshop (such as "Jane got a solid draft of her project outline using Copilot in OneNote")? These stories are valuable evidence of impact.

- **Follow-up usage metrics** In the weeks after, if you have any way to measure Copilot usage (such as the number of Copilot prompts or active users), see if there's an uptick in the group that attended. Even a rough indicator, like increased queries to the internal Copilot support channel, counts as positive engagement.

- **Community growth** If you set up a Copilot user group or channel, track membership and activity post-event. Active questions or shared tips from attendees indicate that the promptathon succeeded in sparking ongoing interest.

- **Feedback loop to planning** Hold an internal debrief with the event team. Review what went well and what didn't. Check the feedback survey for common themes. Use this to refine future beginner-level sessions or to inform the content for the intermediate promptathon. Also, celebrate your team's accomplishment; this was the first step in a larger journey!

- **Alignment with goals** Finally, evaluate against the initial goals. If the goal was Copilot awareness, did awareness increase? You might find that now those employees can at least describe what Copilot does, whereas before, they couldn't. If the goal was getting them to try Copilot, did they? If they attended the session and participated in the exercises, then that's progress.

Document these results to demonstrate value to stakeholders. It will also help justify resources for running additional beginner prompathons for more teams, as well as securing the buy-in necessary to progress to intermediate and advanced promptathons. Microsoft's official guidance emphasizes measuring outcomes and engagement after events to plan the next steps in adoption.

By carefully evaluating the impact of the beginner promptathon, you'll gather data and momentum to fuel the next phase. Now that employees have learned to "crawl" with Copilot, they'll be ready to "walk" and take things up a notch in intermediate promptathon events.

Microsoft 365 Copilot intermediate promptathon playbook

In this appendix, you will:

- Learn how to run an intermediate-level promptathon to help employees deepen their Copilot skills and take their prompts to the next level.

- Discover strategies to create a learning experience to engage intermediate Copilot users across departments in your organization.

This playbook outlines how to organize intermediate-level internal promptathon events to accelerate Microsoft 365 Copilot adoption. The beginner promptathon playbook outlined how to run events for beginners to build capability for and spark interest in Copilot. At the intermediate level, employees are already familiar with Copilot and ready to do more. In intermediate promptathons, participants will deepen Copilot skills, explore real-world use cases, and foster collaboration with their peers. The format is more interactive and challenge-oriented, often a team-based prompt competition or workshop where participants apply Copilot to solve problems. They will walk away with intermediate prompt engineering abilities and practical Copilot workflow solutions.

Intermediate promptathons

As with beginner promptathons, before running an intermediate promptathon, it's important to spend time defining the goals and objectives that are driving the event. What outcomes do you want to achieve? How will you know you have been successful? Goals and outcomes might include:

- **Expand Copilot proficiency** Move beyond the basics into more nuanced uses of Copilot. Attendees will learn to craft more effective prompts and sequences for complex tasks. For example, they might practice multistep prompting and iteratively refining an output or using Copilot across different apps in one workflow. Participants will learn and apply a toolkit of prompt strategies, like getting Copilot to adopt a specific tone or break down a request into smaller parts for better results.

- **Apply to real business scenarios** Whereas beginner promptathons focus on simple tasks, intermediate promptathons tackle real departmental or business scenarios. The goal is to generate practical Copilot use cases or mini-solutions with tangible value. For instance, a team might figure out how to use Copilot to auto-generate a project status update from notes or create a first draft of a client proposal using company data. By the end of the event, each team or participant will have produced at least one solution or use-case example with the help of Copilot (a prompt or set of prompts) that addresses a work-related challenge.

- **Encourage collaboration and peer learning**   Promptathons enable peer-to-peer learning by having participants work together in small groups. Gaining new and different perspectives by pairing people in different areas, such as someone from finance with someone from IT, can lead to creative uses of Copilot. This results in strengthened internal networks and a culture of co-creating AI solutions. Participants share tips and tricks among themselves, elevating the overall knowledge. This might also help identify Copilot champions—individuals with enough know-how to mentor others.

- **Highlight innovative use of Copilot**   People will likely discover inventive ways to use Copilot or note its limitations as they experiment. One of the goals of the intermediate promptathon is to capture these insights. Perhaps as a list of best practices, tips, and new ideas. This might form the basis of an internal prompt library or knowledge base. It also sets the stage for advanced-level promptathons by identifying promising areas to explore further.

- **Increase engagement with AI**   Another goal is maintaining momentum and enthusiasm for AI adoption. Giving intermediate users a platform to shine reinforces the message that the organization values innovation and continuous learning. When participants feel more invested in Copilot's success and growth, they're more likely to become advocates in their teams.

Focus for an intermediate promptathon

To design a promptathon experience that will ensure you achieve the goals and outcomes you've set, focus on setting an engaging theme that will inspire people to take part. This could be a half-day or full-day event where attendees form small teams or work in pairs to tackle prompt-based challenges. The intermediate promptathon format typically includes:

- A brief refresher or advanced tips presentation at the start to introduce new concepts like prompt chaining, using context effectively, or addressing AI limitations.

- Forming teams, if they haven't been formed ahead of the event. Teams of 3–5 people work well to get a good mix of skills and keep everyone engaged.

- A series of prompt challenges or a mini-hackathon where teams choose a problem to solve using Copilot. Allocate several hours for teams to develop and test their approach.

- At the end of the promptathon, teams present their solutions—the prompt or Copilot usage they devised and the result it achieved. Optionally, judges or peers evaluate to pick the "best solution," adding a friendly competitive element to the event.

Theme ideas for intermediate promptathons

Choosing a unifying theme or a set of tracks for your promptathon can help to focus participants' creativity. Select a theme that will resonate with your organization, and if possible, align with your AI vision and strategic objectives. Consider theme ideas such as:

- **"Boost productivity"** Where each team finds a way to save time in a standard process using Copilot.

- **"Department challenges"** Departments like finance, HR, sales, and so on, each come up with a Copilot use case for a typical task in their function. This works well if you group participants by department.

- **"Copilot saves the work day"** Cross-functional teams share broad daily work challenges and pick one to solve with Copilot, such as reducing meeting overload, improving customer responses, or managing email inbox chaos.

- **"Prompt battle"** A more gamified theme where teams get a set of predefined challenges like "Using Copilot, create a five-slide PowerPoint summary of a 10-page report" and see who can get the best result. This prompt competition format is great if the focus is to develop skills through a more playful approach rather than working on solutions for specific organizational challenges.

Ensure the theme is broad enough that everyone can contribute, but specific enough to give direction. For instance, "Explore different Microsoft 365 Copilot capabilities" is a bit vague; framing it as "Learn effective Copilot prompting techniques for scenarios like report writing, data analysis, and inbox management" gives people a clear idea of what to expect to learn during the promptathon.

Content focus for intermediate Copilot users

The intermediate promptathon content builds on the foundational concepts covered in the beginner promptathon and introduces more complex Copilot concepts such as:

- **Effective prompt refinement** Show examples of refining a Copilot response. For example, start with a basic prompt and then demonstrate how adding context or constraints improves it. Teach techniques like asking Copilot to format the output in a specific way or to take on a role such as "Act as a communications expert…".

- **Chaining and multiturn prompts** Demonstrate how Copilot can be used in a conversational multiturn manner. For instance, have Copilot draft something, and then ask it to improve a specific section or to provide alternatives. This sequential prompting is key to solving complex tasks and producing high-quality outputs. It is a step toward "prompt chaining," which is used in advanced AI tasks.

- **Handling unexpected outputs** Address issues like AI hallucinations. Explain why Copilot might sometimes fabricate information. Give guidance on how to fact-check Copilot outputs or how to phrase prompts to minimize incorrect answers. For example, if Copilot's answer seems off, try rephrasing the question or double-check against source data. Also, cover using the "undo" or revert if Copilot's changes in a document aren't suitable.

- **Context and data usage** Highlight how to provide context to Copilot. For example, provide a specific document or data set within the prompt by telling Copilot to reference an attached file or using the context of an email thread. Clarify what internal data Copilot has access to in their Microsoft environment. For instance, it can access the documents and emails you have permissions for. Encourage prompting with relevant data rather than asking overly general questions.

- **Cross-application scenarios** Since Copilot spans multiple Microsoft 365 apps, show an example of using it in a workflow across apps. For instance, use Copilot in Teams to summarize a chat, then use Copilot in Word to draft a document based on that summary. Or use Copilot in Excel to analyze data and then Copilot in Outlook to draft an email with the findings. This illustrates the breadth of capabilities and inspires participants to consider integrated use cases.

- **Ethical and secure use** At an intermediate stage, it's important to remind participants to honor ethical boundaries when using Copilot. Make time for discussions on broad standards like Microsoft's responsible AI principles as well as the specifically relevant policies for your organization. Essentially, this is a reminder not to ask Copilot to do things it's not designed for, like accessing customer information that isn't relevant to your job, writing personal performance reviews, or any policy-violating content. Be mindful of data sensitivity and keep exploration responsible.

Overall, the focus is on problem-solving with Copilot. By focusing on a particular task or challenge, teams work out how to get the best outcome using clever prompting. Encourage teams to document the prompts they tried and what worked or didn't because this is valuable learning to capture and share.

Example promptathon activities

Depending on the format, here are two possible structures:

- **Challenge stations** You could set up "stations" or topics for people to move between. For example, station 1 might focus on "writing and editing with Copilot," station 2 might focus on "data analysis with Copilot," and station 3 might focus on "creative brainstorming with Copilot." Teams rotate through each station and do a small challenge to provide hands-on learning in several different contexts. This could be facilitated either in person or virtually with breakout rooms and timed rotations.

- **Mini-hackathon** Give teams 2–3 hours to identify a challenge or opportunity for a specific scenario. Teams work together using Copilot to craft prompts that help solve the challenge—whether reducing the resources needed or creating value for the organization. Mentors and coaches are available to help teams as they work. After the allotted time, each team presents their prompt or solution. This approach can yield diverse solutions and gives people a chance to practice coming up with prompts for specific scenarios. For the intermediate promptathon, it's a good idea to constrain the scope so that participants can come up with a solution in the given time.

- **Add a competitive element** Introduce a friendly competition to boost engagement. For example, announce that there will be awards such as "Most Innovative Copilot Use", "Biggest Impact Idea", or simply award first, second, and third place. Make judging criteria clear and keep prizes modest. The emphasis is still on learning and sharing, not winning. Prizes could be fun items like company swag or "bragging rights," announced in a newsletter. Competition can drive teams to push harder and add excitement to the presentations.

Ensure the format and activities allow teams to see what other people have been working on. Not only does it give recognition to those who have worked hard on their innovative ideas, but it also allows everyone to learn from each solution. Encourage teams to articulate their prompt approach and any challenges they overcame. This peer learning is one of the most valuable outcomes of intermediate promptathons.

Delivery formats: In-person, virtual, hybrid

Intermediate events can be more complex to coordinate, especially with team activities, but they can succeed in any format with planning. Choose the delivery modality that is most likely to achieve your goals within any resource constraints you might have.

In-person delivery

Running your intermediate promptathon on-site can energize teams and make collaboration easy. People can huddle around a laptop and brainstorm, scribble ideas on whiteboards, and quickly consult with others. In-person can also facilitate easier communication within teams. Ensure that a comfortable space is provided for each team, such as individual breakout rooms or separate tables in a large meeting room. Have plenty of whiteboards or flip charts for idea sketching or mapping out prompt flows.

Kick off the day together in a common area. Use this space to form teams and give them their instructions, but let teams spread out during work time to avoid noise issues. Come back together afterward to hear each group present their solutions. Provide refreshments to keep energy up. A physical scoreboard or agenda timeline on the wall can help everyone keep track of time.

Virtual delivery

Virtual delivery requires different tools for collaboration. Ensure you have an online space for teams to communicate. For example, set up separate Teams channels or private virtual meeting rooms for each team to work together. Use a main meeting for the kickoff and wrap-up presentations. Virtual whiteboarding tools like Microsoft Whiteboard or Miro can be used to brainstorm ideas and map solutions, just as teams collaborating in person would use a whiteboard. Assign each team a mentor who can pop into their call to observe or assist if they're stuck.

Keep the main communication channel open and have someone moderate a group chat throughout the promptathon where reminders, updates, or tips can be posted. To mimic the buzz of an in-person event, encourage teams to post screenshots or short updates in the group chat, such as "We just got

Copilot to auto-generate an FAQ from our policy doc!". This keeps a sense of community even though they are physically apart.

If participants are spread out, be mindful of time zones; you might shorten continuous working time but allow offline work in between if needed.

Hybrid: In-person and virtual

A hybrid approach can combine the best of both delivery types, but it requires effort to create a level playing field for all participants. It can work well to form teams of all in-person attendees or all remote attendees to simplify interactions. Hybrid teams where some people are located together in-person and others are participating virtually can work, but tend to disadvantage the remote members unless technology is used well and people are mindful about including their virtual teammates. Ensure that remote teams can present their screen and be heard clearly by those in the room. Use a large screen and good audio in the physical room to include remote presenters, especially during the demo session. If possible, have a dedicated facilitator for remote participants' needs.

Even for hybrid promptathons, you could consider taking a "virtual-first" approach where in-person folks use the same digital collaboration tools as remote ones. For example, everyone uses a shared OneNote or Teams channel to document their project, so outputs are collated in one place. If the in-person participants are joining from a large room and resources allow, you might have a camera on each in-person team that remote folks can check in with or a roving webcam to give a sense of the room's activity.

Hybrid promptathons are undoubtedly more challenging to facilitate well, so if the group is not too large, you might opt to do separate events for different locations or stick to all virtual or all in-person for this intermediate stage.

Regardless of format, lay out clear ground rules and schedules at the start. Make it clear when to start and stop working, how to ask for help, and how final presentations will happen. With several moving parts, it's important to be clear on instructions and expectations.

Recommended duration

An intermediate promptathon often runs as either a half-day or a full-day event, typically between 4 to 6 hours. This gives enough time for short training, a decent block of work time, and presentations. For example, a typical structure might be one hour of introductory content, followed by two hours for teams to work on their prompting and solutions, followed by one hour for presentations and feedback. You would also need to allow for breaks in that time. You can extend this to a full workday, about 8 hours including breaks, if tackling bigger challenges. A sample one-day agenda for an intermediate promptathon might include:

- **9:00–9:30 AM**   Intro, team formation, and theme briefing.

- **9:30–12:00 PM**   Work session 1 (with mentors checking in).

- **12:00–1:00 PM**   Lunch break (optional: tech talk or informal discussion during lunch).

- **1:00–2:30 PM**   Work session 2 (teams finalize solutions).

- **2:30–3:30 PM**   Presentations and judging.

- **3:30–4:00 PM**   Wrap-up, awards, next steps.

This is just an example. Adjust the timing to fit your needs (and keep sessions shorter if they are virtual to avoid fatigue).

Shorter Options: If taking people away from work for a full day is difficult, consider a two-part event:

- **Day 1 (perhaps a 2-hour session):** Kick off, form teams, and introduce the challenge. Then, allow teams to work on their own time (with a 2–3-day window where they can meet as they wish).

- **Day 2 (2-hour session a few days later):** Teams reconvene to present their results to each other and the judges.

This split approach reduces continuous time commitment and gives flexibility, but it requires teams to be self-directed and meet and work offline. It can simulate an asynchronous hackathon. When it comes to timing and duration, it's a good idea to consider:

- **Breaks**   Schedule regular short breaks to keep everyone fresh. A 15-minute break mid-morning and mid-afternoon, plus lunch if it's a full-day event, works well. Encourage people to step away from screens and get some fresh air if possible.

- **Flexibility**   Be prepared to adjust the schedule as you go. If teams are ready, you can start presentations sooner and offer everyone the benefit of finishing early. Conversely, if several teams need more time, and it's feasible, you can extend the solution time—but be mindful of overall timing and communicate any changes clearly to avoid confusion.

- **Judging time**   If you're conducting a competition, remember to allocate time for judges to deliberate if needed. You could do this during a scheduled break and then announce the winners at the closing. Do this by scheduling a short break for judges to confer and analyze projects and then holding a feedback session to highlight each proposal's strengths. This is a great approach to ensure teams get constructive feedback, not just a ranking.

Whatever the duration of your intermediate promptathon, try not to stretch it over too many days without touchpoints, or momentum can drop. Keep some pressure with deadlines; a bit of time constraint often spurs creativity and focus.

Planning checklist and team roles

Planning an intermediate event involves more moving parts than the beginner stage. Start early to coordinate teams, judges, and content. This guide provides the steps you should take in the weeks before, and an overview of roles in the organizing team.

Four to six weeks before the promptathon

Start planning your event four to six weeks in advance so that you can secure the necessary sponsorship and support. Clarify the specific goals for this event; for example, develop five new use-case ideas or train power users. Decide on the theme or challenge prompts and align with any business needs, perhaps by speaking with department heads about pain points that Copilot could address to seed challenge ideas. Appoint an event lead who will own the planning and be responsible for organizing the event. Form a small core team, including:

- **Content lead/facilitator** Designs the training segment and hosts the promptathon.

- **Logistics/producer** Handles venue or virtual setup, registrations, and communications.

- **Technical mentor lead** Someone well-versed in Copilot and AI who can align mentor support and create example solutions.

- **Scribe/communications** Optional but helpful to capture outcomes and manage postevent documentation.

- **Management sponsorship** Inform relevant managers or department leads that their team members may join a half-day or full-day event. Early buy-in helps avoid last-minute business priority conflicts. Emphasize the value to the manager: employees will come back with skills and solutions that can benefit their team.

When choosing a date and time for the intermediate promptathon, ensure it doesn't clash with major company events or deadlines. Consider the timing of any beginner promptathons the same audience may have been part of—give people time to absorb the basics, but not so long that enthusiasm fades. A few weeks in between usually works well. If in-person, reserve a large room plus breakout spaces. If you expect many teams, ensure enough rooms or areas for each to work without disturbing others. If virtual, decide on the collaboration platform, like Teams channels, and test the breakout room process with a small group.

Three weeks before the promptathon

Announce the intermediate promptathon, invite attendees, and recruit mentors and judges.

- **Invite participants** Announce the intermediate promptathon to those who are ready to move beyond a basic use of Copilot. The intermediate audience might include those who attended the beginner event, or generally any employees who are using Copilot regularly. Describe it as a next-step opportunity for Copilot curious people. Clearly state the time commitment and what they will do (collaborate in teams to build solutions). If space is limited, create a registration form to cap the number of teams.

- **Promote benefits** Highlight the benefits for participants in communications: improving prompting skills, solving real problems, networking with peers, and having fun. If there will be recognition or prizes, mention those to entice signups.

- **Participant preparation**   Encourage participants to sign up individually or in teams if they prefer. If you want cross-functional collaboration, you could deliberately assign people from different departments to each team—ask for department information on the signup form to assist with this.

- **Identify team mentors**   Reach out to a handful of Copilot "power users" or champions in the organization who can act as mentors during the intermediate promptathon. These might be folks from IT or early adopters who are proficient Copilot users. Aim for one mentor per 2–3 teams. Brief them on their role: they should roam (physically or virtually) to answer questions, guide teams who are stuck, and push teams to consider edge cases or refine their approach. Mentors can make a big difference in elevating the quality of solutions.

- **Secure competition judges**   If you plan to judge and award the best solutions, you'll need 2–4 judges. Ideally, include a mix of technical experts, who understand what's impressive or not with AI prompts and outputs, and business stakeholders, who know what solutions would be valuable for the organization. Judges will need to be present during final presentations. Share the judging criteria with them in advance and with participants so everyone knows how things will be evaluated.

- **Logistics and tools**   Finalize how teams will collaborate and present. Prepare any accounts for any collaboration tools you plan to use, like an online whiteboard. Decide how teams will submit their prompts and prepare any necessary resources like submission forms or templates.

If in-person, arrange supplies like notebooks, markers, and name tags. If virtual, add attendees to the Teams channels and assign participants to private channels once teams are set.

One or two weeks before the promptathon

In the final weeks before the event, focus on preparing the promptathon materials and building excitement among attendees. Steps in this stage include:

- **Send participants a detailed agenda**   Include the timing of each segment so participants know when they'll be busy with heads-down work versus when they need to be focused. Also, share any prework, such as "Think of a work challenge you'd like to solve" or "Familiarize yourself with how to use Copilot in Excel to help with analysis".

- **Prepare the intro presentation**   This might include a recap of foundational concepts for those who need a refresher, and then the new intermediate concepts. Keep it brief and practical.

- **Define challenges**   If you set specific challenge prompts for the teams, finalize them now. Alternatively, if the challenge is open-ended, have a few suggested ideas ready to share in case teams struggle to pick a problem on the day.

- **Mentor and judge orientation**   Hold a short call or send a brief to mentors and judges. Clarify the schedule, their roles, and the tools being used. Assign mentors to teams. Confirm how judges will score presentations and whether they will also participate in giving feedback to each team after presentations.

- **Technical dry run** Test out the technology from a participant's perspective. For example, if using Teams, ensure each participant has access to Copilot and any shared resources. If in-person, double-check WiFi capacity and test the projection and audio equipment.

- **Communications** Send a reminder to get teams excited about the upcoming promptathon. Reminders should be upbeat and positive, such as "Only a week to go! Start brainstorming ideas to bring up. What repetitive tasks do you do that Copilot might handle? We'll form teams and tackle these together." If appropriate, build some friendly competitive hype: "Which department will develop the most innovative Copilot prompt?"

Final preparations: 1 day before or day of event

Make the most of all the work that has gone into organizing the promptathon by getting the final preparations right. Ensure that everything is ready to go, including:

- **Printing any materials** Agenda posters, judging criteria, and evaluation sheets. Prepare prize certificates or goodies if you have them. If virtual, ensure all links are readily available to resend if someone can't find them.

- **Team assignments** If you are preassigning teams, communicate team lists and team-specific breakout meeting details. Or if teams will form on the spot, ensure the method is ready, whether random draw or perhaps self-selection by interest.

- **Prepare to open the promptathon** Create a clear script that explains the rules and timeline. Encourage teams to designate a spokesperson and keep notes on their solution development. Be prepared so you can bring energy and excitement to the opening address.

Remind everyone that the goal is to learn and achieve useful outcomes, not just to win. Mention that even partial solutions or failed attempts are okay; they teach valuable lessons to share so that everyone can learn together. Start on time and keep things moving according to schedule. Time management is key in a hackathon scenario.

Day of the promptathon: Roles and responsibilities

Make sure you have the right people in the room supporting your intermediate promptathon. Some of these roles have been covered earlier in this playbook, but as a reminder, key roles include:

- **Event lead/facilitator** Runs the show, keeps time, and ensures everyone knows what to do. Kicks off the promptathon, checks in periodically, and leads the closing ceremony. They also handle any adjustments to the agenda as needed.

- **Team mentors** Float among teams to answer questions about Copilot's capabilities, give hints, and encourage deeper thinking. Mentors should be proactive—if a team seems stalled, a mentor can steer them with questions like "Have you tried breaking the prompt into smaller parts?"

- **Judges**   Observe the final presentations and evaluate based on the criteria. It's often useful if judges interact with teams informally during the promptathon to see how they work together. In the presentation Q&A, judges can ask clarifying questions.

- **IT support**   Have someone on standby to solve technical problems or Copilot license assignment issues. Hopefully, they won't be busy, but it's a good idea to have them standing ready to help.

- **Communications/photographer (optional)**   If you plan to document the promptathon for internal news, assign someone to take photos or screenshots, gather quotes, and note key outcomes from the event. This person can later create a highlight reel or article for internal or external blogs.

- **Participant team roles**   Encourage each team to have one or more prompt developer(s) to craft and test the Copilot prompts and a scribe to write down what the team tried and what worked. Assign a presenter to represent the team during the final presentation and a time-keeper to keep everyone on track. Small teams may have people wearing multiple hats, but identifying these responsibilities helps them organize themselves.

Allow creativity and learning to take center stage by planning thoroughly and assigning clear roles.

Technical setup and support requirements

A few extra technical considerations come into play at the intermediate level, given that teams will push Copilot's usage further than in the beginner promptathon. Confirm again that every participant's account has Copilot access across the necessary Microsoft 365 apps. Participants might use Copilot in various apps, such as Word, Excel, PowerPoint, Outlook, and Teams, at this stage. Ensure none of these services are disabled for them. If certain Copilot features are in preview or not enabled in your tenant, communicate that so teams can pick feasible ideas.

If teams work with company data, provide guidance on what is allowed and safe. Since Copilot respects data security within Microsoft 365, there may be no additional measures required. However, caution teams to use only data they have the rights to, and which is appropriate to share in a demo. If a team's solution involves summarizing a sensitive document, they should not show the content during the final presentation but talk abstractly or use a sanitized example. If you want a safer sandbox, you could provide sample data sets or documents for them to test on (such as a SharePoint site for use in the promptathon or a fictitious data set in Excel). However, using real scenarios is often more engaging.

Tools for collaboration

Aside from Copilot itself, ensure teams have the necessary tools to work together. If in-person, do they each have laptops? Or will they gather around one machine? Ideally, each member can try things in parallel and share with the group. If remote, set up private team channels or meeting rooms as noted earlier in this playbook.

Provide a common knowledge repository for participants to access during the promptathon with Copilot tips or links to the Microsoft Learn Copilot documentation so teams can self-serve answers to some questions. At the intermediate level, teams often start to push the limits of Copilot, such as prompt or input length limits or inability to access certain types of content. Have the mentor team briefed on known limitations to guide teams to answers and workarounds if relevant.

Encourage teams to test their final prompts before presenting to ensure they work as expected. If a team's demo relies on a live Copilot response, be prepared that network or service delays could happen. It might be wise for teams to capture screenshots of successful runs as a backup in case the live demo fails or is slow.

For final presentations, make sure the technology allows each team to share what they have worked on in their own environment. If they will demo Copilot live, ensure screen sharing works whether in-person by connecting their computer to a projector or virtual by ensuring participants have permission to share their screen on the Teams call. If multiple teams need to present from the same machine (in-person scenario if there's one projector), collect their materials (slides, etc.) in advance on that machine, or have them use a portable laptop that you can easily switch to the projector. Test audio if any team plans to play a video or something (unlikely at this stage, but check).

Highlight any corporate compliance guidelines relevant to AI usage. For example, some industries require humans to review AI-generated content before publishing. In an internal promptathon, that's not likely to be an issue, but may be relevant when considering the broad application of any of the prompts developed. Instruct teams not to connect to any external AI services outside of Copilot to keep everything within approved tools—all work should be done with Microsoft 365 Copilot unless connecting to third-party services is explicitly allowed.

Capture data during the promptathon so that you can measure the technical success of the event, such as the number of prompts executed or any system performance issues encountered. This can feed into the evaluation and impact of the promptathon and inform how the technical execution could be improved for future events.

Technology should be an enabler, not a blocker, for creativity. Ensuring everything is set and tested means teams can focus on innovation rather than troubleshooting.

Engagement strategies: Before, during, after

Maintaining enthusiasm through an intermediate promptathon can be a challenge. These participants are more invested but likely busier, so you want to keep up the momentum to retain their commitment, time, and energy throughout the event.

Pre-event engagement

Before the event, build excitement through regular communications and make it easy for participants to understand how the promptathon will run. Pre-event engagement ideas to consider:

- **Idea teasers**   In the lead-up to the event, communications should encourage people to start thinking creatively. You could share one or two example use cases to spark ideas. Real case studies or hypothetical use cases can inspire participants to imagine what they might do.

- **Team dynamics**   If teams are known beforehand, encourage them to meet briefly to prepare so that they can hit the ground running on the day. If teams aren't set until the day of the promptathon, consider creating a space like a Teams channel where attendees can introduce themselves and share what areas they're interested in using Copilot for.

- **Preparation resources**   Share learning resources for those who want to brush up on their Copilot knowledge. For example, share a link to a Microsoft Learn module on Copilot or an internal cheat sheet on prompting from the last event. Frame it as optional but helpful. Enthusiastic participants often appreciate the chance to prepare a bit, and some might even test a few things in advance.

- **Build excitement**   Use a countdown to the event or spotlight a particular challenge or topic. Introduce mentors and any speakers to build interest in the content and excitement about the learning opportunity. If any senior leaders are going to judge or attend, highlight that, too, so that people are prepared to prioritize the time.

Engagement during the event

Kick off the intermediate promptathon with high energy. Play upbeat music as people join and welcome them to the event. Thank everyone for coming, and emphasize that this is about experimenting and learning—remind people that it's okay if not every idea works out. The goal is to push Copilot's limits and have fun. Consider these ideas to keep people engaged during the promptathon:

- **Mentor interaction**   Encourage teams to utilize mentors. Sometimes, teams hesitate to ask for help, so consider a structure like scheduled mentor check-ins where each mentor proactively visits their assigned teams to ask how it's going. This ensures that every team gets attention. Mentors can share anonymized tips across teams. Sharing common problems and solutions during the event via the main chat or an announcement can help all teams.

- **Progress updates**   Send periodic broadcast updates to maintain momentum and help teams keep to time. For example: "We're halfway through and by now, you should aim to have a rough solution. If you're still brainstorming, try picking the most doable idea and focus there!" or "30 minutes left—time to polish your results and prepare to present!" This keeps everyone on track and injects a bit of urgency. In person, you can announce these on a microphone; virtually, send them to the group chat.

- **Spotlight achievements**   During the work session, if you hear about a remarkable breakthrough on one team, share it with the group. For example, post on the event chat such as "Team Alpha just successfully used Copilot in Excel to model budget scenarios. How's everyone else doing?". This can motivate other teams and create friendly peer pressure to make progress. Ensure you're not giving away a team's secret sauce if competition is fierce, but general achievements are fine.

- **Encourage social sharing** If your company has an internal social network, encourage participants to share snippets of their experience and photos of the event and their work. Use a hashtag if internal social is a thing. It spreads the excitement beyond participants.

- **Keep it fun** The intermediate promptathon should be enjoyable, not feel like hard work. You can incorporate mini-games, like prompt trivia during a break. Encourage people to play; it's a great way to learn and unlock the creative thinking needed to reimagine how we work with Copilot and AI.

- **Food and swag** If in-person, nothing keeps people happy during long working sessions like good food. Provide lunch if it's a full-day event and snacks/coffee throughout. If budget allows, have some themed swag like stickers that say "Intermediate Copilot Promptathon" or t-shirts for participants, which builds a sense of community and accomplishment.

Postevent engagement

After the intermediate promptathon, it's important to highlight the impact of the event and encourage participants to continue developing their Copilot skills. Do this by:

- **Publicizing what the teams created** You can compile each team's project summary and send it company-wide or to relevant stakeholders. For example, "Team A created a Copilot prompt to extract key points from client feedback surveys automatically. Team B showed how Copilot can help prepare draft financial reports by pulling data from Excel. Team C…" Highlight the winning or most innovative ideas, but capture and share all the ideas since this can spark Copilot innovation and iteration among other employees who didn't attend.

- **Recognizing winners** If you have winners, ensure they get prizes and a shout-out in a visible forum such as an all-hands meeting or an intranet news post. All promptathon participants should be praised for their contributions. Perhaps each participant receives a certificate or badge (digital is fine) for being an "Intermediate Copilot Prompter" or similar. This gamifies the program and encourages them to get to the next level.

- **Implementing promising ideas** One powerful engagement tool is to follow through on the best ideas. For one or two top solutions, announce a plan to implement them in practice. For example, if a team develops a great prompt workflow for customer proposals, integrate that into the standard process or template. You might form a small project or task force to produce the idea or share the prompt with the relevant department for immediate use. This shows that the promptathon output will drive real change and increase buy-in.

- **Collect learnings** Hold a postmortem with the organizers and mentors to gather what was learned about Copilot. Often, intermediate users will uncover limitations or clever tricks. Document these to inform training materials for the next event.

- **Continue the conversation** Just as with the beginner stage, keep the community interaction going. You likely have a cohort of more proficient Copilot users—encourage them to share their expertise company-wide. Perhaps organize a "Copilot Showcase" session where the promptathon teams demonstrate their solutions to a broader audience beyond the event judges.

Teaching others what they have learned reinforces their knowledge and helps disseminate Copilot best practices.

- **Bridge to advanced**   As enthusiasm peaks from this intermediate promptathon, invite the most engaged and skilled participants to consider the next challenge—the advanced promptathon. This sets expectations that there is a progression path and that they can aspire to even bigger projects.

Evaluation metrics and feedback mechanisms

To assess the success of the intermediate promptathon, gather ideas for improvement, and inform content for the advanced promptathon, consider the following metrics and feedback channels:

- **Participation and retention**   Note the number of initial signups vs. actual participants. If the challenge was team-based, how many teams took part and completed it? Compare attendance to the beginner level promptathon—how many participants attended both, indicating sustained interest? Also, track representation across departments. Was there a diverse mix (a good sign of broad appeal), or was there mostly one department represented?

- **Quality of solutions**   Evaluate the outputs from a functional perspective: How many distinct use-case solutions were developed? Judges' scores or ratings can be aggregated to see overall quality. For instance, if using a 1–5 scale on creativity, look at the average to understand whether teams overall show high levels of creativity. Identify common themes in solutions. If multiple teams chose similar problems, that signals a high-priority area in the company that Copilot could address, which is a valuable insight for management. Were there any particularly innovative prompt techniques seen? These can be documented as emerging best practices.

- **Team feedback**   Conduct a postevent survey or debrief with participants to understand how much they learned about Copilot—did they discover new features or techniques? Ask if they plan to use Copilot more regularly after this event. If their intent is high, that's a win for adoption. Refine the format based on what people liked or wanted more of. Maybe they loved collaboration but wanted more time or struggled with the virtual tool. If they say they would participate again or recommend it to colleagues, that's a strong outcome.

- **Usage metrics postevent**   Similar to the beginner promptathon, monitor whether Copilot usage increases following the intermediate promptathon event, especially in the projects or departments represented. If a team built a solution for creating meeting summaries, look for more usage of Copilot in Teams for meeting notes in the following weeks. It may be subtle, but any spike in Copilot engagement in the participant group can be attributed to the promptathon.

- **Follow through on solutions**   Track what happens to the ideas. How many of the hackathon ideas were adopted or further developed? Even if not formally tracked, anecdotally check with teams a month later—did they continue using/refining their Copilot prompts? This indicates a lasting impact.

- **Mentor and judge observations** Have a quick roundtable with mentors and judges. They often see things that participants don't articulate. For example, a judge might note, "Many teams tried to get Copilot to do X and failed; maybe we need to provide training or tools for that capability." These observations can highlight areas to focus on in the advanced promptathon or additional training. Mentors can share common questions they fielded, which might suggest where intermediate knowledge is lacking or where documentation is unclear.

- **Community growth** Check the membership and activity in the Copilot user community after the event. Did new people (beyond participants) join discussions because they heard about it? Are participants more active in helping others now? A vibrant internal community is a key success factor for Copilot adoption.

- **Business impact estimates** While this is early for concrete return on investment (ROI), you can estimate the potential impact of the solutions presented. For example, if Team A's solution could save an hour per week in a particular process and 10 people could use it, that's about 10 hours saved weekly. Tally such estimates from all solutions. This gives leadership a sense of the promptathon's value. You can phrase it like, "Promptathon teams identified ideas that could collectively save about 50 employee hours per month if implemented." It sets the stage that investing in Copilot and in these promptathon events has a real payoff.

- **Compare to goals** Review the outcomes against the goals for the intermediate promptathon. If the goal was to generate at least one use case per team, record the actual outcomes. If a goal was collaboration, record the number of different departments represented. Reporting on performance against these goals validates the event design and makes it easier to get leadership buy-in for future events.

Use all the above insights and results to inform your advanced promptathon plans. For instance, if feedback indicates that more time is needed to work on solutions, consider a longer duration for the advanced event. If people want to involve more technical integration, perhaps plan for a mix of coding or integration in the advanced promptathon.

Celebrate successes

Before moving on to the advanced promptathon, take time to analyze the evaluation results and celebrate the success of the event. Share a brief report with sponsors and, in internal communications, highlight the impact, from the number of people who took part to the departments represented, and the increased use of Copilot to save resources and create value for the organization.

By thoroughly evaluating the intermediate promptathon, you ensure continuous improvement and gather evidence of momentum. Your organization's Copilot adoption journey is well underway, setting a strong foundation for the advanced promptathon, where impact and value creation go to the next level.

APPENDIX D

Microsoft 365 Copilot advanced promptathon playbook

In this appendix, you will:

- Discover how to run an advanced promptathon for people in your organization with high levels of Copilot proficiency so that they can innovate with AI.

- Understand how a promptathon series of events can provide a pathway for your teams to become experts in using Copilot to solve problems and evolve processes.

The advanced promptathon event format is the culmination of the Microsoft 365 Copilot promptathon series, which aims to support organizations on the journey from crawling, to walking, and to running with Copilot adoption. At the advanced level, the event format is designed for people who have already developed the mindset and habit of integrating Copilot into their daily work. This event is for advanced users who want to collaborate with other Copilot innovators and champions to design agents or solutions for scaled impact. At this level, employees are not just using Copilot for individual tasks; they're pushing the boundaries, combining Copilot's capabilities in creative ways, possibly integrating it with broader workflows or data, and focusing on high-impact innovations. This event is larger in scope, highly collaborative, and aimed at producing prototype solutions or deep insights that can be adopted organization-wide.

Advanced promptathons

As with the beginner and intermediate promptathons, the first step is to define your goals for running an advanced promptathon. What are you trying to achieve, and how do you know if you've been successful? Common objectives for advanced promptathons might include:

- **Drive innovation and breakthrough use cases** The primary goal might be to unleash creativity to discover new, impactful applications of Microsoft 365 Copilot. Participants should be willing to tackle bigger challenges like automating complex processes, solving pain points with the help of agents, or creating new ways of working with AI assistance. They'll work in teams to prototype solutions or develop concepts that could significantly improve productivity, efficiency, or quality. These might be candidates for real implementation or further development after the promptathon.

215

- **Mastery of Copilot and AI integration** At this stage, participants will demonstrate expert-level Copilot skills and perhaps be exploring extending Copilot with third-party connectors and integrations. They might use advanced prompt engineering techniques, chain multiple prompts or workflows, or combine Copilot with other tools like Microsoft's Power Platform. An advanced promptathon offers participants the opportunity to attain a mastery mindset so they know how to get the most out of Copilot, understand its limits, and work around those limits. This cultivates a group of internal experts who can be invaluable in scaling Copilot adoption and impact.

- **Cross-team collaboration** A significant benefit of promptathons is bringing together people from different parts of the organization to collaborate. In the advanced promptathon, teams should ideally be cross-functional to foster knowledge sharing across departments and teams. This supports new connections between departments, meaning ideas and data that usually stay in one team get shared, and a more open, innovative culture is reinforced. It shifts the company culture toward one that embraces experimentation and collaborative problem-solving.

- **Build internal champions and expertise** The advanced promptathon will identify and further empower Copilot champions. These are individuals who are deeply skilled and passionate about AI solutions. These champions emerge who can lead future Copilot initiatives, mentor others, and form a community of practice. They will be the go-to experts after the event, helping to sustain Copilot adoption. This addresses the "AI skills gap" by bringing more employees to expert status.

- **Tangible business value and executive buy-in** An advanced promptathon should illustrate the tangible value of Copilot to the organization. Solving real problems and possibly prototyping solutions that could go into production shows senior leaders how people can create value with AI. Many companies find promptathon projects feeding into their product roadmaps or internal process improvements. Any doubts among leadership about Copilot's usefulness are alleviated by seeing concrete results from the hackathon.

- **Fun, competition, and recognition** Though this is the most advanced level, maintaining the spirit of fun and competition helps inspire people to continue to contribute to your Copilot community of practice. Participants should feel challenged yet enjoy the process and feel a sense of accomplishment, seeing that their expertise is recognized and valued. The event should conclude with celebrating everyone's hard work and achievements, not just the winners.

Focus for an advanced promptathon

An advanced-level event in this series can be structured like a multiday promptathon or an intensive one-day experience, depending on objectives, scope, and available resources. This event is run much like a traditional hackathon that begins with teams defining problem statements and concludes with presentations where solutions for opportunities or challenges are shared. You can allow teams to choose the problem they want to solve or define specific challenge categories that align with organizational priorities, such as "Improving customer experience with AI", "AI for internal knowledge management", or "Increasing productivity with AI". Some advanced promptathons have a broad scope, meaning that teams have freedom to work on any challenge they choose, but in many cases, having defined categories can provide focus and ensure solutions are impactful. Customize the promptathon format for your organization, considering this guidance:

- **Form teams of about 4-6 people** Aim for interdisciplinary teams that include someone who knows the data or process, someone with strong technical or scripting skills, and someone who is a great presenter. Encourage diversity in skills on each team for the best results. Participants might self-organize around ideas they're interested in, or you can orchestrate team assignments to mix departments.

- **Solutioning time** Provide a substantial block of time for teams to work. This could be continuous, such as a 24- or 36-hour period or two workdays back to back. In an internal environment, continuous overnight working is optional—some may treat it like a marathon, but others might just use work hours. Ensure teams know the deadline for deliverables.

- **Mentoring and workshops** During the hack period, offer optional mini-workshops or office hours on relevant advanced topics. For example, a 30-minute deep dive on using the Microsoft Graph API or connectors with Copilot (if applicable), advanced prompt tuning techniques, or even a session on presentation skills for pitching their project. These break up the solutioning and provide valuable learning opportunities. Have expert mentors available, such as solution architects and data experts, for teams to consult when they hit roadblocks.

- **Submission and presentation** By the end of the promptathon, each team should submit their output. This could be a live demo, a slide deck, and/or a short document describing their solution, including the prompts used, any workflows, and intended impact. This is followed by a presentation or pitch session where each team presents their solution to the judges and audience. Depending on the number of teams, you might do a preliminary round if there are many teams. For example, if more than 10 teams are participating in your advanced promptathon, have two tracks of judging and then a final round for top projects.

- **Judging and prizes** A judging panel, including senior executives and technical leads, evaluates the projects and decides category winners. At this advanced stage, prizes could be bigger to reflect the expected impact. However, as noted earlier, emphasize that the real prize is learning and collaborating to create potential Copilot solutions.

- **Theme** The theme can be broad, like "Copilot for enterprise innovation", but it helps to have tracks or categories. Consider these theme ideas as a starting point:

  - **Process automation**—Using Copilot to automate or streamline a specific business process.
  - **Knowledge and insights**—Using Copilot to extract insights or generate knowledge from company data.
  - **Employee experience**—Using Copilot to improve daily work life.
  - **External impact**—Using Copilot in customer-facing scenarios.

Choose a theme that's aligned with your organization's highest priority areas. Alternatively, the theme could be "Think Big with Copilot" to encourage moonshot ideas that might combine Copilot with other emerging tech. Since this is internal and skill-focused, it's okay if some ideas are futuristic or not immediately deployable.

Content to cover

There isn't a structured "training" session at the advanced promptathon since participants are expected to be already proficient with using Copilot. Instead, focus on enabling them with knowledge and tools. Consider having internal and external experts present sessions on:

- **Latest Copilot features and integrations**   Provide an update on any new Copilot capabilities. Also, clarify what integration points are available. For example, can they use the Microsoft Graph API to feed data to Copilot? Is there an SDK or Power Automate connector they can leverage? Give an overview of technical possibilities so teams know what they can attempt. Expand their solution space by informing them of all the tools at their disposal.

- **Datasets and APIs**   If you want teams to use company data creatively, ensure they understand what's accessible. For instance, provide access to a sanitized data set or a sample knowledge base if relevant. If appropriate, allow teams to use Power BI, Dataverse, or other internal data sources along with Copilot. Some advanced promptathons involve building a quick pipeline, perhaps using Power Automate to gather info and then Copilot to summarize it. Internal technical experts should join the promptathon to explain to participants what they need to know and ensure they have documentation or support for those integrations.

- **Advanced prompt engineering**   While advanced participants know how to prompt, consider having a session to introduce high-end concepts like using few-shot learning within prompts by giving Copilot examples within the prompt to shape its output, or writing prompt chains where the production of one prompt becomes the input to another, either manually or via a tool. Encourage participants to share advanced prompting tips and tricks amongst their peers.

- **Understanding retrieval-augmented generation (RAG)**   If your organization has the capability, teams might incorporate a strategy to retrieve information and feed it to Copilot. Some might do this manually; advanced teams might script something. A session explaining the concept of RAG can inspire more technical solutions. Not every team will go that route, but it plants a seed for those inclined.

- **Quality, ethics, and governance**   Since projects could be intended for real use, briefly discuss ensuring quality and ethical AI use. That means, for example, validating Copilot's output with users, avoiding biases, and compliance with regulations. If your organization has an AI council or governance group, invite them to present at the promptathon to advise what teams should consider in their solution design.

- **Innovative inspiration**   Share a few inspiring examples of AI-driven solutions from other promptathons or industries. Real examples from internal case studies, if you have them, or Microsoft case studies, if not, can stir ambition and spark ideas.

One challenge in advanced promptathons is teams overscoping and not finishing. Encourage teams to be ambitious but realistic. Remind people to aim for a minimum viable product (MVP) or even a simple prototype by the end of the promptathon. It's better to have a working core concept than a grand vision that isn't realized. Suggest they identify the riskiest part of their idea and tackle it first. If it fails, they can pivot to a more feasible approach with the remaining time.

Competition and gamification

Whereas beginner and intermediate promptathons encourage optional competition, the advanced promptathon is structured as a competition to develop the most impactful solutions with Copilot. You can also add fun sub-competitions such as:

- A prize for "Best Team Name."

- Spot prizes during solutioning, such as "Night Owl" for the team that stayed online the latest, or a "Helper Award" for a participant who was seen assisting other teams.

- Set meaningful award categories, such as Most Innovative, Best Use of Data, Greatest Business Impact, or Crowd Favorite. Allow one team to win multiple awards if truly deserving, or spread out if you want to reward more teams.

- If your advanced promptathon theme has several categories, let participants know if you plan to have distinct category winners.

Since this is the pinnacle event in the promptathon series, executives should be more involved and visible. Have an executive give an inspiring opening talk about the role AI will play in the organization's future and attend the final presentations. When leadership sees what employees create during advanced promptathons, it often boosts support for AI initiatives. It also gives participants a chance to shine in front of a leader, which is motivating. If an executive is on the judging panel, that adds even more weight.

Let teams know that the end of the promptathon is not necessarily the end of their project. If they're passionate, they may continue refining it. Schedule a follow-up showcase a month later to see the progress teams have made. Or incorporate top ideas into the AI roadmap. This helps frame the event as part of a larger innovation process, not a standalone experience.

The advanced promptathon is like a traditional hackathon that brings together technical experts and business users, but tailored to Copilot and the organization's context. It should be intense, collaborative, and engaging—allowing participants to run free with their imagination and skills as they formulate an impactful solution.

Delivery formats: In-person, virtual, hybrid

An advanced promptathon can be run in-person, virtually, or as a hybrid event. Consider that it's lengthier and more complex work compared to the beginner or intermediate promptathons, and choose the delivery mode that suits your workforce best and maximizes participation.

In-person advanced promptathon

This is often the most immersive experience. Participants can work together in one room, brainstorm with whiteboards and sticky notes, and feed off each other's excitement. In-person delivery facilitates quick collaboration and high-bandwidth communication. It's easier to pull someone over to show an output or have an impromptu discussion with the whole team. Serendipitous interactions between teams during breaks also happen more naturally, which can spark cross-pollination of ideas. Ideas for a great in-person experience include:

- **Provide a promptathon space**   A large meeting room or a series of breakout rooms that are available for the event duration. Create a warm environment with tables or desks with comfortable chairs, spaces for rest, and maybe even some bean bags for when people want a break.

- **Supply plenty of food and refreshments**   Typically, promptathon organizers provide meals, snacks, and coffee around the clock. If people stay late or overnight, consider dinner, late-night snacks, and maybe breakfast if it goes into the next day.

- **Arrange for secure access**   If people need to come and go after hours, inform security of the event and give participants badges or passes if needed.

- **Make the space fun**   Use swag, banners, a scoreboard listing teams, and a screen showing an internal social feed of posts about the event.

- **Encourage breaks**   Have a quiet corner if someone needs a power nap. Remind people not to push beyond their limits. Fatigued participants should rest and come back fresh to avoid burnout or accidents.

Virtual advanced promptathon

A virtual promptathon can still be very effective if teams are distributed across several locations or working remotely, though it requires solid coordination and tools for online engagement. For successful advanced promptathons, consider these tips:

- **Use a robust collaboration platform**   For example, set up a dedicated Microsoft Teams channel for the promptathon with a general channel for announcements and socializing, and a private channel per team for discussions and file sharing. Slack or Discord can also work for continuous chat and voice channels.

- **Have a clear schedule**   Communicate it widely and consider the different time zones participants are joining from. Run the promptathon over a longer timeline without expecting overnight work, so people in different time zones can contribute within their daylight hours. If the advanced promptathon is for a global audience, consider extending the hackathon to three or four days, but allow each team to allocate time to work on their solutions as schedules allow.

- **Facilitate "face-to-face" time virtually**   Encourage teams to have video calls at specific check-in points. Also, host daily stand-ups or checkpoint calls for all teams at a common time each day. Everyone in the team joins a call to share progress and blockers in one sentence or two.

- **Virtual fun** Open a "watercooler" channel for off-topic banter, run a Spotify playlist participants can tune into, or do a virtual backgrounds competition to simulate similar camaraderie as people might experience at an in-person promptathon.

- **Provide an easy way for teams to ask for help** Perhaps a "Mentor Help" channel where they can mention a mentor and a mentor will respond, or a scheduling link to book a 15-minute consultation with an expert.

- **Use cloud-based collaboration tools** For code or prompt sharing to ensure smooth collaboration. For example, some teams may write sample code for integration, so provide a shared repository. If building a Power Automate flow, ensure everyone in the team has access.

- **Rehearse presentation transitions** Decide who shares the screen first and how to handle Q&A. Possibly have teams prerecord demos as a backup so they could be played during the live session with team commentary if it's not feasible to demonstrate the solution.

Hybrid advanced promptathon

This is the toughest to execute, but it is sometimes necessary if some participants are colocated and others are remote. If running a hybrid advanced promptathon, consider this advice:

- **Strive to create one unified experience** For example, even if some participants are attending in-person, they might still use the same online channels as everyone else to document progress.

- **Connect in-person and remote teams with quality tools** For instance, if one team has both in-person and remote members, set them up with a dedicated meeting station that includes a camera and speaker so the remote person can always be "present" at the table via a screen.

- **Group people by location for team formation** Structure teams so that participants are either fully colocated or all joining virtually. This avoids the worst challenges of mixing, though it also means less cross-geography diversity within teams. If your goal is to mix global teams, invest in excellent collaboration tools.

- **Host joint events thoughtfully** Facilitate the kick-off meeting, presentations, and awards celebrations in an equitable way, ensuring that remote folks aren't worse off. For example, the main presentations could all be done via Teams, even if judges and some audience sit together in a room watching a big screen. The participants are still present through Teams so that remote judges and audiences see the same thing.

- **Assign a hybrid facilitator** This person is responsible for ensuring remote participants are heard and included. They periodically check in with remote folks and relay their questions in the physical room if needed.

A hybrid approach can work if done carefully. It can allow global participation while still giving local clusters the benefit of face-to-face work.

Regardless of format, certain support elements remain constant. Make sure that you provide participants with real-time communication channels and that clear documentation and resources are accessible to all. Consider how to ensure judges can fairly evaluate all teams. As much as possible, strive to level the playing field and ensure everyone feels included in the advanced promptathon. It's worth noting that many companies have successfully run global innovation hackathons and promptathons virtually. The key is to encourage and facilitate continuous engagement, even if physically apart.

Recommended duration

The duration of advance promptathons is determined by the objectives of the event, the availability of the audience, and the resources allocated to run it. Between one to three days is typical for internal promptathons. Some ideas to consider when setting the duration of your event include:

- **One-day advanced promptathons**   This format can be very intense. It works if the challenges are narrowly scoped or participants are experienced and can move fast. The day would start early in the morning and end with judging and awards in the evening. Often suggested as a way to accelerate Copilot adoption in one day, but keep in mind that this short duration may limit the depth of solutions.

- **Two-day advanced promptathons**   This is a popular format. It allows organizers to give teams a full day for solving and extend that time to day two as required. Then, presentations and demonstrations can start as teams are ready, and judging can take place in the afternoon. This gives teams at least one overnight; even if they don't work through the night, the extra time to incubate ideas helps. It also allows any issues on day one to be resolved by day two. Start day two with a short check-in or allow teams to pivot if they hit a dead end on day one.

- **Three-day (or more) advanced promptathons**   If participants can dedicate more time to the advanced promptathon, the extra time can yield more polished outcomes. Some internal hackathons even last a full five-day working week, but not all teams work full-time on solutions. They might spread their effort across time. A three-day event might start on a Wednesday and end on Friday, giving ample time for development, especially if projects involve integrating systems or creating more complex demonstrations.

Scheduling considerations

Have participants released from regular duties during the advanced promptathon. Management support is crucial here—make sure everyone is on the same page so that participants can step away from routine work to focus on the innovation process. This dedicated focus time allows rapid progress. Without it, teams might get distracted and fail to complete the challenge. When putting the schedule together, consider:

- **Intensity and breaks**   Communicate the expected intensity so that participants are prepared. For example, if they are expecting to fit their usual work around the event, they may struggle. In an on-site 24-hour promptathon, participants often self-regulate with some pushing through late into the night and others opting to go home so they can rest and return refreshed in the morning. Provide a schedule but allow flexibility for each team's working style. If fully remote and longer than a day, encourage teams to set their own working hours, but with certain agreed-upon checkpoints like daily stand-up meetings.

- **Interim deadlines** For multiday events, introduce interim milestones to keep teams on track. For example, by the end of day 1, teams should have a clear plan and a proof-of-concept of the core idea. To ensure progress, there should be a mid-promptathon check-in, such as a quick review with a mentor or submitting a one-page concept paper. This prevents the scenario of teams scrambling at the last minute because they attempted too much.

- **Presentation time allocation** Work backwards from the end of the promptathon to determine what time to start the final presentations and judging. For example, if you have 10 teams and give each 10 minutes (including Q&A), that's about 2 hours for presentations. Factor in judge deliberation time, allow 15-30 minutes, and another 15 minutes for the award ceremony. Ensure the solution phase ends with enough buffer to set up for presentations. Set a clear deadline for teams to have finalized presentations and submitted their solution documentation. Some promptathons have teams submit their materials an hour before presentations to avoid delays.

- **Buffer for technical issues** In any event, something might go wrong with technology at the last minute—a video doesn't play, or the code breaks just before the demo. If time permits, a short buffer between each presentation or having a "troubleshooting" laptop available can save the day. Alternatively, ask teams to prerecord a demo video as backup. Schedule a bit of extra time in case the event timeline slips.

- **Optional extension** Sometimes teams need just a little more time. Whether you allow this is based on how it might impact judging fairness and other knock-on impacts of giving teams more time. Generally, try to hold the line to be fair to those who manage time well. But if it's a minor extension and all teams unanimously want it, you could extend solutioning by 30 minutes, perhaps by shortening the break before presentations. Use with caution. Clear, consistent communication is key when making any scheduling changes.

- **Post-promptathon celebration** The promptathon might formally end with awards, but consider scheduling a casual after-event gathering (even if virtual, like a social call). This lets everyone decompress and share stories, reinforcing connections made during the promptathon. It could be something like a team dinner if in-person or a virtual happy hour if remote. This isn't required, but it's often appreciated after an intense effort.

Choose a duration that matches the expected complexity of the challenges teams will be trying to solve, and based on the availability of participants. Many organizations find a full two days is a good balance for internal advanced promptathons because it provides enough time to get results but not too long to disrupt business. Whatever the duration, ensure every minute is used effectively through good planning and time management.

Planning checklist and timeline

Organizing an advanced promptathon is a huge project in itself that requires a lot of work up front and on the day to make it a success. This section provides a week-by-week comprehensive checklist and breakdown of roles needed to support the promptathon.

Four to six weeks before the advanced promptathon

Secure executive sponsorship for the event early. This might involve putting together a brief proposal that outlines the objectives of the advanced promptathon and required resources. To win executive support, emphasize the strategic value the event delivers—innovation, upskilling, and potential solutions to burning issues. Make it clear what you're asking for, whether budget for prizes, time off regular duties for participants, and for a senior executive to be the "champion" of the event. If they are willing, ask them to open the advanced promptathon and serve as a judge.

In addition to buy-in from senior leaders, at this point you need to gather a core organizing team for the advanced promptathon. Establish a committee to handle various aspects of running the event, including roles like:

- **Hackathon director or event lead**   Responsible for overall planning and execution of the advanced promptathon.

- **Project manager**   Leads on logistics and handles scheduling, venue/virtual arrangements, catering, and supplies.

- **Technical lead**   Ensures that technical resources, such as Copilot access, sample data, and development tools, are ready, coordinates mentors, and can also design technical challenge starter kits.

- **Communications lead**   Manages invitations, updates, promotional content, and possibly internal/external coverage of the event. They craft the messaging and keep everyone informed.

- **Judging coordinator**   Recruits judges, defines scoring criteria, prepares score sheets or judging platforms, and moderates the judging process.

- **Volunteer coordinator**   If you have many mentors and volunteers to help during the promptathon, assign someone to coordinate their schedules and roles.

Some people might take on multiple roles in a smaller event, but define the responsibilities clearly to ensure that everyone knows what they need to do.

Some key activities and decisions should be made at this point, including

- **Date and venue**   Choose a date, or dates, to run the advanced promptathon. Avoid overlap with critical business cycles, events, or public holidays. If running a multiday event, aim for midweek so that people are more energized. Book the venue and breakout spaces if it's an in-person promptathon. If virtual, decide on the collaboration platforms and work with IT to acquire any special licenses needed.

- **Define challenges and promptathon focus**   Decide if you will provide specific problem statements or allow open innovation. If exact, start gathering those challenges now by talking with department heads to see where Copilot could add value. If open, perhaps still outline a few example topics to inspire teams.

- **Plan the budget**   Consider food, swag, prizes, and any software costs. Also, factor in if you want to give all participants something such as a t-shirt to commemorate their participation in the advanced promptathon. If hybrid or remote, maybe send them a "promptathon kit" with some goodies to enjoy during the event.

Four weeks before the advanced promptathon

It's time to announce the advanced promptathon and recruit participants. Identify your target audience who has been developing their advanced Copilot skills. Send a save-the-date and call for participants as an email or a post to your internal social network.

Make it exciting and convey that this event is the pinnacle promptathon experience. You could produce a short promo video or a poster for internal communications. Be clear on who should attend. Unlike the beginner promptathon, a basic Copilot experience won't cut it for the advanced event. Participants should ideally be those with some Copilot experience or interest in AI. Highlight that exceptions could be made for anyone who is passionate about improving organizational processes to join a team with technically proficient Copilot users. Explain the commitment, such as "Two full days of focused innovation, away from regular duties," and get managers to approve their team members' participation. Other details to include in the announcement:

- **Sign-up process**   Decide if anyone can join or if you need to cap the number of participants. If there is more interest than spaces, you might require teams to submit ideas and then select the best or award spaces on a first-come-first-serve basis. Alternatively, you could limit to a certain number per department. Use an internal form to capture sign-ups. Ask about participants' skills and interests to help with team formation.

- **Team formation**   You can let participants form teams ahead of time or facilitate it at the promptathon kickoff if you expect last-minute sign-ups. Ideally, teams should be formed, and project ideas should be defined before the event starts so participants can come prepared. Consider organizing a pre-promptathon meetup or an online forum for idea pitching. Aim for balanced, cross-functional teams with representation across departments and skill sets. For example, matching a business analyst with a developer and a data expert. This diversity sparks creativity and ensures that each team knows the problem domain and technology. Avoid last-minute scrambles; having teams and ideas set in advance prevents chaos at kickoff and lets teams possibly do some early brainstorming or data gathering.

- **Pre-promptathon workshops**   In the weeks before the advanced promptathon, consider offering preparatory sessions to boost skills. For example, host an advanced Copilot techniques workshop or a tutorial on using Microsoft Graph API or Power Automate with Copilot. You could also share resource kits that might include documentation, prompt tips, or API guides so eager team members can study or start experimenting early.

Two weeks before the advanced promptathon

Finalize all details for the advanced promptathon. Confirm the participant list and team assignments. If teams are too small or missing a skill, adjust by merging teams or asking people to join another team. Send out the detailed advanced promptathon agenda, including start/end times, checkpoint times, and presentation slots. Also, share the judging criteria with participants in advance—this helps teams focus on what matters. For example, if "business impact" is 40 percent of the score, they need to consider that when selecting a challenge to work on. Other activities to complete in this stage include:

- **Logistics check** For in-person promptathons, confirm catering orders, room setups, and equipment like projectors, extra monitors, adapters, plenty of power strips, and reliable WiFi. For virtual promptathons, ensure all Teams links are set and test any tools like shared workspaces with a small group.

- **Mentor and judge briefings** Review the event flow with mentors and judges. Provide judges with the scoring rubric and clarify their roles. For example, let them know if they should visit teams during solutioning or only see final presentations. Mentors should get an overview of likely technical challenges and a roster of teams to familiarize themselves with team compositions and proposed ideas (if known).

- **Data and technology preparation** Make sure any data sources or sandbox environments are ready for teams. For example, if you've created a dummy SharePoint site or sample database for them to use, populate it now. Ensure participants have access to all necessary systems and test that permissions on any shared data are correct.

- **Communications** Send an enthusiastic reminder to participants about the upcoming advanced promptathon. Include any last-minute instructions or information they might need. Build excitement by highlighting a coveted prize like an extra day off or time with a respected judge.

One to three days before the advanced promptathon

Perform final checks and set up for the advanced promptathon. If on-site, set up the venue the day before: arrange team seating, post signage like team name placards, event schedule posters, WiFi info, and set up a help desk station. Prepare any welcome kits, such as t-shirts, notepads, or badges, to distribute as participants check in.

If virtual, send calendar invites for all key sessions, such as kickoff, any progress check-ins, final presentations, and awards, to ensure they're on everyone's calendar with the correct meeting links. Consider a test call to troubleshoot any screen-sharing or VPN issues.

Send a final email reminder. Encourage participants to get a good night's rest and reiterate what's expected of them during the advanced promptathon and what they need to have on hand (installed software, access credentials). If teams have submitted project briefs or intros, share that document with all participants to build cross-team awareness and spark friendly competition. Remind people to show up on time and be ready to go when the executive sponsor or host shares opening remarks, and make sure that judges and mentors know when and where to show up.

Day of advanced promptathon

The organizing team should arrive early to check that everything is ready for participants as they arrive. Throughout the advanced promptathon, the organizers should:

- Keep time and announce transitions (start, breaks, deadline reminders).

- Facilitate a mid-event checkpoint, a brief check-in where each team gives a one-minute update on their progress. This fosters accountability and allows teams to share any quick tips or identify whether they need to pivot.

- Ensure support coverage by rotating mentors or IT support so someone is on hand to answer questions quickly, even at odd hours.

- Observe team dynamics and be ready to assist if a team gets blocked or demotivated. A gentle nudge or connecting them with a needed expert can right-size a project.

- Gather content for storytelling and amplifying the impact of the advanced promptathon. Capture photos of teams working together, screenshots of solutions in development, and participant quotes. These will be useful for postevent communications and celebrating success.

- Before presentations, verify that all presentation materials are loaded or that teams are ready to share screens. To streamline, assign an order for teams to present ahead of time.

- Enforce time limits during presentations. Have a timer visible or a moderator gently cut off speakers if necessary, so the schedule stays on track.

- During judges' deliberation, consider how to keep participants engaged. You could run a fun poll for the "People's Choice" award or facilitate a quick roundtable where everyone shares a key insight they learned. This keeps the energy up while judges evaluate the submissions.

- Have prizes and recognition ready. It's good to award the overall winner and recognize other efforts like most innovative, best technical solution, and best teamwork, so multiple teams get kudos. Even if prizes are symbolic, the recognition is highly motivating.

Close on a high note by congratulating everyone and reinforcing how much value they've created in a short time. Ideally, have the executive sponsor reiterate their gratitude and commitment to helping bring the best ideas to life.

Post-promptathon activities

Immediately collect all project artifacts—prompts used, code, slides, videos. An easy way to do this is to have teams upload to a shared folder or DevOps repository. Other key activities at this stage include:

- Within 24 hours of the advanced promptathon ending, send a thank you email to participants, mentors, and judges. Recap the winners and include any highlights from the event.

- Prepare a postevent report summarizing outcomes and lessons to share with leadership and participants. Include metrics like the number of participants, projects, details on the winning ideas, and quotes or survey feedback.

- Schedule follow-up meetings for promising projects as relevant. For example, a pitch to the IT steering committee or AI council.

Recognize participants' efforts publicly, such as with shout-outs in a company-wide meeting or newsletter. This not only rewards the individuals but also highlights the value of these innovation programs to the organization.

Promptathon team roles and responsibilities

Advanced promptathons are a true team effort, requiring clear role definition and expectations. Some of these roles have been highlighted already, but are listed here as a checklist for organizers to help ensure all roles are covered and communicated. Promptathon roles include:

- **Organizing committee** Coordinates the promptathon, troubleshoots issues, and keeps the event running.

- **Executive sponsors** Provide vision and support, help kick off and close the event, and ensure outcomes have a path forward. This could be a CIO, CTO, or other leader who is passionate about innovation.

- **Judges** Typically, 3–5 people, including senior leaders and experts. They evaluate projects based on preset criteria like Innovation, Business Value, Feasibility, Quality of Prompt/Technique, and Presentation. They should be objective and provide constructive feedback. Share an evaluation form or scorecard for consistency and have a brief calibration discussion among judges beforehand to agree on what each criterion means.

- **Mentors and technical advisors** Experienced experts in AI, Copilot, or organizational processes. They roam during solutioning, answering questions, and guiding teams. Mentors might help teams refine their ideas or overcome roadblocks (without doing the work for them). Having dedicated support teams for different aspects, such as one for logistics, one for technical queries, and one for data queries, can greatly enhance the experience for participants.

- **Participants (team members)** Each team will self-organize, but encourage them to assign a team captain (primary contact), a lead presenter, and specialist roles like prompt engineer, data wrangler, and quality assurance tester, depending on the project. This helps ensure that everyone contributes and that key tasks are covered. In advanced promptathons, teams might split work, like one person focusing on prompt design while another may write a script or prepare sample data.

- **Support staff** If in-person, have volunteers or staff to manage practical needs like registering attendees, replenishing food, and handling AV equipment. If virtual, have a moderator for the chat and someone recording sessions as needed.

- **Observers or scribes** Sometimes, having neutral observers take notes on each project can help in judging or postevent reporting. They can note what tools were used and what worked well so they can feed those insights back into adoption plans.

Having these roles defined and people assigned to them ensures the advanced promptathon runs smoothly. These roles mean that everyone knows who to turn to for what, which is crucial in the frenzy of the event when dozens of people are engaged in intense work.

Technical setup and support requirements

The advanced promptathon will push the technical environment to its limits, so prepare accordingly. Ensure all participants have Microsoft 365 Copilot enabled and fully functioning on their accounts across all needed apps. If your tenant has a limit on the number of Copilot users or any throttling, coordinate with Microsoft or your IT admin to accommodate the promptathon usage. You don't want anyone locked out mid-event.

Consider which developer tools are needed. While projects should center on Microsoft 365 Copilot, teams may attempt integrations like using the Microsoft Graph API, Power Automate, or custom code to feed data to Copilot. Make sure they have access to the necessary tools. If using Power Platform (Power Apps, Power Automate) to build something around Copilot, check licenses and environment access. Share the process to enable any relevant API permissions if teams want to call external data. For instance, they might use an API to pull data from a company database and then paste it into Copilot for analysis. Check that code editors and relevant software is installed or available. Common ones might be VS Code for scripting or Postman for calling APIs. If participants use their own laptops, they likely have their preferred tools ready to go; if providing computers, consider preloading them with useful software.

Other technical setup considerations include:

- **Test environment**   If there are concerns about using production data or systems, set up a sandbox environment. This could mean a separate M365 demo tenant loaded with synthetic data where Copilot is enabled (Microsoft may be able to provide one) or simply clearly instructing teams to use only nonsensitive data. Internal promptathons can proceed with production environment access as long as data is accessed acceptably, but it's wise to double-check your organization's policy. If using real data, teams should anonymize or limit what they show in a demo.

- **Data resources**   Provide easy access to any data sets that could spur solutions. For example, an export of anonymized help desk tickets, a set of sample sales reports, or employee handbook documents. Teams might incorporate these into prompts to demonstrate how Copilot solves a real problem (like analyzing common support questions). If you have a data lake or search index, see if teams can query it. If not, encourage them to bring sample data to demonstrate their idea.

- **Remind about data labeling**   If using actual internal documents, ensure they heed confidentiality labels. Copilot will warn or refuse to use data labeled confidential. This is a good thing, but teams should know to either use properly labeled documents or use only publicly shareable info in demos.

- **Infrastructure and connectivity** For on-site promptathons, provide robust WiFi or wired Internet to support promptathon teams that will be simultaneously making API calls and using cloud services. For virtual, ensure VPN or remote access issues are sorted out. Some corporate VPNs might slow down Copilot; maybe advise participants to use a direct connection if possible during solutioning. Have an IT admin on call who can quickly address access issues.

- **Technical support channels** Set up a clear system for participants to get support during the event, like a dedicated "Tech Support" chat channel where participants can post issues and get quick responses or an FAQ document that covers standard Copilot troubleshooting like what to do if Copilot times out or how to handle specific errors.

- **Identify go-to experts for different domains** For example, assign one person for Copilot functional questions, one for data access questions, and one for Power Platform questions. Share this list so teams know who to contact for what.

Have contingency plans if the Copilot service has an outage or limitation. If the Copilot service is slow or down, teams could use the time to work on their presentation or solution logic. This ensures the promptathon isn't wasted. While unlikely, it's good to mention that the idea can still be demonstrated conceptually if the tool fails.

Encourage teams to save outputs and interactions. For instance, screenshot if they get a great result from Copilot during solution development. This way, if the same prompt doesn't yield the exact result later, since large language models (LLMs) can vary responses, they have evidence of what they achieved. It's also useful for their presentation to show the evolution of their prompt.

Security and privacy considerations

Since advanced promptathon projects might push boundaries, it's important to remind teams of ethical AI use, including that:

- They should not attempt to jailbreak or misuse Copilot. The event is about productive use, not attacking the AI.

- Any customer or employee data used should be handled in line with policies, and personal data should be avoided unless it's part of an approved data set.

- If they integrate external services, those services should be approved. Avoid teams secretly using some noncompliant AI tool as a workaround to get a result.

- Keep the hackathon "white hat" by focusing on positive, sanctioned AI innovation.

Ensure everyone has the necessary hardware to securely work on their projects during the promptathon. If someone's device isn't powerful enough to run multiple apps, have a few spare loaner laptops available. Copilot itself is cloud-based, so the computational load is minimal, but if someone's machine is old and struggles with Teams screen-sharing and having multiple Office apps open, that could hold them back. Before the event, test the Copilot features that might get heavy use. For example, if you think many will use Copilot in Excel for large data sets, try it on a large file to see performance. If a particular feature is known to be preview/beta (and possibly unstable), warn the participants so they can avoid relying on it.

Plan to maintain access to development environments after the event. Some promptathons disable special access immediately afterward. However, if possible, allow participants to retain access to the environment they used for a few days to show their department leaders or colleagues. If relevant, it would also allow them to refine their projects for internal showcases.

Ensure the technical canvas is ready to help teams be as creative as possible. By removing roadblocks like access issues and providing sample data, and being prepared to solve problems on the fly, you allow advanced participants to focus on innovation rather than infrastructure.

Engagement strategies: Before, during, after

For the advanced hackathon, engagement is about sustaining energy over a more extended period and amplifying the excitement across the organization about the impact that advanced AI solutions have for people and processes.

Pre-event engagement

Promote the hackathon in the company as a significant innovation event. Even those not participating directly should be aware that it's happening and interested in the outcomes. Use internal newsletters, team meetings, and executive communications to promote the advanced promptathon. This not only helps recruit participants but also indicates the organization's commitment to advancing the use of AI and Copilot. Build buzz through:

- **Countdown and teasers**   In the lead-up to the event, send regular countdown updates and share the promptathon themes (or problem statements). Introduce teams as they are confirmed, perhaps highlighting a few team names and ideas to spark friendly rivalry. Feature short interviews or quotes from participants on why they're excited to take part to build a connection and encourage participation.

- **Executive encouragement**   Have a senior leader send a note to all participants a few days before, highlighting the value of the advanced promptathon to the organization as a key part of the AI enablement strategy. Encouragement from the top can be very motivating.

- **Social media**   If your company is open to it, encourage participants to share their excitement on internal or external social platforms using an event hashtag. For example, an employee might share their challenge in a post on LinkedIn and highlight the upcoming promptathon and what they hope to learn. This can enhance employer branding as an innovative place to work.

- **Pre-event orientation**   Conduct a short orientation webinar for advanced promptathon participants a couple of days before kickoff. Cover final logistics, give people an opportunity to ask questions, and have a past promptathon winner share their advice. Getting everyone together before the big day helps build community and ensures everyone is on the same page.

Make sure remote participants or those from smaller offices feel just as included. For hybrid events, mention that in communications, and highlight that every site or remote individual is a full part of the promptathon. If a social gathering is happening after the event, share the arrangements and extend the invite to anyone who wants to attend.

Engagement during the event

Treat the start of the hackathon like an important event. Play intro music, have the executive sponsor give an enthusiastic speech about innovation, and perhaps show a short inspirational video about AI and the future of work. Creating a spectacle energizes participants and signals that this is a big deal. If virtual, you can still do fun things like encourage everyone to set a virtual background with their team name. Other ideas for an engaging promptathon include:

- **Real-time updates**   Share progress updates with the broader company (if appropriate) throughout the promptathon. For example, post an update on the intranet at the end of day one. Include some photos of teams working or screenshots of virtual teams. This shares the excitement and can spur late interest from people dropping by the venue or tuning into final presentations.

- **Mentor moments**   Have mentors or organizers periodically broadcast general tips or encouragement. For example, post common questions and answers on the group chat, or simply encouraging messages like "All teams are doing great—hang in there, and don't forget to submit your demo concept by 3 PM!" This assures teams that the organizers are engaged and here to help.

- **Wellness checks**   Promptathons can be intense. Encourage short breaks, such as a "Copilot stretch break" where everyone stops coding for five minutes to stretch or walk around. You could even incorporate quick, fun activities like a group photo session or post a trivia question in chat for a small prize. Remind participants to stay hydrated and eat, things people can sometimes forget when deep in problem-solving mode.

- **Capture stories**   During the promptathon, if a team has a breakthrough or a funny moment, document it. They make great anecdotes to share later in newsletters or at the closing ceremony.

- **Cross-team collaboration**   Although it's a competition, encourage teams to help each other and share noncritical insights for everyone's benefit. This builds community and doesn't detract from the competition since each great idea ultimately has the potential to positively impact the organization. You can facilitate this by highlighting how a team overcame an issue if others might benefit from hearing about it (without giving away their core idea).

Include some fun elements to surprise and delight participants. For example, you could hold a spontaneous mini challenge like a "meme challenge," telling participants to create a meme in the next hour about your hackathon experience and share it in the chat. The best meme gets a special snack delivered! These minor diversions can re-energize tired minds and remind people to have fun.

Encourage leaders, who are not judges, to drop by physically or in virtual team rooms to cheer teams on. A director popping in to say, "Hey, team, love what you're doing; keep it up!" can give a boost. Just ensure they don't inadvertently disrupt teams' focus by coordinating supportive brief visits. Also, keep leadership updated on notable developments so they share the excitement and talk up the impact of the promptathon.

Postevent engagement

If possible, have a little celebration after the final presentations. A huge amount of effort and energy goes into running and participating in advanced promptathons, so it's important to celebrate the milestone. In-person, this could be a small party or happy hour for participants, judges, and mentors to unwind together. In hybrid promptathons, a video montage of the best moments and a short group debrief can provide closure. Celebrating immediately while the excitement is high leaves a lasting positive impression. After the event, make sure to:

- **Communicate results** Announce the winners to the wider organization. For example, in an email or intranet post, highlight what was achieved and credit all teams who took part. Encourage employees to contact these innovators to learn more. This disseminates the knowledge and recognizes the effort broadly.

- **Reward and recognition** Besides prizes also consider formal recognition. Participants could receive an internal award certificate or badge (perhaps an "AI Innovator" badge in whatever internal recognition system exists). If your company has a rewards program, give points or perks to participants. The winners might get an opportunity to present to the executive team or at the next all-hands meeting, which offers the reward of kudos and exposure across the organization.

- **Next steps for projects** Communicate what will happen with the advanced promptathon ideas. It's demotivating if projects vanish after the event. Instead, outline a plan to assess how to implement the best ones in production. Team members might be invited to contribute to these implementation projects. Then, make sure to follow up. If there is no formal path, at least encourage teams to continue using their solution informally and gather results.

- **Participant feedback** Survey the participants one or two days after the promptathon. Ask what they liked about the event, what they learned, and what could be improved. Also, ask how it affected their view of Copilot, for example, "Do you feel more confident advocating for AI solutions in your daily work now?" Use suggestions to improve future events or the overall Copilot adoption program.

- **Community building** Leverage the camaraderie built. Invite people to join the Copilot champions program, or start one if you don't already have a community of practice for Copilot. That way, advanced promptathon participants can continue to exchange tips and help drive adoption in their respective teams. These folks are now your internal experts—give them a platform to continue shining and share their knowledge. They might host lunch and learn sessions to show others what they built or share Copilot tips on internal forums.

- **Publicize externally** Share a sanitized event summary on external social media or a company blog if company policy allows. This positions your company as an AI-forward, innovative organization. This not only celebrates employees but can also attract talent interested in a workplace that offers opportunities to develop AI proficiency.

- **Tie back to business goals** Articulate how the promptathon outcomes align with your organization's objectives. This helps leadership see the concrete value created during events like promptathons. It also sets the stage for securing funding or resources to implement the ideas or run more events.

By continuing to engage beyond the advanced promptathon, it becomes more than an event. It will be seen as a moment when the organizational culture evolved. It broadcasts a strong message organization-wide: we are innovating, we are learning, and everyone can be part of our AI journey.

Evaluation metrics and feedback mechanisms

The advanced promptathon is likely the most resource-intensive of the three, so measuring its impact is even more necessary than with beginner or intermediate promptathons. Evaluate both the immediate promptathon outcomes and the broader promptathon program success by evaluating:

- **Participation metrics** The number of participants, teams, and representation across departments or business units. If most major departments participated, that would be a win for broad engagement. Note the mix of roles to demonstrate cross-functional collaboration.

- **Completion rate** How many teams delivered a workable demo or concept by the end? A high completion rate indicates that the event support was sufficient, and the scope was well managed. If some teams didn't finish, note why as a learning for next time. Were they overly ambitious in scope, or did they stumble at technical hurdles?

- **Mentor/support utilization** Track how often mentors were consulted and how many questions were asked on support channels. If support was rarely used, seek specific feedback to understand whether participants were overly self-reliant or support wasn't advertised enough. If it was heavily used, it shows the value of that setup and perhaps indicates a need for more pre-event training.

- **Project outcomes** Review the quality of the projects submitted by advanced promptathon teams:

  - **Innovation and feasibility scores** Use judges' scoring sheets to analyze trends. If innovation scores were high but feasibility scores lower, perhaps allocate more time for feasibility checks or include an implementation planning segment in the next advanced promptathon.

  - **Common themes** Identify if multiple teams tackled similar problems to understand pressing areas that are worth following up. Also, see if certain Copilot features were especially popular or if any feature gaps were identified by teams. Share these insights about what users want with Microsoft and your IT department.

- **Prototype quality**   How many projects are practically implementable? Judges or a follow-up committee can evaluate ideas, for example, into categories like ready for immediate deployment with minor polishing, promising but need further development, or exploratory/learning with less immediate applicability. This ratio helps quantify the tangible output.

- **Return on investment (ROI) estimates**   Estimate the potential impact of the top ideas. For instance, if a solution automates a task that currently takes 10 hours a week for a team, that's about 520 hours saved per year. Providing these numbers gives a notional concept of "value created." These are prototypes, but provide a ballpark of what's at stake if implemented. Companies have found that promptathons can yield solutions that improve operations significantly.

- **Skill development and behavior change**   Consider how the promptathon series has contributed to raising AI literacy across the organization by looking at:

  - **Copilot upskilling**   Survey participants on their Copilot proficiency before and after events. If most report a large improvement, that's a key indication that capability has increased at scale. Also, ask if they learned to use new tools. Perhaps someone learned to use Power Automate in service of their Copilot project—that's a bonus skill acquired.

  - **Confidence and AI mindset**   Ask if participants are more likely to experiment with AI at work after taking part in a promptathon. Do they feel empowered to lead AI initiatives? This can be qualitative feedback. It aligns with the idea that promptathons shift culture and help overcome the "AI skills gap" by providing opportunities for hands-on experience with Copilot.

  - **Champion identification**   Note if any participants naturally took on leadership or mentoring roles during the promptathon. These individuals could be great contributors to the ongoing champion program or future promptathon facilitators. It's a success if the program not only built solutions but also surfaced new leaders in innovation.

  - **Adoption and usage metrics**   Monitor Microsoft 365 Copilot usage in the weeks and months after the promptathon series, especially in areas related to promptathon projects. For example, if a project was about using Copilot for project status reports, see if more people start using Copilot to draft status emails or documents. It might be subtle to trace, but any uptick coinciding with promptathon participants' influence is notable. Track how many participants (or their close colleagues) become active Copilot users if they weren't before. Internally, you might have metrics like the number of monthly Copilot prompts per user. If hackathon folks go from near-zero to dozens of prompts a week, that's a big adoption win. If you created a prompt library or knowledge repository during the program, measure its contributions or accesses. Are people reusing hackathon-developed prompts or ideas?

Follow through to extend promptathon impact

Within 3–6 months, check the status of top ideas that came out of the promptathon series. Keep track of how many have been implemented or are in progress and whether any encounter barriers, such as technical, compliance, or budgetary, that stopped them from being implemented. Document these as lessons. Record any measurable benefits from any implemented projects. Even a single project making it to production can often justify the effort, especially if it yields ongoing savings or new capabilities. Highlight these wins in reports and future pitches for continuing the Microsoft 365 Copilot promptathon program.

Reflect on the success of the program and highlight the impact with leaders by evaluating:

- **Engagement growth**   How many people engaged with at least one event? Some may have joined at the beginner promptathon and not progressed, while others might jump in at the intermediate or advanced stage later as awareness spreads. If the number of active Copilot users in the company increased significantly while running these events, that's a strong indicator of success.

- **Adoption rates**   Compare Copilot adoption metrics like licenses active and frequency of use before and after the program time frame. The promptathon series should correlate with a boost in adoption and proficiency.

- **Qualitative culture shift**   Gather anecdotes from leadership and employees. For instance, a manager might report, "After the hackathon, my team has been much more proactive in automating tasks with Copilot". These stories can be more influential than formal training programs in driving culture change.

- **Sustained communities**   Is there now a self-sustaining Copilot or AI community in the organization? Perhaps a champions community or even active forums where regular knowledge sharing happens. The existence of a vibrant community suggests that the promptathon program succeeded in seeding continuous learning.

- **Repeatability**   Did new ideas for future use cases or training emerge? If the events uncovered enough interest that departments requested targeted promptathons for their teams or requested it to be an annual program, that's a sign that the series had a big impact in driving AI curiosity and use.

Compile the evaluation into a comprehensive report or presentation for stakeholders. Use data and quotes to tell the story of how a crawl-walk-run approach drove Copilot adoption. Share this report in an open forum or town hall to close the loop with the community involved. Recognize the efforts of organizers and participants and celebrate the results to reinforce the value of these events.

Finally, consider this question: Did the promptathon series meet its objectives of increasing Copilot skills, innovation, engagement, and adoption? Based on the metrics above, you should be able to answer with a resounding yes and have the data to back it up.

As a result of beginner, intermediate, and advanced promptathon events, Microsoft 365 Copilot adoption will be accelerated as users are enabled to discover new scenarios and learn from each other, leading to more frequent and effective use of Copilot in daily tasks. The organization benefits from improved productivity and innovative solutions, and employees benefit from growth opportunities and reduced time spent on mundane tasks.

The "crawl, walk, run" adoption journey starts at the beginner level to build awareness and foundational skills. Then, encourages practice and intermediate mastery, and finally, unlocks advanced AI innovation. The outcome is a workforce that not only adopts Copilot but also continuously finds creative ways to create value with it. With careful planning, robust support, and a focus on continuous learning, your internal promptathon series will drive immediate engagement and long-term transformation in how your organization works with AI.

Microsoft AI innovation challenge playbook

In this appendix, you will:

- Understand what an innovation challenge is and how you can use this event format to engage nontechnical people across your organization in AI innovation.

- Learn how to prepare for and run a successful innovation challenge and create a backlog of ideas for problems that can be solved with the help of Copilot.

An innovation challenge is a powerful way to engage stakeholders across your organization who might not typically get involved in technology projects but have valuable and innovative ideas on how AI can be used to improve processes. This is especially helpful in the early stages of rolling out Copilot to spark creativity and uncover impactful ideas from people for whom technology is not their core focus.

This playbook guides you through organizing a Microsoft AI Innovation Challenge where teams of business stakeholders pitch problems that they would like solved with the help of Copilot and AI. These challenges generate fresh solutions, energize employees, and reinforce a culture of innovation. Use the strategies in this playbook to help you plan, execute, and maximize engagement for an AI-focused innovation challenge.

Planning timeline and event structure

It's important to dedicate sufficient time to planning so that you achieve the goals you've set for running your Microsoft AI innovation challenge. You'll want to focus pre-event activities on getting the right buy-in and creating buzz for the event, so that you can give participants enough time to form ideas and maximize the experience on the day.

Step-by-step planning

This section outlines the planning steps you could take from 30 days before a one-day challenge, right up to the day of the event, to run a successful innovation challenge.

- **30 days before the event**   Executive green-light
  - Secure an executive sponsor, budget, and a firm event date.

- Book the venue, create the Teams channel and Live event for the innovation challenge, and hold the slot on the corporate calendar.
- Confirm a judging panel and outline prize funding.

- **28 days before the event**   Craft the innovation challenge brief

  - Write a two-page brief covering the theme for the Microsoft AI innovation challenge, any rules, judging rubric, prizes, and timeline.
  - Avoid technical jargon—the audience is business users.
  - Share an early draft with the executive sponsor for sign-off.

- **25 days before the event**   Build and test the Microsoft Form for event registration

  - Create an 'Idea Intake Form' to capture interest and ideas from participants. Once you've built the form, save a copy as a template so you can reuse it for future innovation challenges. Form fields might include:
    - ❑ Idea title (short).
    - ❑ Submitter name (can be auto-captured).
    - ❑ Short description of the problem (about 50 words)
    - ❑ What are the pain points in the current process?
    - ❑ What should the future process look like?
    - ❑ Data sources and connectors you think we'll need.
    - ❑ Team members (names, roles, and departments).
    - ❑ Can this idea be applied outside your area?
    - ❑ Business units affected.
    - ❑ Region (if your organization has more than one location).
    - ❑ Average effort per employee on current process (hours/week).
    - ❑ Number of people currently doing this task.
    - ❑ Potential value to the organization if fully developed.
    - ❑ Estimated percent of effort reduction if the idea is implemented.

> **Tip**   Keep the form to one page and use branching sparingly to avoid overwhelm. Enable optional file upload for early sketches and auto-generate a confirmation email that summarizes the entry so teams can see and refine their estimates before the day of the innovation challenge. Use Copilot in Microsoft Forms to help you build the form quickly.

- **21 days before the event**   First participant communications

  - Send a "Save the Date—Join us for a Microsoft AI Innovation Challenge" email to relevant teams and departments.

- Post the same email on your internal comms channels, such as Viva Engage, and put it in the new Teams channel that you created for the innovation challenge.
- Include the event registration link and encourage people to sign up. Keep the narrative inspirational—explain the purposed of the innovation challenge and briefly outline how it works.

■ **18 days before the event**   Run an introductory webinar

- Host (and record) a 30-minute intro to the Microsoft AI innovation challenge format, including a high-level overview of what's possible with Microsoft's AI platform for nontechnical staff.
- Take time for Q&A, drawing out questions people might have about whether they are qualified to attend. Remove barriers and make it clear that the innovation challenge is for people with problems to solve; they don't have to come with solutions.
- Post the recording to the Teams channel to amplify the reach of this message.

■ **14 days before the event**   Optional ideation workshop

- Run a one-hour brainstorming session, either in-person or virtually, with digital collaboration tools like Klaxoon, Miro, or Microsoft Whiteboard.
- Invite volunteer mentors so teams can double-check early ideas.
- This can be a great way to spark ideas and create buzz for the event.

■ **10 days before the event**   Idea-submission window opens

- Share the "Idea Intake Form" via email, internal social networks, and the innovation challenge Teams channel.
- Encourage people to share ideas and remind staff that even a rough outline is acceptable; they can refine it later.

> **Tip**   Ask your executive sponsors and supportive managers to highlight the importance of the innovation challenge. Encourage them to take this opportunity to get visibility to solve some of the most painful challenges their teams face.

■ **7 days before the event**   Build buzz and gather ideas

- Send an upbeat reminder email: "One week left—need help with ideas?"
- Share an anonymized example of a strong, concise submission to set the bar.
- Announce follow-up office hours for last-minute questions.

■ **5 days before the event**   Mentor office hours

- Hold a drop-in Teams call or an in-person huddle, where mentors answer questions about ideas, provide advice on value estimates, and demystify AI tool choices.

- **3 days before the event**   Team roster freeze and final call for ideas

  - Lock in final team names and member lists to set pitch order and print agendas.

  - Double-check IT/AV needs if you plan to live stream pitches.

- **2 days before the event**   What to expect on the day

  - Email every team the detailed agenda, pitch order, judging rubric, and slide/video submission instructions.

  - Include tips on recording a 5–10 minute pitch either in PowerPoint or Teams.

- **1 day before the event**   Tech dress-rehearsal and judge preview

  - Collect all Form responses and export them to Excel for the judges to review.

  - Run a quick AV test of the live stream or projector setup.

  - Share anonymized idea summaries with judges.

  - Brief executive sponsors so they can plan to show support for the event.

- **The day of the event**   Microsoft AI innovation challenge day

  - Have the organizing team arrive early for final checks and preparation.

  - Partner with Microsoft, IT, and executives to capture as much value as possible throughout the day.

Innovation challenge day breakdown

Depending on the theme of your innovation challenge and the scale of the teams taking part, the agenda you set might differ from this sample. It's helpful to break the day into morning and afternoon sessions and provide clear guidance on how teams should use the time in each session.

Morning session

Start with a high-energy kickoff by the most senior and visible executive sponsor. The goal is to outline the organization's objectives and the vision for how AI can help drive those goals.

Teams then split off into their own spaces, either in person or via Microsoft Teams, to refine their ideas and prepare their PowerPoint presentation and video pitch. Have mentors or coaches float between the teams to answer any questions.

Share clear timings with the teams and schedule reminders, for example, "One hour to go until you need to submit your presentations and videos." It's a good idea to set a hard deadline of midday for all teams to have uploaded their files to the Teams channel. This ensures everyone gets the same amount of time to work on their pitch, and also gives the organizers a chance to check that all the videos are working before the pitch broadcast after lunch.

Breaks and lunch

Instruct teams to take breaks as they need to. Given the short time frame to build out their innovative idea and craft a compelling pitch, many teams will be tempted to work through. Provide snacks and drinks stations so that they can quickly grab food if they want to keep working.

Afternoon session

Straight after lunch, get into the pitches. This works by broadcasting the prerecorded pitch videos to those gathered in the room, or via Teams if running the event remotely or for a hybrid audience. (More on the event format is in the next section.) Play the videos in the order defined by the agenda.

Judges deliberate while participants grab refreshments and take a chance to talk about their ideas and what they have learned with their colleagues. Bring everyone back together for the awards ceremony. Make it a celebration, with feedback and photo-ops. Thank the executive sponsors and include an announcement of what happens next to take the winning ideas forward.

After the challenge

Don't lose the momentum that your innovation challenge creates. After the event, send a highlight reel via email and Teams posts. Celebrate the winners and share fun stats and photos from the day. Issue a quick feedback survey to participants and judges to see what people loved about the event and what they'd like to see improved. Kick off a lightweight incubation plan with IT or an innovation squad for the top ideas.

Issue digital badges, or if budget allows, ship swag or certificates to all participants to reinforce recognition and encourage awareness for future events.

Getting the format right

If you can, the most impactful Microsoft AI innovation challenges are run as hybrid events. This allows anyone in the organization to participate regardless of location. Each team chooses their area to work from and joins a Microsoft Teams breakout room to brainstorm ideas and prepare their pitch. Once the idea and solution are defined, hybrid teams can use Microsoft Teams to record their pitch.

Choose the right collaboration platforms

Microsoft 365 provides collaborative online platforms such as Microsoft Teams and SharePoint. Typically, to run an innovation challenge, you'll use:

- A communication hub like Microsoft Teams with channels for announcements and team discussions
- Video conferencing for a live kickoff session at the start of the day, and to enable hybrid teams to work together in small groups

- A submission tool, which could be as simple as a SharePoint or Teams folder or a Microsoft Form on your intranet where teams upload their presentations and videos

- An idea brainstorming tool like a Miro board or Teams Whiteboard, where teams can collaborate visually while forming their ideas

Creating community atmosphere

Create a fun, engaging environment for the innovation challenge. One that makes people who hear about it or walk past want to stop and get involved. Borrow ideas from tech hackathons—provide sustenance and swag. Supplying food and drinks (think pizza, coffee, snacks) keeps the energy up throughout the intense working sessions. Play upbeat music during work periods or breaks. You might decorate the venue with posters or banners related to the theme. This should feel like an exciting event, not just another meeting. Emphasize that standard work rules are relaxed: encourage creative thinking, brainstorming on whiteboards, and cross-team mingling.

Have organizers, mentors, or coaches available to assist teams. They should drop into the team's breakout room to offer help. For an AI challenge with noncoders, mentors could be IT staff or data scientists who clarify what Microsoft AI tech might do ("Yes, Azure Cognitive Services could automate that task") without building it for them. Your Copilot champions would also make incredible mentors and coaches for this event. Their presence can inspire teams and help shape viable ideas.

Consider global time zones if your workforce is distributed. For live webinars or meetings, try to pick reasonable times across key regions or record sessions for those who can't attend live. Avoid low energy times of the week, like Friday afternoons. Keep virtual or hybrid teams engaged by replicating the interactivity of an in-person event. Just as you would walk past a team at an in-person event and offer encouragement, jump into virtual rooms to celebrate milestones: "We're halfway through—great ideas coming in!" This consistent engagement prevents drop-off in a virtual setting.

It can be harder for team members to collaborate remotely, especially if they don't usually work together. Encourage the use of video calls for team brainstorms. If participants are shy, consider an ice-breaker at kickoff to create a sense of community. Also, enforce a code of conduct—remind everyone to be respectful and inclusive online. This ensures a safe, welcoming virtual space for everyone.

Don't forget to leverage the advantages of virtual collaboration. Virtual facilitation allows you to include more people, potentially hundreds, since there is no physical space limit. It also saves costs on venues or food. Use that budget instead to cover prizes or swag that can be shipped direct to participants. Another benefit is that you can easily bring in guest speakers or mentors from anywhere. A Microsoft AI expert could give a short talk via Teams to inspire participants. Embrace these opportunities that an online format offers.

Guidelines for participants: Craft a winning AI pitch

This section guides participants in developing a compelling pitch that checks all the boxes. Share these tips with all teams—perhaps as a one-pager or briefing at kickoff—to help them focus on what matters.

Understand the judging criteria

Participants should know how their ideas will be evaluated upfront. Provide a submission template so that they can see what key areas judges care about. This often includes:

- Team presentation
- Problem statement
- Solution concept and business value
- Business value measures
- Social impact

Make sure teams understand each category in detail. The pitch should clearly describe the role they see AI or Copilot playing in the idea and articulate why it's innovative. This section outlines what the judges are looking for in each part of the presentation.

Team presentation

Introduce the team and their background. A brief slide with team names, member names, and departments represented gives context. Diverse teams with a mix of roles from different departments often produce well-rounded ideas, so encourage cross-functional teaming. Judges won't score based on job titles, but showing that the concept has input from different perspectives can be a plus.

Keep this section short—enough to humanize the team, but the focus should remain on the idea.

Problem statement

Clearly articulate the problem or opportunity your idea addresses. Who experiences this problem, and what is the impact? A strong problem statement should succinctly convey what issue exists and why it's worth solving. Participants should describe the current pain points or inefficiencies in concrete terms (such as, "It currently takes 5 days to compile this report, causing delays in decision-making").

Emphasize why it's an excellent opportunity to fix this now; maybe new AI capabilities make it feasible now. Be brief and clear—ideally, two or three bullet points hitting what, who, and why. A compelling problem statement grabs the judges' attention early.

Solution concept and business value

Describe your proposed solution—what is it, and how does it leverage Microsoft AI to solve the problem? Then, articulate the business value it would bring. This is the heart of the pitch. Participants should focus on benefits and outcomes rather than technical jargon. Explain how the solution would improve things. Will it save time? Cut costs? Increase revenue? Improve customer or employee satisfaction?

An example might outline that "Using an AI chatbot to handle routine inquiries, our solution could free up 20 percent of call center agents' time, allowing them to focus on high-value calls." Tie the value to company goals like efficiency, accuracy, growth, or strategic initiatives whenever possible. Provide specifics or examples where possible. Judges will look for a clear link between the concept and tangible business impact.

Business value measures

If teams can quantify the impact, it dramatically strengthens the pitch. Encourage participants to estimate metrics—even rough numbers—that illustrate potential return on investment (ROI) or savings of time or resources. For instance, "We estimate this AI tool could save about 5,000 hours of manual work per year." Show your work. How did you arrive at the figure? A simple formula to calculate hours saved could look like:

$$\textit{Annual hours saved} = \textit{(number of people doing the task)} \times \textit{(hours each person spends per occurrence)} \times \textit{(frequency of the task per week)} \times \textit{(weeks per year)}$$

To get the numbers to insert in this formula, you need to:

- Count how many employees perform the process.

- Measure (or estimate) how long it currently takes each time.

- Note how often it happens (daily, weekly, and so on).

- Multiply those three numbers, and then multiply by 52 (or the relevant number of weeks) to get an annual total.

Once your proposed AI solution is in place, repeat the same equation based on the new process, then subtract to find the net hours saved.

Other business value measures might capture error rate reduction or customer satisfaction score improvements. While this section is optional, it differentiates great pitches from good ones. Advise teams to make reasonable, supportable assumptions (they can mention any baseline data they used). Judges will appreciate the effort to back up claims with numbers.

Social impact

This section of the presentation is usually optional but encouraged. If an idea has a positive social or environmental impact beyond pure business value, teams should highlight it. Does the solution contribute to sustainability by reducing paper or energy use? Does it improve inclusivity, accessibility, or benefit employee well-being? While this may not be the primary judging criterion (unless your challenge specifically emphasizes social impact), it can be a tiebreaker or an "extra credit" factor. Plus, it aligns with many companies' values and environmental, sustainability, and governance (ESG) goals. Encourage sincerity—only include this if relevant, not as fluff. A genuine social benefit, even a small one, can add depth to the idea.

Include visual elements

Show, don't just tell. A visual element helps bring the idea to life. Teams do not need to develop a working prototype, especially since this is a pitch challenge, but they can include mock-ups, sketches, or diagrams to illustrate how the solution might work. For example, a mock-up of an app screen, a flowchart of the AI input and output process, or even a storyboard of a user scenario. This makes the concept more concrete for the judges. If a team has the capability, a short demo in their pitch video, even an imagined scenario, can be very impactful. Remind participants that visuals should complement the narrative; prioritize clarity over artistry. A simple PowerPoint graphic can do the job if it conveys the user experience or process.

Tell a compelling story

In preparing their 5–10 minute video pitch, teams should aim to tell a cohesive story: present the problem, introduce the solution, show its value, and conclude with a strong finish; maybe you could include a vision of the future if this idea is implemented. Encourage a conversational, engaging tone in the video. Business stakeholders can leverage their communication skills here.

Teams might use a slide recording in PowerPoint or record in Teams with members talking through slides/screens. It doesn't need to be Hollywood quality; judges look more at content than video editing. However, good pacing (not rushing or dragging) and an audible and clear voice-over are essential. Suggest that teams rehearse a few times and ensure they stay within the time limit. It helps to simulate a "pitch" as if speaking to company executives or the judging panel live. This prepares them for any live Q&A and tends to produce a crisper video.

> **Tip** Record your pitch rehearsals in Teams with Copilot transcription turned on. Then, once the transcription is completed, ask Copilot to summarize your key message and highlight the innovative elements of your idea. Refine based on the feedback to maximize your communication and the impact of your idea.

Judges won't expect a fully detailed implementation plan since these are ideas from nontechnical teams. However, it boosts credibility if the team thinks about the feasibility of their solution, for example, does the needed data exist in the company, or would this require new data collection? Is the idea something that could realistically be piloted in a year? Encourage teams to mention any obvious requirements or steps (like "we'd need to partner with IT to integrate this into our CRM system"). They don't need to solve it all now, but showing awareness of what it would take can impress judges that this idea is realistic.

Finally, encourage participants to be creative and bold. Judges love to see innovative thinking that differentiates the idea or excites people. This could be an unexpected use of AI, a clever twist on a process, or a novel problem being tackled. A good question for teams to ask themselves: "What's the most innovative aspect of our idea?" and make sure that it shines through in the pitch. Even if the idea is simple, the approach or impact may be inspiring, so be sure to highlight that. Passion and enthusiasm come across in a pitch, so teams that believe in their idea should let it show.

These guidelines will help participants nail their submissions. You can even provide a Template presentation deck and a checklist based on the above so that all teams know what's expected of them. The goal is to help every team put their best foot forward, regardless of technical skill, focusing on clear problem-solving and business outcomes.

Judging criteria and scoring rubric

Defining transparent judging criteria is crucial for fairness and helps teams understand how they'll be evaluated. For the Microsoft innovation challenge, judges should ideally come from both business and technical backgrounds. For example, the judges could be a mix of business unit leaders, an IT/AI expert, and maybe an external innovation coach or Microsoft partner. This ensures a balanced perspective when assessing ideas for business viability and appropriate use of AI. Provide judges and participants with a rubric that broadly aligns with the submission sections and overall goals of the challenge.

Key judging criteria with possible weighting or scoring guidelines could include:

- **Problem clarity and significance (15 percent)**   Is the problem or opportunity significant and clearly defined? Judges look for a clear articulation of the problem and its importance to the organization. A top score here means the team identified a real pain point or opportunity area that resonates.

- **Innovation and solution creativity (20 percent)**   How creative or innovative is the proposed solution? Does it cleverly or effectively leverage Microsoft AI technologies? The idea should stand out in its originality and innovative use of tech. Judges will favor ideas that are not just copycats of existing solutions. The valuate is based on the unique value created by the solution, not the technical complexity.

- **Use of Microsoft AI (15 percent)**   Evaluate how well the idea harnesses the capabilities of Microsoft's AI platform. Is the choice of AI tool appropriate to the problem? This prevents ideas from being "AI-washed" and allows judges to determine whether AI is an integral solution enabler rather than a tacked-on buzzword.

- **Business value and impact (20 percent)**   How much value could this idea deliver to the organization if implemented? Judges consider both the magnitude of the benefit and how well the team articulated it. High scores are awarded for ideas that promise significant ROI or strategic advantage and back them up with reasoning or data. Even smaller-scale ideas can score well if they convincingly address a niche but important problem.

- **Measurability of outcomes (10 percent)**   Did the team provide metrics or a measure of success? Judges aren't expecting detailed financial models, but some quantifications like hours saved or percentage improvement on core KPIs show the team did its homework. This criterion rewards teams that take the time to evaluate their solution's impact.

- **Feasibility and practicality (10 percent)** Given the company context, how feasible is the idea to implement? An idea that requires completely unrealistic resources or assumes perfect data might score lower, whereas an idea that could be piloted with accessible data and tools would score higher. Judges weigh whether the solution seems technically achievable (with available AI tools) and is likely to gain organization-wide adoption. This doesn't mean the simplest idea always wins, but truly outlandish ideas might lose points here. Mentors or an IT judge can help assess this.

- **Presentation and demo quality (10 percent)** How well did the team communicate their idea? This includes the clarity of the presentation, the quality of the video pitch, and the effectiveness of any visuals or demonstrations. A well-structured, engaging pitch that tells a story can edge out a similarly good idea that was poorly presented. Judges will award points for clear and compelling pitches. Strong communication reflects the team's understanding of and belief in their idea.

- **Social impact (bonus points)** If social impact is a stated goal of your challenge or a value for your organization, you can include it as a bonus points category. For instance, "+5 points for significant positive social or sustainability impact." This way, teams that don't address it aren't penalized, but those that do can be rewarded. If the social impact is core to the challenge, make it a weighted criterion instead, but in a general corporate challenge, it might be more appropriate as a bonus.

Each criterion can be scored on a numeric scale and weighted as suggested to compute a total score for each team. For simplicity, many internal competitions use a 5-point scale per criterion, where 1 = poor and 5 = excellent. Ensure judges share a common understanding of what each score means. It's often helpful if judges make short notes justifying scores, especially for close calls or to provide valuable team feedback.

Judging process

Decide if the judging will happen individually, where each judge scores all submissions individually and then scores are aggregated, or via a panel discussion where judges view pitches and then confer to decide winners. A hybrid can work well. Have judges do initial scoring independently to reduce bias, then hold a meeting to discuss top entries and finalize winners. Emphasize fairness and consistency; every team should be evaluated on the same criteria. If possible, use a scoring sheet or an online form that tallies scores to simplify this process.

Also, consider allowing a "People's Choice" vote separate from the main judging. For instance, employees or audience members can vote for their favorite idea via an internal poll. This can be an additional award recognizing the crowd favorite, fostering more engagement with the challenge, and amplifying the impact by encouraging people to watch the pitch videos if posted internally. Make it clear that the judging panel decides the official winners, but a People's Choice award is a fun supplement that gives insight into what people care about.

Once judging is complete, prepare feedback for teams. Even if you don't share detailed scores with everyone, it's good practice to let teams know how they did and why the winners won. For example, announce the winners with a summary: "Team X won for their innovative approach to Y that judges felt had a high business impact and clear ROI. Team Z was runner-up due to the creativity of their AI solution tackling a major pain point." This transparency helps all participants learn and feel that the process was merit-based.

Prizes and incentives

The right prizes can drive participation and show that the organization values innovation. When choosing prizes, tailor them to your audience's interests. Since participants are business stakeholders, and likely internal employees consider incentives that reward them personally or within the corporate context. Motivating prize ideas could include:

- **Monetary rewards**   These could be cash bonuses, gift cards, or a budget for a team outing. Even a modest cash prize can motivate employees, though money isn't the only motivator. Some companies also offer stock or shares as a prize for big innovation wins, aligning the reward with the organization's success. Ensure any cash or stock prize complies with HR policies for fairness.

- **Executive recognition**   An opportunity for the winning team to present their idea to senior executives or at a high-profile internal forum can be hugely rewarding. For example, an opportunity for winners to present to the CEO and leadership team, or get featured in the Company's town hall. This gives participants face time with leadership and recognition as innovators. Even an informal but memorable "coffee chat with the CEO" could be valued by the winners.

- **Incubation and implementation support**   Many participants are motivated by seeing their ideas come to life. Consider making the prize something like "winning idea will be considered for pilot implementation with a $Xk budget" or access to a special innovation fund. Promise resources or project time to develop the idea further with IT or a relevant department. Coupling this with mentorship, where winners get a series of coaching sessions from an AI expert or Microsoft engineers to refine the concept, can also be valuable. It signals that the Company is serious about innovation, not just giving out prizes.

- **Career learning opportunities**   Innovation challenges can highlight talent. A clever incentive could be offering winners or top teams a chance to attend a conference or training program of their choice related to innovation or AI, funded by the organization as an investment in employees' growth. In some cases, outstanding participants might even earn internal promotions or roles in innovation projects. While you shouldn't promise a promotion outright, you can certainly involve HR in leveraging the innovation challenge to identify and reward high-potential employees.

- **Experiences and perks**   Internal competitions often reward winners with unique experiences. If travel policies allow, some companies have offered paid travel to another office or innovation hub, like visiting Microsoft's campus or a tech center.

  - Tickets to industry events, tech expos, or fun events like sports games or concerts.
  - Extra vacation days or an "Innovation Day Off" to relax after the intense work.

- Team celebration dinner or team outing sponsored by the organization.

- **Bragging rights and swag**   Don't underestimate the value people place on simple rewards, such as a nice trophy, plaque, or certificate for the winning team, as a lasting reminder of their achievement. Feature winners and participants in the company newsletter or on the intranet homepage. Public recognition can be cherished as much as a physical prize. You could also give participants something to commemorate the event, like a t-shirt, mug, or medal, which makes everyone feel like a winner and incentivizes participation next time.

If your challenge has multiple finalist teams or category winners (such as "Most Innovative" or "Biggest Business Impact"), prepare prize tiers. For instance, the grand prize might be the implementation budget plus $100 gift cards for each team member, and perhaps second-place team members each get $50 gift cards and a small trophy. Spreading prizes encourages more teams. Also, consider a spot prize for anyone who submitted a valid entry to reward participation. This could be a smaller item like a new gadget, tablet, or a popular piece of branded swag. It signals that you had a chance at something even if you didn't win.

Ensure prize decisions align with company policies, given that some firms have caps on gift values or rules about equity for contest rewards. Work with HR and Legal early to clear your approach to prizes. Budget for prizes in advance to ensure you get approval as part of planning.

Finally, when announcing the innovation challenge, hype the prizes appropriately. Emphasize the intrinsic rewards, too: participating is a chance to learn new skills, network across departments, and positively impact the organization. Sometimes, framing the challenge as contributing to a greater good for the organization or society in general can be highly motivating beyond the prize incentives. Use prizes to attract interest but sustain engagement by appealing to participants' passion to learn, innovate, and be recognized.

Driving engagement and excitement

Even the best-planned challenge needs active engagement to succeed. This section covers tips to create buzz, sustain momentum, and ensure participants have a positive, memorable experience. High engagement leads to more and better ideas and strengthens your innovative culture. These strategies will help drive engagement and excitement:

- **Leadership sponsorship**   One of the strongest motivators for employees is seeing leadership backing the innovation challenge. Secure an executive sponsor to champion the event, or for a large-scale event, involve several sponsors. Ask them to send the initial invite or speak at the kickoff, expressing why this challenge matters to the organization. Throughout the challenge, get leaders to proactively encourage teams. This assures participants that their efforts are valued at the highest levels. Leadership involvement can also nudge hesitant participants to join the challenge.

- **Effective promotion**   Treat the challenge like a product you're marketing internally. Use multiple channels to spread the word: emails, intranet banners, internal social networks like Viva Engage, or digital signage in offices. A short promo video can be effective, especially featuring leaders or past innovation challenge highlights. Keep messaging upbeat and inclusive: make it clear it's for everyone, not just tech folks. Invite people to join and clearly communicate:

- The purpose of the event: to innovate with AI to solve our business challenges.
- What's in it for me? (WIIFM) for staff—prizes, skill building, recognition
- How to participate.

- **Build community**   Fostering a sense of community and competition will energize participants. Set up an online community space like a Teams channel, as mentioned, and encourage sharing. You could have a "Team Spotlight" where you introduce one team each day. Encourage peer interaction; the more people feel part of a movement, the more engaged they'll be.

- **Gamify the experience**   Gamification can create excitement. You might give points or badges for specific actions: forming a team early, attending a workshop, submitting on time, or helping another team. While not everyone is driven by points, it adds an element of fun. If you have the means, a live leaderboard (even showing the number of ideas submitted by each department) can stimulate friendly rivalry.

- **Support and mentor access**   Participants will be more engaged if they can overcome obstacles. Set up support systems like an "AI help desk," office hours, or a channel where an expert will answer questions daily. If possible, assign a mentor to each team. These could be volunteer technical folks or past innovation challenge winners who check in with the team regularly and provide advice. Bringing in expert guides (external or internal) significantly helps nontechnical participants and boosts productivity. Mentors keep teams from getting discouraged and can inspire new ideas, keeping engagement high.

- **Interim milestones and feedback**   Create interim milestones to prevent a drop in energy halfway through the innovation challenge. For example, ask teams to share a one-page idea summary in the middle of the morning session. This serves two purposes: it forces teams to firm up their concept early and allows you to give them feedback. Judges or organizers can review these short summaries and send encouragement or tips. This feedback loop shows teams you're invested in their success and keeps them engaged in working towards the final submission.

- **Proactively address low engagement**   Despite best efforts, if you notice low sign-ups or teams struggling to progress, take action. Common reasons could be a lack of time, unclear instructions, or intimidation by the topic. Counter these by reiterating leadership support, offering quick training sessions, and reminding everyone that all ideas are welcome. If only a few teams are participating, contact other departments to encourage them personally. Sometimes, a direct nudge or identifying a problem for them can spur more involvement. Keep the tone positive and invitational. Double down on communication and support if engagement is lagging.

- **Leverage success stories**   Throughout and especially at the end, shine a spotlight on success. Share testimonials or short interviews from participants to inspire others and validate participants' efforts. If a particular team finds a great insight or even discovers something the organization can implement (even if they didn't win), make sure they are acknowledged and celebrated. Seeing tangible outcomes keeps the innovation momentum going beyond the event itself.

Not everyone will win, but everyone should enjoy participating. The journey should be as rewarding as the destination; participants who have fun will spread positive word of mouth and join your next challenge. Implementing these strategies will create an engaging experience for participants. The excitement is infectious—if you, as the organizer, show passion and celebrate every small win, participants will mirror that energy.

Communication templates and examples

Clear communication is vital at every stage of the innovation challenge. These suggestions provide ideas for key communications you'll need as a starting point. Customize for your organization, using the language that feels most relevant to your culture. You might also find it helpful to announce the challenge at a meeting and follow up with an email with these details, as it's a lot of information to cover. Remember to keep the tone friendly and encouraging; we aim to excite people, not intimidate them.

Challenge Invitation

The innovation challenge announcement and invitation email covers the essentials: what, who, when, how, and why. The tone should be enthusiastic and informative. Adjust the level of detail based on your organization's culture, but keep it friendly and direct. You're asking people to register for the challenge, so highlight that link to ensure people can find it easily.

Subject: Join our AI Innovation Challenge—We need your ideas!

Hi team,

We are excited to announce the *[organization name]* AI Innovation Challenge! This is a fun and competitive event where teams of 1–6 people will pitch innovative ideas leveraging Microsoft AI technologies to solve our business challenges. If you have a creative idea, we want to hear it! No coding skills are required.

Why participate?

- **Make an impact:** Tackle a real problem or opportunity in our business and propose a solution. Your idea could shape our future.
- **Learn and innovate:** Discover the latest in AI—we'll provide resources and support—and develop new skills in creativity and problem-solving.
- **Prizes and recognition:** Exciting prizes await—think gadgets, gift cards, and a chance to present to our executive team.
- **Have fun:** Step out of your day-to-day routine and work with colleagues in a high-energy, supportive environment.

Challenge overview:

Theme: Innovate with Microsoft AI—"*[your theme tagline]*"

Who can join: All employees at *[Organization]*, technical or not. Cross-functional teams are encouraged. Don't have a team? We can help you find one!

Format: In person or via Teams.

Key dates:

- **Launch/kickoff:** *[Date & Time]*. Join us at *[venue/link]* for the kickoff event, which will feature a special intro by *[leader's name]*.
- **Team registration deadline:** *[Date]*. (This is just so we know who's participating; you can still refine your idea after this.)
- **Final submissions due:** *[Date & Time]*. Submit your pitch deck and video for judging.
- **Awards and winners announced:** *[Date]*. The winners will be revealed [at the event/via live stream].

How to register:

- Form a team of up to six people.

Tip: Diversity in skills makes a strong team!

- Choose a team name.
- Register your team by filling out this short Form at *[insert link]* by *[Registration deadline]*. We'll then share the submission template and more info.

If you want to join but need help finding teammates, reply to this email—we'll connect you with others.

Resources: [Add a link to Participant resources, including the submission template, judging criteria, and Microsoft AI idea starters.]

We'll also hold an optional "AI Basics" workshop on *[Date]* to inspire your thinking.

This is your chance to showcase your creativity and help drive *[Organization]* forward. Let's innovate together with the power of AI.

Ready to accept the challenge? Click *[here]* to register your team now. If you have any questions, please contact *[Organizer Name]*.

Game on, and good luck to all innovators!

— *[Your Name]*, Innovation Challenge organizer

Reminders on the day

On the day of the innovation challenge, schedule reminders to be sent at key points throughout the day. For example, at the halfway point, send an encouraging message with a reminder of the time remaining before the submission deadline. In addition to that, use the Teams channel to share updates throughout the day, perhaps highlighting exciting developments as teams work on their ideas or share tips to help the teams bring their pitches together. Highlight the available support channels for any teams who might be stuck.

Include submission instructions in several reminders and updates on the day, especially the scheduled emails. Make it easy for teams to find and follow the instructions, even if they're rushing to submit before the deadline. Include explicit details, such as:

- Finalize your presentation using the provided PowerPoint template. Save it as *[TeamName]_[ProjectName].pptx*. Aim to keep it under 10 slides.

- Record a video pitch 4–10 minutes long. This could be a screen recording of your presentation with voiceover, a webcam video of your team presenting, or a mix. Save the video as *[TeamName]_[ProjectName]_pitch.mp4*.

> **Tip** In PowerPoint, you can use "Record Slide Show" to easily narrate and export a video of your deck. Ensure your team name is on your slides and mentioned in the video intro.

- Upload your submission at *[insert link]* (often a SharePoint folder). Upload your PowerPoint and video files. Once uploaded, you should see your files listed. If you have trouble uploading, email them to *[organizer's name]* as a backup.

- Fill out the submission form at *[insert form link]* to officially submit. You'll enter your team's name and a one-paragraph abstract of your idea, and attach your files or provide the SharePoint file names. You will receive a confirmation email when you are done.

- Submissions are due by *[insert time/timezone]* on *[insert date]*. Late submissions may not be accepted, so please plan to upload a bit early. You can submit multiple times before the deadline, but only the last submission will be considered.

Schedule another email reminder one hour before the submission deadline, reminding teams to upload their PowerPoint and video pitches to the submission location before the deadline. Give teams a way to ask for help if they're having trouble with their recordings and submissions. You might want to flag that only the judges and organizers can access submitted materials, and confirm the timeline for judges to review the submissions and announce winners. Congratulate the teams on all their efforts and explain that they can enjoy a break and some refreshments while the judges prepare for the pitch broadcast.

The goal with these communications is to provide clear, step-by-step guidance for participants. Notice that they reference both the template and the video, aligning with what the challenge requires. Always test the submission process yourself and ideally ask someone else to follow your instructions to ensure it's smooth and the steps are documented correctly based on your organization's technical setup. Provide a contact for help and assign mentors to proactively check in with teams throughout the challenge. Repeating these steps in multiple communications, like announcement packets, chat messages, or reminder emails, reduces the chance of a team failing to submit correctly.

Ideas to action

With the strategies and resources in this playbook, you'll be well on your way to running a successful Microsoft AI innovation challenge. The goal is to engage people across your business and surface impactful ideas for how Copilot and AI tools can create value. Remember to plan thoroughly, communicate clearly, and foster an environment where creativity and collaboration thrive.

Many organizations have found that innovation challenges become a highlight of the year when executed effectively. They energize employees and generate ideas that can create real business value. Unlock the immense innovation potential in your organization by combining Microsoft's AI capabilities with your employees' domain expertise. Good luck with your challenge, and enjoy watching ideas turn into action!

Index

A

Plug into learning at

MicrosoftPressStore.com

The Microsoft Press Store by Pearson offers:

- Free U.S. shipping

- Buy an eBook, get multiple formats – PDF and EPUB – to use on your computer, tablet, and mobile devices

- Print & eBook Best Value Packs

- eBook Deal of the Week – Save up to 60% on featured title

- Newsletter – Be the first to hear about new releases, announcements, special offers, and more

- Register your book – Find companion files, errata, and product updates, plus receive a special coupon* to save on your next purchase

P Pearson